FOCUS ON

Grades 9–12

HIGH SCHOOL

CHEMISTRY

Rebecca W. Keller, PhD

with illustrations by

J. Moneymaker and D. J. Keller

Cover design: David Keller
Opening page: David Keller
Illustrations: Rebecca W. Keller, PhD, Janet Moneymaker, David Keller

Focus On High School Student Textbook (softcover)
ISBN: 978-1-936114-94-8

Published by Gravitas Publications, Inc.
www.gravitaspublications.com

Chapter 10 molecular images were created by David J. Keller using POV-Ray.

I would like to thank Susan Searles for copy editing and critical reading of the manuscript. I would also like to thank Christopher Keller, Kimberly Keller, and Kathryn Keller for their help with the text material and their willingness to eat many crock pot meals so mom could publish this book. I would also like to thank Jennifer Gockley, Mary Pierce, Randy Pierce, Karen Wood, Marianne Hughes, Roy Hughes, and Hope Garcia for review of the final draft. Finally, a special thanks goes to Gaeth McLean for valuable input.

Rebecca W. Keller, PhD

Printed in United States

The Periodic Table of Elements

Legend:
- Alkali metals
- Alkaline earth metals
- Metalloids
- Metals
- Non-metals
- Synthetic elements (unconfirmed)

— Transition metals

Noble gases

Halogens

Element	Name	Atomic mass
1 H	Hydrogen	1.0079
2 He	Helium	4.003
3 Li	Lithium	6.941
4 Be	Beryllium	9.0122
5 B	Boron	10.811
6 C	Carbon	12.011
7 N	Nitrogen	14.0067
8 O	Oxygen	15.9994
9 F	Fluorine	18.9984
10 Ne	Neon	20.1797
11 Na	Sodium	22.9898
12 Mg	Magnesium	24.3050
13 Al	Aluminum	26.9815
14 Si	Silicon	28.0855
15 P	Phosphorus	30.9738
16 S	Sulfur	32.066
17 Cl	Chlorine	35.4527
18 Ar	Argon	39.948
19 K	Potassium	39.0983
20 Ca	Calcium	40.078
21 Sc	Scandium	44.9559
22 Ti	Titanium	47.867
23 V	Vanadium	50.9415
24 Cr	Chromium	51.9961
25 Mn	Manganese	54.9380
26 Fe	Iron	55.847
27 Co	Cobalt	58.9332
28 Ni	Nickel	58.693
29 Cu	Copper	63.546
30 Zn	Zinc	65.38
31 Ga	Gallium	69.723
32 Ge	Germanium	72.64
33 As	Arsenic	74.9216
34 Se	Selenium	78.96
35 Br	Bromine	79.904
36 Kr	Krypton	83.80
37 Rb	Rubidium	85.4678
38 Sr	Strontium	87.62
39 Y	Yttrium	88.9059
40 Zr	Zirconium	91.224
41 Nb	Niobium	92.9064
42 Mo	Molybdenum	95.96
43 Tc	Technetium	(98)
44 Ru	Ruthenium	101.07
45 Rh	Rhodium	102.9055
46 Pd	Palladium	106.42
47 Ag	Silver	107.8682
48 Cd	Cadmium	112.411
49 In	Indium	114.82
50 Sn	Tin	118.710
51 Sb	Antimony	121.757
52 Te	Tellurium	127.60
53 I	Iodine	126.9045
54 Xe	Xenon	131.29
55 Cs	Cesium	132.9054
56 Ba	Barium	137.327
57 *La	Lanthanum	138.9055
72 Hf	Hafnium	178.49
73 Ta	Tantalum	180.9479
74 W	Tungsten	183.84
75 Re	Rhenium	186.207
76 Os	Osmium	190.2
77 Ir	Iridium	192.22
78 Pt	Platinum	195.08
79 Au	Gold	196.9666
80 Hg	Mercury	200.59
81 Tl	Thallium	204.3833
82 Pb	Lead	207.2
83 Bi	Bismuth	208.9804
84 Po	Polonium	(209)
85 At	Astatine	(210)
86 Rn	Radon	(222)
87 Fr	Francium	(223)
88 Ra	Radium	226.0254
89 **Ac	Actinium	227.0278
104 Rf	Rutherfordium	261
105 Db	Dubnium	262.11
106 Sg	Seaborgium	263
107 Bh	Bohrium	264.12
108 Hs	Hassium	269.13
109 Mt	Meitnerium	266
110 Ds	Darmstadtium	269
111 Rg	Roentgenium	(272)
112 Cp	Copernicium	277
113 Uut	Ununtrium	(284)
114 Uuq	Ununquadium	(285)
115 Uup	Ununpentium	(288)
116 Uuh	Ununhexium	(289)
117 Uus	Ununseptium	(291)
118 Uuo	Ununoctium	(293)

Lanthanide series (Elements 58–71):

Element	Name	Atomic mass
58 Ce	Cerium	140.116
59 Pr	Praseodymium	140.9076
60 Nd	Neodymium	144.24
61 Pm	Promethium	(145)
62 Sm	Samarium	150.36
63 Eu	Europium	151.964
64 Gd	Gadolinium	157.25
65 Tb	Terbium	158.9253
66 Dy	Dysprosium	162.50
67 Ho	Holmium	164.9303
68 Er	Erbium	167.26
69 Tm	Thulium	168.9342
70 Yb	Ytterbium	173.054
71 Lu	Lutetium	174.967

Actinide series (Elements 90–103):

Element	Name	Atomic mass
90 Th	Thorium	232.0381
91 Pa	Protactinium	231.0359
92 U	Uranium	238.0289
93 Np	Neptunium	237.0482
94 Pu	Plutonium	(244)
95 Am	Americium	(243)
96 Cm	Curium	(247)
97 Bk	Berkelium	(247)
98 Cf	Californium	(251)
99 Es	Einsteinium	(252)
100 Fm	Fermium	(257)
101 Md	Mendelevium	(258)
102 No	Nobelium	(259)
103 Lr	Lawrencium	(260)

*The lanthinide series: Elements 58–71

**The actinide series: Elements 90–103

GRAVITAS

REAL SCIENCE 4 Teens

http://www.gravitaspublications.com

CONTENTS

CHAPTER 1 MATTER, MASS, AND MOLES

1.1 INTRODUCTION

1.1.1 Chemistry happens every day

Chemistry is the science of atoms and how they combine to form molecules. In many ways, it is the science that is most important to our everyday lives. Everything around us—the air, the ground, the chair we sit in, our clothes, and even our own bodies—is composed of atoms and molecules. Many of the things we do, such as running, swimming, jumping and eating involve chemical reactions. For example, when we eat a piece of chocolate or a bowl of pasta, chemical reactions inside the body convert these foods into energy. Most of that energy is used to keep our cells alive and to keep us warm, but we use some of the energy to play, think, breath, and even study chemistry! Chocolate contains fat and sugar molecules that can be chemically "burned" to produce useful energy. For example, molecules in your mouth called enzymes [en'-zīmz] begin breaking the food molecules into smaller pieces (proteins, fats, sugars). These smaller pieces are then used to make a host of other molecules (such as ATP—adenosine triphosphate [ə-de'-nə-sēn trī-fäs'-fāt]—and Acetyl CoA [ə-sēt'-əl kō-ā]) that enter complex metabolic pathways inside your cells. One such pathway is the citric acid cycle which uses Acetyl CoA to make the energy molecule ATP, the basic "fuel" used by all living things.

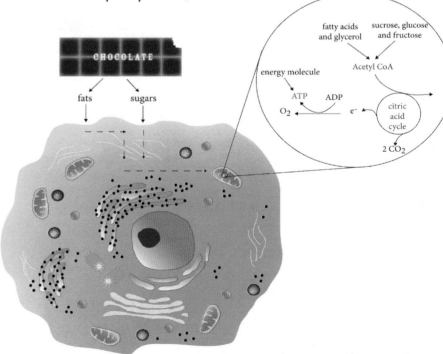

Figure 1.1: Diagram of a cell showing a simplified metabolic pathway.

1.1.2 What is chemistry?

Chemistry is the study of atoms and molecules, which are the smallest bits of matter that can undergo chemical reactions. At the simplest level, an atom is depicted as a little ball, and a molecule is shown as one or more atoms bonded together into a cluster of balls. A chemical reaction is a change in the way the atoms are bonded together. Chemistry is concerned with the properties of atoms and molecules and the way they react with each other.

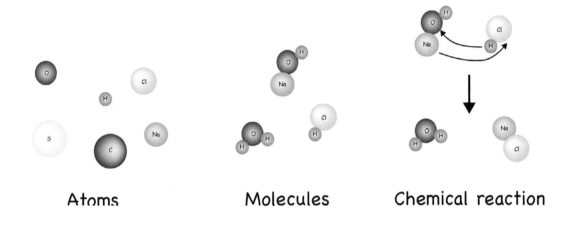

Figure 1.2: Atoms, molecules, and a chemical reaction.

1.1.3 Where did we get chemistry?

Today we know a great deal about the chemistry around us and inside our bodies, but it wasn't too long ago that chemistry was not very well understood. Where did the science of chemistry come from? How did we find out about chocolate, fats, sugars, enzymes, ATP, Acetyl CoA, acids, bases, water, proteins, carbohydrates, and everything else? The knowledge we have today about chemicals and their properties has accumulated over many centuries, beginning with the early Greek, Egyptian, and Chinese peoples. The word *chemistry* comes from the Greek word *chemeia*, which means "preparation of gold and silver." Much of modern chemistry has its roots in the work of artisans and alchemists of ancient Egypt, China, and Greece. Later in Europe, where the purification of gold and silver was of prime importance, one aim of the early alchemists was to turn lead into gold. They experimented with different kinds of chemicals hoping that one day they would get rich! They never succeeded (do you know why?), but they did learn a great deal about chemicals and their properties.

Over time, the basic knowledge for the science we now call chemistry proved much more valuable than gold. Until the 1700s, chemistry was haphazard at best, but beginning with the investigations of Antoine Lavoisier, Joseph Priestly, and Robert Boyle, chemistry slowly developed into a powerful systematic science. The most important early experiments taught chemists how to separate mixtures from pure substances and how to weigh and measure the products of chemical reactions.

Today chemistry is divided into at least four main areas: analytical chemistry, synthetic chemistry, physical chemistry, and biochemistry. Analytical chemistry deals with what kinds of chemicals compose various substances. The word *analytical* comes from the Greek word *analeuin* which means "to resolve." Analytical chemists can determine, or resolve, the chemical makeup of a number of different and complex samples such as contaminated dirt, tissue samples from patients, or cloth and blood samples from a crime scene.

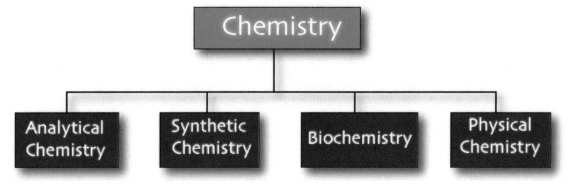

Figure 1.3: The major divisions of chemistry.

Synthetic chemistry deals with making new kinds of chemicals or chemicals not found naturally. The word *synthetic* comes from the Greek prefix *syn* which means "with or together," and the Greek word *thesis*, which means "to place or put." So synthetic chemists use their knowledge of how molecules react with each other to *synthesize* or put together new molecules. Nylon is a fiber used in clothing that was designed by synthetic chemists.

Physical chemistry focuses on how chemical reactions and other properties arise from the basic laws of physics. The word *physics* comes from the Greek word *physis*, which means "nature or natural growth." So physical chemistry is concerned with how natural forces are involved in molecular bonding, for example, or how some chemical reactions give off or absorb heat. Biochemistry is concerned with the complicated chemistry that takes place inside living things. The prefix *bio-* comes from the Greek word *bios*, which means "life," so biochemists study the chemistry of life. For example, biochemists have figured out how chocolate is turned into energy!

1.2 ATOMS

1.2.1 Protons, neutrons, and electrons

Atoms are the smallest distinctive chemical units of matter. They are made of three smaller particles: protons [prō′-tonz], neutrons, [nü′-tronz] and electrons [i-lek′-tränz]. Protons and neutrons make up the center of an atom, called the atomic nucleus. Even though the nucleus is very tiny (it would be invisibly small if it were shown at its real size in Figure 1.4), it contains essentially all the *mass* of the atom. Mass is different from weight and is a property that makes matter resist being moved (see section 1.2.2). The electrons occupy the space surrounding the nucleus, called the electron cloud. Even though the cloud is large (compared to the nucleus), it has almost no mass. Figure 1.4 shows a simple electron cloud, but the electron cloud is really made up of several smaller clouds, called orbitals. Some orbitals have odd shapes; they are not simple and round as shown in the diagram. We will learn more about the different kinds of orbitals in Chapter 2 (see Section 2.2).

Helium atom

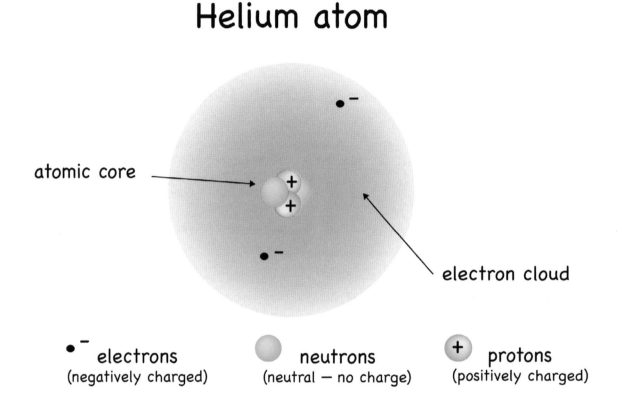

atomic core

electron cloud

•⁻ electrons
(negatively charged)

neutrons
(neutral — no charge)

+ protons
(positively charged)

Figure 1.4: A helium atom showing the atomic core (with two protons
and two neutrons) and the electron cloud (with two electrons).

Every proton in the nucleus of an atom carries one unit of *positive* electric charge, and every electron carries one unit of *negative* electric charge. Neutrons have no electric charge. (They're neutral, that's why they're called neutrons!) The negative charge of one electron can cancel the positive charge of one proton, and *vice versa*. Every atom must have a zero electric charge overall. Therefore...

the number of electrons equals the number of protons.

For example, a hydrogen atom has 1 electron and 1 proton, a carbon atom, which has 6 protons, also has 6 electrons and a gold atom has 79 protons and 79 electrons.

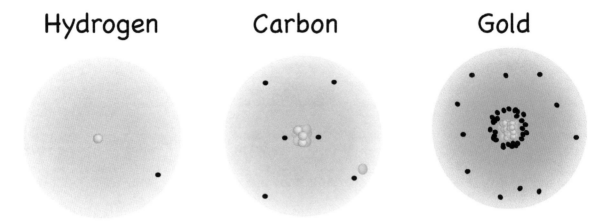

Hydrogen   Carbon   Gold

Figure 1.5: A hydrogen atom with 1 proton and 1 electron, a carbon atom with 6 protons and 6 electrons, and a gold atom with 79 protons and 79 electrons.

1.2.2 Matter and mass

Atoms are one of the most basic forms of matter. Tangerines and automobiles, baseballs and bowling balls, and even the wind and the rain are all made of matter. Everything we can see, touch, taste, or smell is made of matter. But what *is* matter?

Matter is a general term that describes anything that occupies space and has mass. Recall that mass is different than *weight*. Mass is a property that makes matter resist being moved (*intertia*), but weight is a force caused by the earth's gravity. For example, a bowling ball and a feather both have mass but the bowling ball has more mass than the feather. On earth, the bowling ball will *weigh* more than the feather, but in space neither the bowling ball nor the feather weighs anything at all. Now think about taking a bowling ball and shaking it back and forth. It is harder to shake than a feather. Even in space, where neither the bowling ball nor the feather has weight, the bowling ball is still harder to shake. This is because the bowling ball has more mass than the feather. It resists being moved, and it has more *inertia* than the feather.

1.2.3 Atomic mass and atomic weight

Since atoms are a form of matter, they must have mass. We can estimate the mass of an atom just by counting its protons and neutrons. The masses of atoms are most conveniently measured in atomic mass units, or amu.

Each proton and each neutron has a mass of 1 amu.

An electron also has mass, but it's only about ½₂₀₀₀ the mass of a proton or neutron, so its mass is usually ignored in computing atomic mass. A hydrogen atom, with 1 proton and no neutrons, has a mass of 1 amu; a carbon atom, with 6 protons and 6 neutrons, has a mass of about 12 amu; and a gold atom, with 79 protons and 118 neutrons, has a mass of 197 amu. These values are only estimates. The true atomic mass is always a bit different than just the sum of protons and neutrons, but it is usually close.

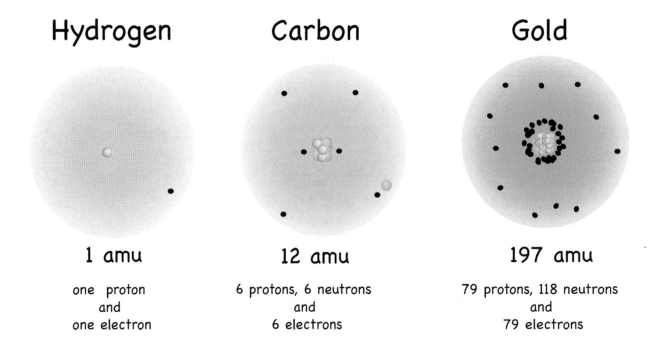

Hydrogen   Carbon   Gold

1 amu   12 amu   197 amu

one proton   6 protons, 6 neutrons   79 protons, 118 neutrons
and   and   and
one electron   6 electrons   79 electrons

Figure 1.6: A hydrogen atom with an atomic mass of 1 amu, a carbon atom with an atomic mass of 12 amu, and a gold atom with an atomic mass of 197 amu.

Mass and weight are different, but on Earth mass always gives rise to weight (the force due to gravity acting on mass). So we often talk about the weight of something when we really mean mass. Very often chemists speak of "atomic weight," but this just means the same thing as atomic mass. The atomic mass (or weight) of each element is listed on the periodic table. For example, the atomic mass of oxygen (O) is listed on your table as 15.9994 amu, and the atomic mass of iron (Fe) is listed as 55.847 amu.

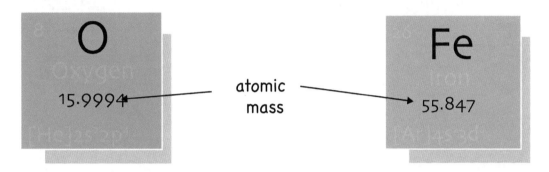

Figure 1.7: The element oxygen with an atomic mass of 15.9994 amu and the element iron with an atomic mass of 55.847 amu as represented on the periodic table.

Atoms are very small, so the mass of one atom is also very tiny. However, if there are enough atoms together they can weigh a lot. *The weight (or mass) of every object around us is just the sum of the masses of all the atoms in it.* A bowling ball has a lot of mass, but it all comes from the masses of the atoms inside. Moreover, if the mass is doubled, the number of atoms is also doubled, as is the weight.

1.2.4 Moles: counting and weighing atoms

The fact that the weight of an object is the sum of atomic masses has one very important consequence: You can count atoms by weighing them! Atoms are *much* too small to count one by one, so chemists count them in big groups, called moles. A mole is defined such that 1 mole of carbon atoms, each with a mass of 12 amu, weighs 12 grams. In general:

A mole of atoms weighs the same (in grams) as its atomic mass (in amu).

For example, a helium atom has a mass of 4 amu, so a mole of helium atoms weighs 4 grams. Two moles of helium atoms weighs 8 grams, three moles weighs 12 grams, and so on. (*How much would half a mole of helium atoms weigh? How many moles are there in 16 grams of helium?*)

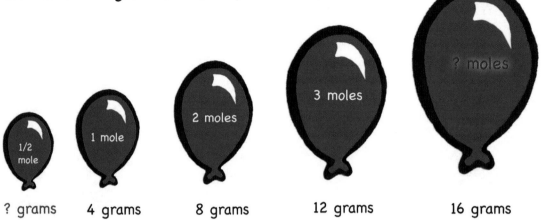

Figure 1.8: Grams of helium increase as the number of moles increases. Since helium has a mass of 4 amu, the number of grams increases by a multiple of 4 for every mole of helium.

An oxygen atom has a mass of 16 amu; a mole of oxygen atoms weighs 16 grams. (How much would two moles of oxygen atoms weigh? How many moles are there in 4 grams of oxygen?)

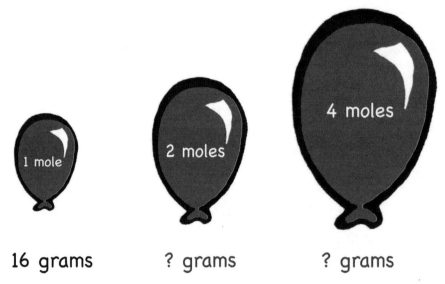

Figure 1.9: Grams of oxygen increase as the number of moles increases. Since oxygen has a mass of 16 amu, the number of grams increases by a multiple of 16 for every mole of oxygen.

A gold atom has a mass of 197 amu; a mole of gold atoms weighs 197 grams. (How much would two moles of gold weigh? four moles?)

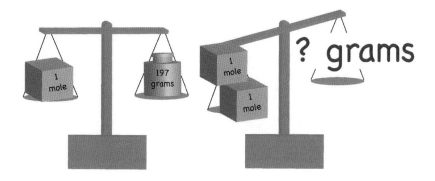

Figure 1.10: The number of moles is balanced by quantity in grams.

A mole is just a name that represents a certain number of atoms, molecules, ions, or even umbrellas. We count things all the time by using names that represent certain amounts.

HALF DOZEN

ONE DOZEN

TWO DOZEN

For example, we count 12 eggs by calling them a dozen. Twenty-four eggs are two dozen; six eggs are a half dozen, and so on. A dozen is just a group of 12, so when you count by dozens, you are counting by groups of 12. In the same way, chemists count by groups called moles.

The only difference is that a mole is a VERY large number:

1 mole = 602,200,000,000,000,000,000,000

(If you are familiar with scientific notation, a mole can also be written in a more convenient form: 1 mole = 6.022 x 10^{23}.) A mole is 6022 followed by 20 zeros. That's such a big number, it won't even fit on most calculators! It's so big that if you had a mole of marbles, it would be bigger than the moon! But atoms are very tiny, so a mole of atoms is a nice, manageable size. A mole of most atoms will fit in the palm of your hand.

It is important to note that one mole of any atom is the same number of atoms, no matter how much the sample weighs. One mole of carbon atoms has the same number of atoms as 1 mole of gold atoms, even though the carbon weighs 12 grams and the gold weighs 197 grams.

The mole is a very important concept in chemistry. It allows chemists to tell how many atoms or molecules they have in their samples just by weighing them. For a pure element, if you know the weight of your sample in grams, then you can find the number of moles in your sample by dividing by the atomic mass.

$$\text{moles} = \frac{\text{weight in grams}}{\text{atomic mass in amu}}$$

Without the concept of the mole, it would be difficult to tell how many atoms you have in a sample, and much of chemistry would not be possible.

1.3 THE PERIODIC TABLE

1.3.1 Introduction

All of the elements are organized into a table called the periodic table of elements. The periodic table lists all the elements and gives some of their properties, such as number of protons, atomic weight, and chemical symbol. More importantly, the periodic table organizes the elements into families according to such chemical properties. By noting where an element is in the periodic table, you can often tell how it will behave when mixed with other elements.

1.3.2 The elements

As we saw in Section 1.2, the nucleus of every atom is made of protons and neutrons, and some nuclei have more protons than others. For example, an atom with only one proton and one electron is a hydrogen atom, but an atom with two protons, two neutrons, and two electrons is a helium atom. An atom with three protons, three neutrons, and three electrons is a lithium atom.

We call the different kinds of atoms elements. There are 92 elements found naturally

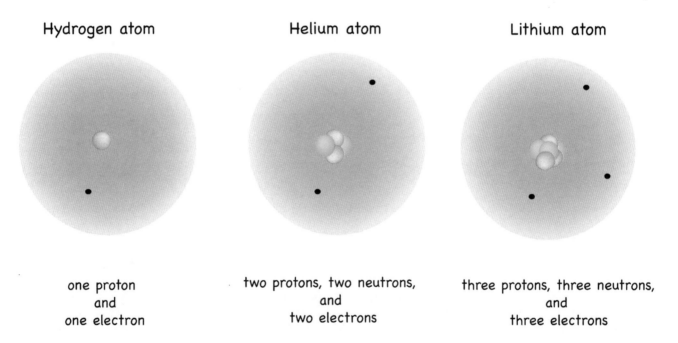

Hydrogen atom   Helium atom   Lithium atom

one proton
and
one electron

two protons, two neutrons,
and
two electrons

three protons, three neutrons,
and
three electrons

Figure 1.11: A hydrogen atom with one proton and one electron, a helium atom showing two protons, two neutrons, and two electrons, and a lithium atom with three protons, three neutrons, and three electrons.

and about a dozen additional elements that have been synthesized artificially by humans. The periodic table lists all the different elements, that is, all the different possible kinds of atoms. Hydrogen, helium, carbon, oxygen, gold, and plutonium are all elements.

1.3.3 Mixtures and pure substances

Matter—which is everything you can see, taste, and touch—is made of different kinds of atoms. Matter can be classified into two categories: mixtures and pure substances. We will learn more about mixtures in Chapters 6 and 7.

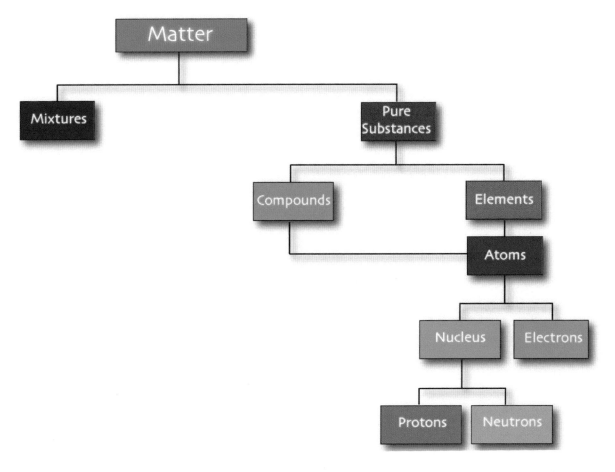

Figure 1.12: Matter can be divided into two categories; mixtures and pure substances. Pure substances can be further divided into compounds and elements. Elements are composed of atoms, which contain a nucleus (with the protons and neutrons) and the electrons.

A pure substance can be either a *compound* or an *element*. Some pure substances are made of only one kind of atom. For example, pure gold contains *only* gold atoms and nothing else. Likewise, pure graphite, such as the graphite in your pencil, contains *only* carbon atoms and nothing else. All pure metals such as aluminum, iron, and copper contain *only* one kind of atom. Pure oxygen gas is made of *only* oxygen atoms, and pure nitrogen gas is made of *only* nitrogen atoms.

We call such substances elemental, as in *elemental gold*, or *elemental carbon*, to indicate that they are composed of only one kind of atom.

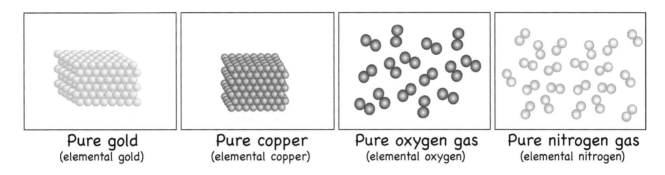

Pure gold
(elemental gold)

Pure copper
(elemental copper)

Pure oxygen gas
(elemental oxygen)

Pure nitrogen gas
(elemental nitrogen)

Figure 1.13: Pure gold, pure copper, pure oxygen gas and pure nitrogen gas are all elemental substances.

Other pure substances contain more than one element but are composed of only one type of molecule. Pure water, for example, is made of two different elements: hydrogen and oxygen. Pure ammonia contains three hydrogen atoms and one nitrogen atom, and pure carbon dioxide contains two oxygen atoms and one carbon atom. Even though they contain more than one kind of atom, they are considered to be pure substances because they are composed of only one kind of molecule. We call such pure substances compounds.

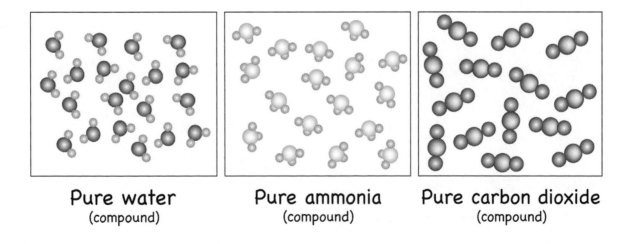

Pure water
(compound)

Pure ammonia
(compound)

Pure carbon dioxide
(compound)

Figure 1.14: Pure water, pure ammonia and pure carbon dioxide are all compounds.

In general, a compound is *two or more atoms bonded together in a fixed ratio.* (For example, there is always one oxygen atom to two hydrogen atoms in a water molecule for a ratio of one to two.) Because the atoms in compounds have a fixed ratio, they are also considered pure substances.

Matter can also exist in mixtures. A mixture is defined as two or more substances physically (but not chemically) combined. The air we breathe is a mixture of nitrogen gas, oxygen gas, and other trace substances. Tap water is a mixture of water molecules and small amounts of metals and chlorine. Unlike a compound, the ratio of the components of a mixture are not fixed. Therefore, mixtures are *not* pure substances.

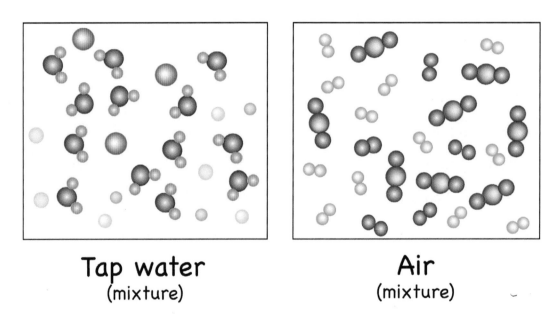

Tap water
(mixture)

Air
(mixture)

Figure 1.15: Tap water is a mixture of water and other ions. Air is a mixture of different gases.

1.3.4 Where did we get the periodic table?

At one point in history, many elements were known, but there was no suitable way to organize them. This problem was largely solved by a Russian chemist named Dmitri Mendeleev [dmē'-trē men-də-lā'-əf]. Mendeleev loved playing card games, and one day he decided to put all of the elements known to him on individual playing cards.

Then, he organized the cards according to their atomic mass and chemical properties. When he did this, he discovered that elements with similar chemical properties fell into a particular pattern or periodicity. He wasn't sure what to do with hydrogen, the lightest element, so originally he left it out. He started with

lithium (Li), and noted that elements, such as sodium (Na) and potassium (K), with chemical properties similar to lithium, were spaced eight elements apart: Li is element number 3 (3 protons, 3 electrons); Na is element number 11 (11 protons, 11 electrons); K is element number 19 (19 protons, 19 electrons), and so on. He lined them up with increasing atomic weight and then grouped them into families with similar chemical properties. An early periodic chart by Dmitri Mendeleev looked something like this:

PERIODIC TABLE: DMITRI MENDELEEV (1834 — 1907)

SERIES		GROUPS							
	O	I	II	III	IV	V	VI	VII	VIII
1		H = 1.008							
2	He = 4.0	Li = 7.03	Be = 9.1	B = 11.0	C = 12.0	N = 14.04	0 = 16.00	F = 19.0	
3	Ne = 19.9	Na = 23.05	Mg = 24.3	Al = 27.0	Si = 28.4	P = 31.0	S = 32.06	Cl = 35.45	
4	Ar = 38	K = 39.1	Ca = 40.1	Sc= 44.1	Ti = 48.1	V = 51.4	Cr = 52.1	Mn = 55	Fe = 55.9, Co = 59
5		Cu= 63.9	Zn = 65.4	Ga = 70	Ge = 72.3	As = 75	Se = 79	Br = 79.95	Ni = 59, (Cu)
6	Kr = 81.8	Rb = 85.4	Sr = 87.6	Y = 89	Zr = 90.6	Nb = 94.0	Mo = 96	(-)	
7		Ag = 107.9	Cd = 112.4	In = 114.0	Sn = 119	Sb = 120	Te = 127	I = 127	Ru = 101.7, Rh = 103
8	Xe = 128	Cs= 132.9	Ba = 137.4	La = 139	Ce = 140	(-)	(-)	(-)	Pd = 106.5, (Ag)
9		(-)	(-)	(-)	(-)	(-)	(-)	(-)	
10	(-)	(-)	(-)	Yb= 173	(-)	Ta = 183	W = 184	(-)	Os = 191, Ir = 193
11		Au= 197.2	Hg = 200.0	Tl = 204.1	Pb = 206.9	Bi = 208	(-)	(-)	Pt = 194.9, (Au)
12	(-)	(-)	Rd= 224	(-)	Th = 232	(-)	U = 239		
	R	R_2O	RO	R_2O_2	RO_2	R_2O_6	RO_3	R_3O_7	RO_4

(1871) ADAPTED TABLE FROM ANNALEN, SUPPL. VIII, 133 (1871); REVISED 1898 AFTER THE DISCOVERY OF RADIUM (Rd, MODERN Ra)

Figure 1.16: An early periodic table. [Redrawn by R.W. Keller from several composite tables.]

1.3.5 The periodic table today

Mendeleev's chart had gaps in the pattern that suggested there should be other elements. So even though he didn't know all of the elements we know today, he was able to predict new elements that would fit into the empty spaces on his chart. He could also tell roughly what atomic mass they would have.

Today, we know all of the naturally occurring elements, and scientists have even been successful in synthesizing many elements that do not occur naturally. The modern periodic table is organized in three ways. First, *each element is identified by the number of protons alone*; the number of neutrons doesn't matter. The number of protons is called the atomic number. The atomic number determines the element. Atomic number 1 (1 proton) is hydrogen, atomic number 2 (2 protons) is helium, atomic number 6 (6 protons) is carbon, atomic number 79 (79 protons) is gold, and so on.

Second, *elements increase in atomic number from left to right across the rows*. The first row has just hydrogen (atomic number 1) on the left side and helium (atomic number 2) on the right side. The second row elements include lithium (atomic number 3) in the left-hand column through neon (atomic number 10) in the extreme right-hand column.

The third row elements are sodium (element 11) through argon (element 18), and so on. Each row is called a period (hence the name "periodic table").

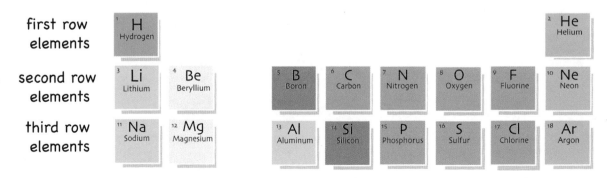

Figure 1.17: The first three rows of the periodic table.

Third, *elements with similar chemical properties are lined up in the same column.* By chemical properties chemists mean "the way the atoms react with each other to form compounds." For example, the elements in the left-hand column (lithium, sodium, potassium, rubidium, cesium, and francium) are called the alkali metals. They are all soft, white metals, and they all react strongly with water. Sodium hisses and fumes when tossed into water, and potassium explodes. It can even cause fires from moisture in the air.

Rubidium and cesium are similar. Similarities in physical properties (like color, hardness, and metallic character) and chemical properties (like reacting with water in similar ways) are examples of the kinds of properties Mendeleev used to create his early periodic tables.

The elements in the next-to-last column (fluorine, chlorine, bromine, iodine, and astatine) are called the halogens. Most are strongly colored and melt or vaporize at low temperatures. Fluorine is a colorless gas, chlorine is a yellow-green gas, bromine is a dark red-brown liquid, and iodine is a dark brown solid. The halogens react with most metals, but they react especially violently with the alkali metals. The reaction between any of the alkali metals and any of the halogens always creates a saltlike compound. For example, sodium and chlorine react to

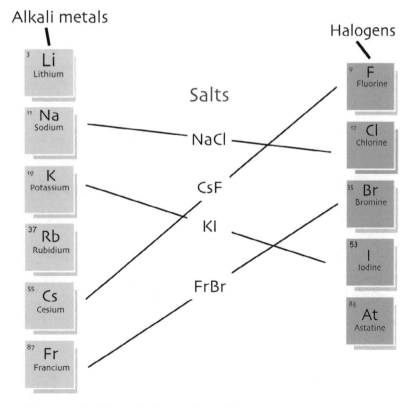

Figure 1.18: The alkali metals and the halogens react to form salts.

form sodium chloride, which is ordinary table salt. Potassium and chlorine form potassium chloride, which is sometimes called "light salt" and is so similar to table salt that you can eat it, and it almost tastes the same. Similarly, lithium reacts with bromine, cesium reacts with fluorine, and so on. All these combinations create saltlike compounds.

The very last column (helium, neon, argon, krypton, xenon, radon) contains the inert gases, or noble gases. As their name implies, they are all gases, and they are all very unreactive (with any element). Only a very few compounds containing the noble gases have ever been discovered.

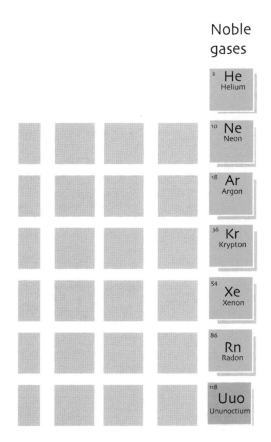

Figure 1.19: The noble gases.

Finally, the periodic table is also divided into two large blocks: the main group and the transition metals (also called transition elements). The main group elements are located on the right-hand and left-hand sides of the periodic table.

The difference between the main group and the transition metals is in the way their electrons are organized. To jump ahead a bit, the main group elements have their outermost electrons (the ones that are responsible for most chemical properties) in s and p shells, while the transition metals have their outermost electrons in d shells. We will learn more about electron shells and how the electrons in atoms are organized in Chapter 2.

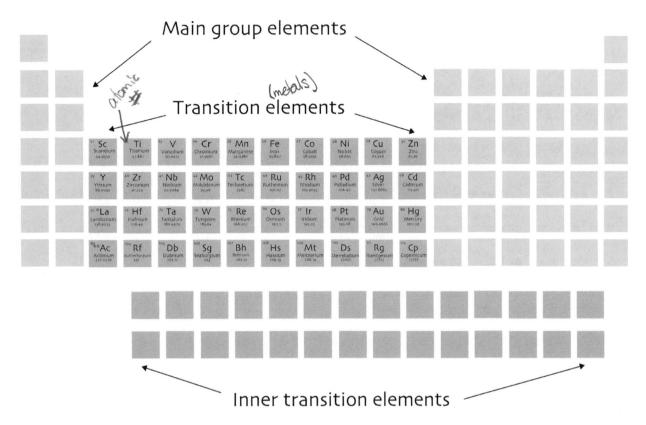

Figure 1.20: The main group elements (blue), the transition elements (orange), and the inner transition elements (pink).

1.4 SUMMARY

- Everything around us is made of atoms. Chemistry is the study of how atoms combine to make molecules and how both atoms and molecules react with each other to form new substances.

- Every atom is made of three basic particles: protons, neutrons, and electrons. The protons and neutrons form a tiny core called the nucleus, and the electrons form a cloud around the nucleus.

- The number of protons in the nucleus is called the atomic number.

- Each atom has a tiny mass equal to the number of protons plus the number of neutrons (in atomic mass units, amu).

- A mole is a specific number of atoms (or molecules). A mole is the number of atoms it takes to make the total weight in grams equal the atomic mass (in amu). The number of moles of atoms can be determined by weighing the sample (in grams) and dividing by the atomic mass (in amu).

- All the elements are gathered together in the periodic table of elements. Each element is listed by atomic number. Each row of the periodic table is called a period, and each column is called a group. The periodic table is organized so that the columns are groups of elements with similar properties.

- Among the most important groups are the alkali metals, the halogens, and the noble gases. The periodic table is also divided into two large blocks called the main group and the transition elements.

1.5 STUDY QUESTIONS

1. What are the three basic particles in an atom? Which of these have electric charge, and what charge does each have? proton (positive charge)   electron (negative charge)   nuetron (no charge)

2. An unknown element is found to have 150 protons in its nucleus. How many electrons does it have?   150 electrons

3. An atom is found to have 24 protons and 30 neutrons in its nucleus. What is its atomic mass (in amu)?   atomic mass = 54

4. Identify each of the following elements and give its atomic symbol:

a. Atomic number 17 *Chlorine Cl*

b. Atomic number 6 *Carbon C*

c. Atomic number 3 *Lithium L*

d. Atomic number 7 *Nitrogen N*

e. Atomic number 80 *Mercury Hg*

5. Which of the following are halogens: atomic number 7, atomic number 12, atomic number 9, atomic number 17, atomic number 35? *# 9, 17, 35,*

6. Which of the following are noble gases: atomic number 10, atomic number 20, atomic number 36, atomic number 2, atomic number 18? *2, 10, 18, 36*

7. Which of the following are alkali metals: atomic number 2, atomic number 3, atomic number 11, atomic number 19, atomic number 21, atomic number 37? *3, 11, 19, 37*

8. How many moles of atoms are in 10.81 grams of boron?

   10.81

9. How many grams would 3 moles of boron weigh?

   32.43 g

10. Ammonia molecules, NH_3, have 1 nitrogen atom and 3 hydrogen atoms. How many grams would 1 mole of ammonia weigh?

   16.03 g

CHAPTER 2 CHEMICAL BONDING

CHEMICAL BONDING — PART B

CHEMICAL BONDING — PART A

2.1 FORMING BONDS

2.1.1 Introduction

We saw in the last chapter that everything is made of atoms. Sometimes the atoms are *free*, meaning not bonded to any other atoms. Noble gases, such as helium and argon, are always found as free, unbonded atoms. Liquid metals, such as mercury or molten iron, are also composed of essentially free atoms. However, most things are made of two or more atoms "bonded" together in clusters. Two or more atoms bonded to each other are called a molecule [mä'-li-kyül]. Water is made of molecules (H_2O), as is ammonia (NH_3), and carbon dioxide (CO_2). As we saw in the last chapter, even the "oxygen" in the air is not free oxygen atoms, but molecules with two bonded oxygen atoms (O_2). Likewise, the nitrogen in the air is made of N_2 molecules instead of loose N atoms.

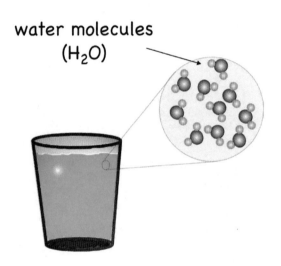

water molecules
(H_2O)

Figure 2.1: Water is made of molecules.

2.1.2 Chemical bonding: basic picture

In this chapter, we are going to learn about chemical bonding, the "glue" that holds molecules together. "Chemical bonding" is just a fancy way to say that atoms like to stick to each other. What is this "glue", and why do atoms like to stick or bond?

The short answer is that atoms bond because...

electrons on one atom are attracted to the protons on another atom.

Protons have positive electrical charge, and electrons have negative charge. One of the fundamental laws of physics is that *opposite electrical charges attract*, so electrons are attracted to protons, and vice versa. (That's why atoms always have equal numbers of electrons and protons in the first place; it's hard to pull electrons and protons apart!) Sometimes atoms "share" electrons, and these shared electrons are attracted to *both* nuclei. This attraction acts like glue to hold the atoms together to form molecules.

At its most basic level, chemical bonding is very simple: It's just the result of the attractions between electrical charges in the atoms. But chemical bonding follows definite rules. Not every atom sticks to every other atom. Some atoms form several bonds, some atoms form only one bond, and some atoms don't form bonds at all! Some chemical bonds are much

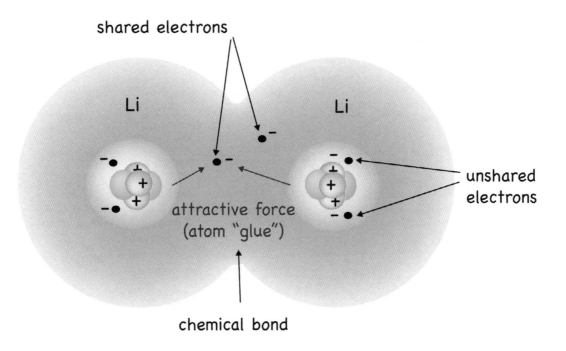

Figure 2.2: Two lithium atoms: a dilithium molecule. The shared electrons are attracted to the positively charged nuclei from each atom. The result is a chemical bond between the two atoms, where the "glue" that sticks them together is the attractive force between the nuclei and electrons.

stronger than others. Learning the rules of chemical bonding will help us understand how the common substances around us (water, air, metals, wood, components of our bodies) are built. Knowing the rules of chemical bonding will also help us understand how molecules react with each other to build new molecules. Before we can learn the rules for forming bonds, we must look at the way in which electrons are arranged in atomic orbitals inside the atoms.

2.2 ATOMIC ORBITALS

In Chapter 1, we saw how electrons are found in a cloud surrounding the nucleus of every atom. We saw earlier in this chapter that these electrons are sometimes shared between two atoms, forming a chemical bond. But when are electrons shared, and when are they not shared? Are all the electrons involved or only a few? Why do some atoms share their electrons differently than others? To answer these questions, we need to learn more about how the electrons are arranged inside atoms.

Electron clouds are not simple balls. Each electron in an atom is in a little cloud called an orbital which can hold up to two electrons, and the overall electron cloud of an atom is built up from these orbitals. The electrons occupy the space inside the orbital like marbles would occupy the space inside a balloon. There are three common kinds of orbitals, each with its own shape and special properties: *s* orbitals, *p* orbitals, and *d* orbitals (there are also *f* and *g* orbitals).

2.2.1 *s* orbitals

The simplest kind of orbital is called an *s* orbital and is shaped like a sphere. *s* orbitals come in several sizes: a 1*s* orbital is small, a 2*s* orbital is bigger, and a 3s orbital bigger still. The largest atoms in the periodic table have 7*s* orbitals.

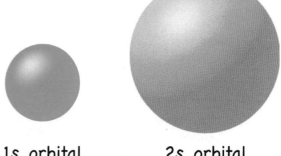

1*s* orbital   2*s* orbital

Figure 2.3: The 1*s* orbital and the 2*s* orbital.

2.2.2 *p* orbitals

The next simplest orbitals are called *p* orbitals. They are shaped a bit like dumbbells, with two lobes and a narrow waist. There are *three* different kinds of *p* orbitals. Each kind points in a different direction, and each one is perpendicular to the others.

Like the *s* orbitals, *p* orbitals come in different sizes: 2*p* orbitals are the smallest, 3*p* slightly larger, 4*p* larger still, and so on. The biggest atoms are those with 6*p* orbitals.

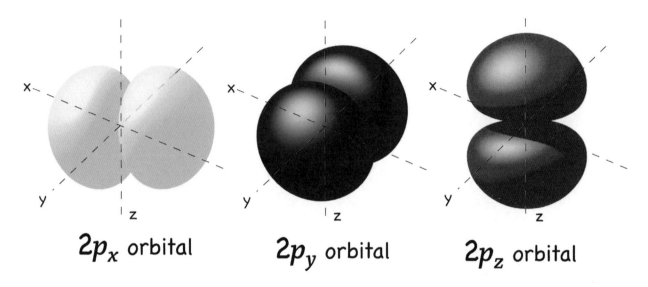

$2p_x$ orbital $2p_y$ orbital $2p_z$ orbital

Figure 2.4: The $2p_x$ orbital (oriented along the *x* axis), the $2p_y$ orbital (oriented along the *y* axis), and the $2p_z$ orbital (oriented along the *z* axis).

2.2.3 *d* orbitals

The most complicated orbitals we will consider are called *d* orbitals. They come in five different shapes, as shown in Figure 2.5. Each of these orbitals has its own name: d_{xy} d_{xz} d_{yz} $d_{x^2-y^2}$ and d_{z^2}. (If you know enough to guess where these weird names come from, you are very wise indeed! All the orbitals, including *s*, *p*, and *d*, come from quantum mechanics, a very difficult, high level mathematics subject. The names of the *d* orbitals come from the details of quantum mechanics. If you major in physics or chemistry in college, you'll learn about quantum mechanics.)

Again, like the *s* and *p* orbitals, *d* orbitals come in several sizes: 3*d* orbitals are smallest, 4*d* next biggest, 5*d* bigger yet. The largest atoms in the periodic table have 6*d* orbitals.

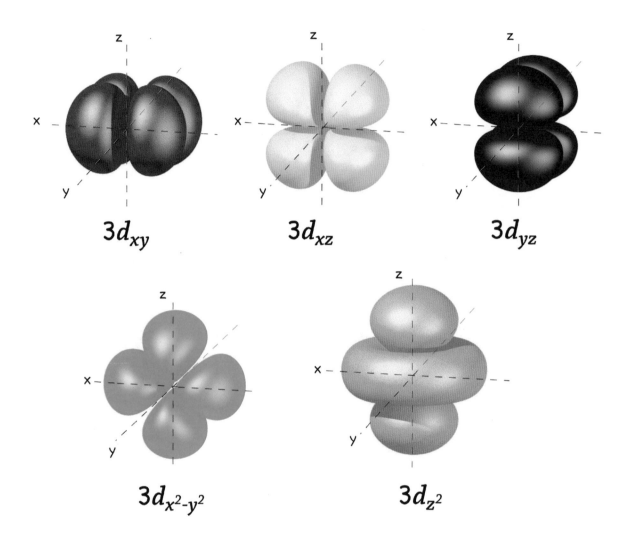

Figure 2.5: The *d* orbitals (the lobes are oriented along the *x*, *y*, and *z* axes).

2.2.4 Subshells

A set of three *p* orbitals of the same size is called a *p* subshell. So the three 2*p* orbitals form a *p* subshell, the three 3*p* orbitals form a *p* subshell, the three 4*p* orbitals form a p subshell, and so on. Similarly, a set of all five *d* orbitals forms a subshell (a *d* subshell), and a single *s* orbital forms its own subshell (an *s* subshell). As we will see later, atoms with all their subshells full of electrons are particularly stable and unreactive, while atoms with unfilled or partially filled subshells are reactive.

2.3 FILLING ORBITALS

2.3.1 The Pauli principle

We can use the *s*, *p*, and *d* orbitals to build the electron clouds for each atom of the periodic table. We take all the electrons in an atom and fill up each orbital, one by one, until we run out of electrons. There are two rules for filling electron orbitals. The first rule is called the Pauli principle. It states that each orbital can hold a maximum of two electrons. So, a single orbital can be empty (0 electrons) or have 1 or 2 electrons, but never three or more.

Rule 1: The Pauli principle: *Each orbital can hold at most two electrons.*

When we put an electron in an orbital, where does it go exactly? Electrons actually spread out to fill all the space inside an orbital. In atoms and molecules, electrons do not act like "points" or "particles," they act like "waves." We say that they are delocalized [dē-lō'-kə-līzd]. This means that the electron has spread out in space and is not *localized* in any one place. So, in an *s* orbital, electrons just occupy the spherical space for the orbital. For *p* or *d* orbitals, do the electrons occupy different lobes? Does one electron occupy one lobe of an orbital while the other electron occupies the other lobe of the orbital? Do both electrons stay in one lobe and leave the other lobe empty? Do the electrons swim around inside the orbital occupying space in both lobes? In fact, the electrons don't occupy a particular place inside the lobes of the orbitals. One electron does not occupy one lobe and the other electron the other lobe, nor do both of the electrons occupy only one lobe. Both electrons occupy the space of both lobes. Chemists refer to this concept as electron density, which means that one electron is *more probable* in some places than in others, but is not located in any one place.

We can illustrate electron density by making a *filled* orbital solid, a *half-filled* orbital partly transparent, and an *empty* orbital more transparent. Figure 2.6 shows the electron density of an *s* orbital.

The solid orbital is filled, the transparent orbital is half-filled, and the ghostly orbital is empty.

full
(has 2 electrons)

half-full
(has 1 electron)

empty
(has no electrons)

Figure 2.6: The electron density for a full, half-full, and empty s orbital.

The same is true for p orbitals. Figure 2.7 shows the electron density for p orbitals that are filled (solid), half-filled (transparent), and empty (ghostly).

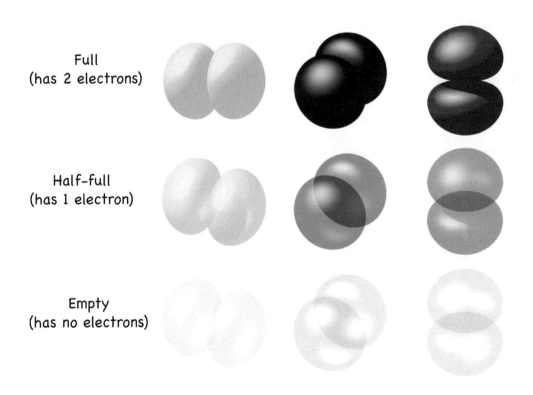

Full
(has 2 electrons)

Half-full
(has 1 electron)

Empty
(has no electrons)

Figure 2.7: The electron density for full, half-full, and empty p orbitals.

2.3.2 The Aufbau principle

The second rule is called the Aufbau principle. It states that the orbitals must be filled in a particular order:

Rule 2: The Aufbau principle: *The orbitals are filled in the order 1s, 2s, 2p, 3s, 3p, 4s, 3d, 4p, 5s, 4d, 5p, 6s, 4f, 5d, 6p, and so on.*

This means that electrons must fill up the 1s orbital before they are placed in the 2s orbital, and electrons must fill the 2s orbital before they are placed in the 2p orbitals and so on. The 1s, 2s, 2p, 3s... order may seem strange at first; it is another (not so obvious) result of quantum mechanics. Notice that the orbitals get bigger and bigger as the order advances. (Compare the size of the 1s orbital to the 2s orbital in Figure 2.3.) This makes sense. The more electrons an atom has, the bigger it should be. The orbitals all overlap each other to make one big electron cloud around the bigger atom. All of the electrons move around in space, but the electrons in larger orbitals are free to move in a bigger space compared to the electrons in smaller orbitals.

2.3.3 Electron configurations of the elements

Now we are ready to see how the electrons are organized inside atoms. Let's consider the simplest atom of all—a hydrogen atom. A hydrogen atom has just one proton and one electron. According to the Pauli Principle, the 1s orbital can hold up to two electrons, so we put the one electron that hydrogen has inside the 1s orbital. The 1s orbital is spherical, so hydrogen has just one electron in a nice spherical electron cloud. Notice that this orbital is "half-filled." That's all there is to it.

Hydrogen

Figure 2.8: A hydrogen atom with one electron in the 1s orbital (half-filled).

Boron

Boron has five electrons: two in the 1*s* orbital, two in the 2*s* orbital, and one in the 2*p* orbital. The first electron to be added to the *p* orbitals can go into either the $2p_x$ $2p_y$ or $2p_z$ orbital. Whichever one we choose, the other two *p* orbitals are empty.

Figure 2.12: A boron atom with two electrons in the 1*s* orbital (full) and two electrons in the 2*s* orbital (full) and one electron in the 2*p* orbitals (half-full $2p_y$; empty $2p_x$, $2p_z$).

Carbon has six electrons: two in the 1*s* orbital, two in the 2*s* orbital, and two in the 2*p* orbital. The second electron to be added to the *p* orbitals must go into one of the empty *p* orbitals. All three *p* orbitals must have one electron in them before they can take a second electron. This means that if the first electron is added to the $2p_y$ orbital, the second electron must go into either the $2p_x$ or $2p_z$ orbitals.

Carbon

Figure 2.13: A carbon atom with two electrons in the 1*s* orbital (full) and two electrons in the 2*s* orbital (full) and two electrons in the 2*p* orbitals (half-full $2p_y$, $2p_z$, ; empty $2p_x$).

Nitrogen

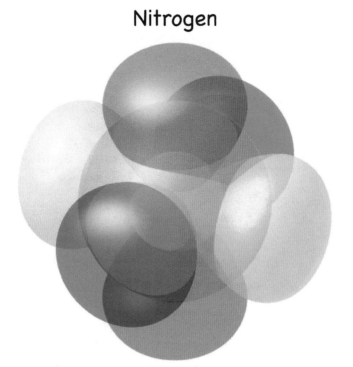

Figure 2.14: A nitrogen atom with two electrons in the 1s orbital (full) and two electrons in the 2s orbital (full) and three electrons in the 2p orbitals (half-full $2p_y$, $2p_z$, , $2p_x$).

Nitrogen has seven electrons: two electrons in the 1s orbital, two electrons in the 2s orbital, and three electrons in the 2p orbitals. The third electron to be added to the p orbitals must go into the remaining empty p orbital. This means that all three p orbitals are now half-full.

Oxygen has eight electrons: two in the 1s orbital, two in the 2s orbital, and four in the 2p orbitals. The fourth electron to be added to the p orbitals can go into any of the half-full orbitals. Now, one of the p orbitals is full and the other two are half-full.

Oxygen

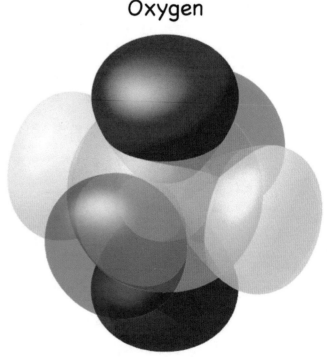

Figure 2.15: An oxygen atom with two electrons in the 1s orbital (full) and two electrons in the 2s orbital (full) and four electrons in the 2p orbitals (full $2p_y$, half-full $2p_z$ and $2p_x$).

Fluorine

Figure 2.16: A fluorine atom with two electrons in the 1s orbital (full) and two electrons in the 2s orbital (full) and five electrons in the 2p orbitals (full $2p_y$ and $2p_z$ with half full $2p_x$).

Fluorine has nine electrons: two in the 1s orbital, two in the 2s orbital, and five in the 2p orbitals. The fifth electron to be added to the p orbitals cannot go into the full p orbital, but goes into one of the two half-full orbitals. Now only one p orbital is half-full.

Neon

Neon has 10 electrons: two in the 1s orbital, two in the 2s orbital, and six in the 2p orbitals. The last electron to be added to the p orbitals goes into the remaining half-full orbital. Now all of the p orbitals are full.

Figure 2.17: A neon atom with two electrons in the 1s orbital (full) and two electrons in the 2s orbital (full) and six electrons in the 2p orbitals (full $2p_y$ $2p_z$ and $2p_x$).

By now you can see the pattern: As we go across a row of the periodic table, each new atom has all the electrons of the previous atom, plus one more. The full list showing all the electrons in their orbitals is called the electron configuration of an atom.

The electron configuration is given by listing the orbitals in the same sequence as they were filled. For example, the electron configuration for hydrogen can be represented as $1s^1$ (pronounced "one"-"es"-"one"), where the "1s" represents the first *s* orbital and the superscript 1 indicates how many electrons are in that orbital. Helium is $1s^2$ (pronounced "one-"es"-"two") and lithium is $1s^2 2s^1$ (pronounced "one"-"es"-"two," "two"-"es"-"one"), and so on. Figure 2.18 shows all of the first and second row elements, their atomic orbitals, and their electron configurations.

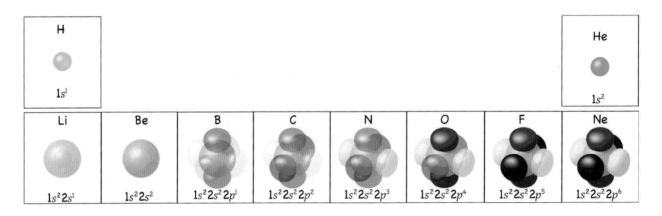

Figure 2.18: The electron configurations for the first and second row elements.

It can become tedious to write out every shell and its electrons. To simplify, the filled shells are often represented using brackets and the symbol for the noble gas of the previous row. For example, lithium can be written as $[He]2s^1$, Beryllium as $[He]2s^2$, Boron as $[He]2s^2 2p^1$ and so on. The electron configurations can be written this way

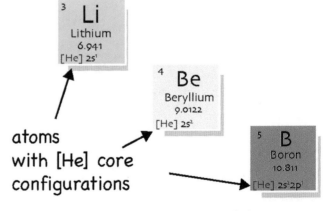

atoms with [He] core configurations

Figure 2.19: The elements lithium (Li), beryllium (Be), and boron (B) from the periodic table, showing the [He] core configuration.

because all of the second row elements have the same electron configuration as helium plus some extra electrons. Likewise all of the third row elements have the same electron configuration as neon plus some extra electrons. All of the fourth row elements have the same electron configuration as argon plus some extra electrons, and so on. These "extra" electrons play a very important role in

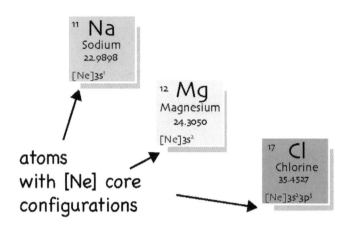

Figure 2.20: The elements sodium (Na), magnesium (Mg), and chlorine (Cl) from the periodic table, showing the [Na] core configuration.

chemistry, so they have a special name of their own; they are called valence electrons. The other electrons buried inside the [He] or [Ne] subshells are called core electrons. Valence electrons are responsible for all chemical bonding. Core electrons do not participate in chemical bonding. We will learn more about chemical bonding and valence electrons in Chapter 2, Part B.

2.4 THE PERIODIC TABLE

The Chemistry Level II Periodic Table, found in the front of this book, shows all the atoms with their electron configurations. Now that we know about orbitals, the structure of the periodic table is clearer.

2.4.1 Noble gases: all subshells filled

First, notice that all the elements in the last column (the noble gases) have *all their subshells completely filled*. For example, helium has two electrons in the 1*s* orbital, so the *s* subshell is completely filled. Neon has a completely filled 1*s* orbital, a completely filled 2*s* orbital, and all three of its 2*p* orbitals completely filled. Krypton has completely filled 1*s*, 2*s*, 2*p*, 3*s*, 3*p*, 4*s*, 3*d*, and 4*p* orbitals, so all its *s*, *p*, and *d* subshells are filled. The electron configurations of the noble gases, with all subshells filled, are very unreactive. That's why the noble gases rarely, if ever, form chemical bonds with other atoms. They are "happy" just as they are, and don't share their electrons with anyone.

2.4.2 Alkali metals: one extra electron

Noble gases

2 **He** Helium 4.003 $1s^2$
10 **Ne** Neon 20.1797 $[He]2s^2 2p^6$
18 **Ar** Argon 39.948 $[Ne]3s^2 3p^6$
36 **Kr** Krypton 83.80 $[Ar]3d^{10}4s^2 4p^6$
54 **Xe** Xenon 131.29 $[Kr]5s^2 4d^{10}5p^6$
86 **Rn** Radon (222) $[Xe]6s^2 4f^{14}5d^{10}6p^6$

Figure 2.21:
The noble gases

Now consider the first column of the periodic table, the alkali metals. Each alkali metal atom has the same electron configuration as the nearest noble gas atom, *except for one extra electron in an* s *orbital.* For example, lithium has two electrons in its 1s orbital, the same as helium, plus one more electron in its 2s orbital. The next element down the column, sodium, has filled 1s, 2s, and 2p orbitals, the same as neon, plus one more electron in its 3s orbital. Potassium is the same as argon (1s, 2s, 2p, 3s, 3p all filled), plus one 4s electron.

In every case this extra *s* electron is very reactive. *If the alkali metal atoms could lose the extra* s *electron, they would be left with only filled subshells, like a noble gas atom.* In fact, in most chemical reactions, that's exactly what the alkali metals do. The alkali metals usually give up (or "donate") an electron to some other atom. That's why they all have similar chemical properties. The chemical properties of the alkali metals are determined by their lone *s* electron.

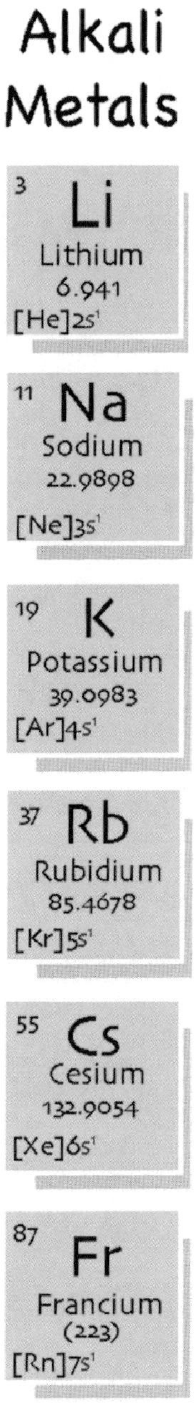

Alkali Metals

3 **Li** Lithium 6.941 $[He]2s^1$
11 **Na** Sodium 22.9898 $[Ne]3s^1$
19 **K** Potassium 39.0983 $[Ar]4s^1$
37 **Rb** Rubidium 85.4678 $[Kr]5s^1$
55 **Cs** Cesium 132.9054 $[Xe]6s^1$
87 **Fr** Francium (223) $[Rn]7s^1$

Figure 2.22:
The alkali metals

Halogens

F
Fluorine
18.9984
[He]2s²2p⁵

Cl
Chlorine
35.4527
[Ne]3s²3p⁵

Br
Bromine
79.904
[Ar]4s²3d¹⁰4p⁵

I
Iodine
126.9045
[Kr]5s²4d¹⁰5p⁵

At
Astatine
(210)
[Xe]6s²4f¹⁴5d¹⁰6p⁵

117

Figure 2.23:
The halogens

2.4.3 Halogens: one missing electron

Look at the next-to-last column, the halogens. Each of these atoms is just one electron short of the nearest noble gas. Fluorine has all of its 1s and 2s electrons, but is missing one 2p electron compared to neon in the next column. Similarly, chlorine has one less 3p electron than argon, bromine has one less than krypton, and so on.

If the halogen atoms could *gain* another electron, they would have all their subshells filled like a noble gas atom, so that's what they usually do. Most reactions of the halogens involve picking up (or "accepting") one electron from another atom. The chemical properties of the halogens are determined by their "missing electron."

2.5 SUMMARY — PART A

- Chemical bonding is the "glue" that holds atoms together to form molecules.

- This "glue" is a result of electrons of one atom being attracted to the protons of another atom.

- The electron cloud surrounding the core of an atom is called an orbital.

- There are different types of orbitals, each with different shapes. *s* orbitals are spherical, *p* orbitals are dumbbell shaped and *d* orbitals are butterfly shaped, donut shaped or dumbbell shaped.

- The Pauli principle (Rule 1) states that each orbital can hold at most two electrons.

- The Aufbau principle (Rule 2) states that electrons fill orbitals in a particular order, beginning with the 1s orbital.

- The periodic table is organized according to the electron configuration of elements. The *periodicity* reflects how elements in a given column share similar chemical properties because of the similarities in their electron shells.

2.6 STUDY QUESTIONS — PART A

1. List the three types of orbitals.
   S orbitals   p orbitals   d orbitals

2. Name and draw the three 2p orbitals.
   2px, 2py, 2pz

3. Name the five 3d orbitals.
   3dxy, 3dxz, 3dyz

4. Describe the Pauli principle.
   only 2 electrons per orbital. (at most)

5. Describe the Aufbau principle.
   electrons fill orbitals in a particular order.

6. Describe the electron configuration for nitrogen.
   2 e in 1s orbital   3 e in 2p orbital
   2 e in 2s orbital

7. Describe the electron configuration for sodium.
   3s¹, 3s², 3s²3p⁵

8. What is special about the orbitals for noble gases?
   all subsells are filled

9. How are the orbitals for the alkali metals different from the noble gases?
   All noble gas orbitals are filled. Alkali have an extra

10. How are the orbitals for the halogens different from the noble gases?
    Halogens have one missing electron.

Helium

Helium has two protons and two electrons. The 1s orbital alone can hold both electrons, so helium has its two electrons, both in the spherical electron cloud of the 1s orbital. Notice that the 1s orbital is now "full."

Figure 2.9: A helium atom with two electrons in the 1s orbital (full).

Lithium

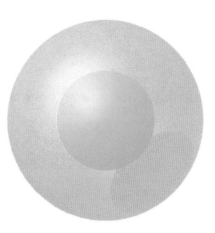

Lithium has three protons and three electrons. According to the Pauli principle, we can put the first two electrons into the 1s orbital, and according to the Aufbau principle we should put the remaining electron in the 2s orbital. The 2s orbital is still spherical, but a bit bigger than the 1s orbital. The 1s orbital is "full," and the 2s orbital is "half-full."

Figure 2.10: A lithium atom with two electrons in the 1s orbital (full) and one electron in the 2s orbital (half-full).

Beryllium

Similarly, beryllium (atomic number 4) has four electrons. Two electrons go into the 1s orbital, and two go into the 2s orbital. Notice that both the 1s orbital and the 2s orbital are "full."

Figure 2.11: A beryllium atom with two electrons in the 1s orbital (full) and two electrons in the 2s orbital (full).

CHEMICAL BONDING — PART B

2.7 MOLECULAR BONDING

2.7.1 Introduction

In Part A, we discussed two important points about chemical bonding. First, we saw that chemical bonding (the sticking together of atoms) is always caused by attractions between electrons (negatively charged) of one atom and protons in the nucleus (positively charged) of the other atom. Second, we saw that electrons in atoms occupy orbitals and that the most favorable electron configurations are those of the noble gases (He, Ne, Ar, Xe...). We will now use these two points to understand how chemical bonding works. We will focus on only a few groups of atoms, since most of the essential elements for chemical bonding are illustrated within these groups.

To take a closer look at chemical bonding, we will focus on the following three important groups of atoms: (1) the alkali metals (Li, Na, K...) and the alkali earths (especially Be, Mg, and Ca); (2) the halogens (F, Cl, Br, I...); and (3) the atoms H, C, N, O, P, and S. This last group does not have a special name, but it is responsible for a very large part of all known chemistry. This group is especially important for the chemistry of life. We will call it the "HCNOPS" group. Most of the relevant information about chemistry can be investigated by looking at the ways in which these three groups of atoms bond to form molecules.

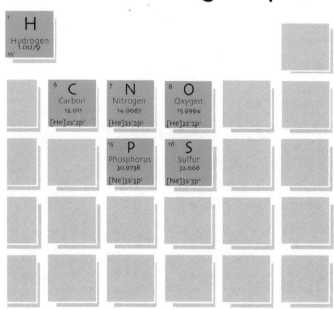

Figure 2.24: The HCNOPS group; hydrogen (H), carbon (C), nitrogen (N), oxygen (O), phosphorus (P), and sulfur (S).

2.7.2 Core and valence electrons

As we saw in Part A, core electrons are the electrons that occupy the same orbitals as the nearest smaller noble gas atom. All other electrons are valence [vā'-ləns] electrons. The word *valence* comes from the Latin word *valere*, which means "to be strong" or "capacity." Hence, the valence electrons are those that have the capacity to form strong bonds. Valence electrons are the "outer" electrons, or electrons that are placed into atomic orbitals last. Typically, these electrons are said to occupy the "outer shell."

For example, the electron configuration for carbon is $1s^2 2s^2 2p^2$. The nearest smaller noble gas atom is helium, He, with electron configuration $1s^2$. So for carbon, the core electrons are its two 1s electrons, and the valence electrons are the $2s^2 2p^2$ electrons.

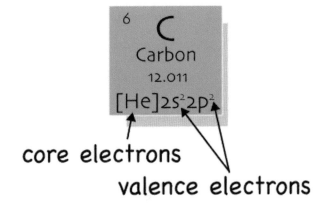

Figure 2.25: The element carbon as shown on the periodic table with a [He] core and four valence electrons.

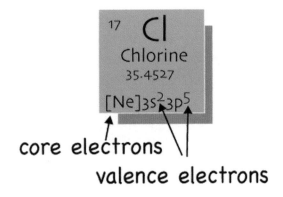

Figure 2.26: The element chlorine as shown on the periodic table with a [Ne] core and seven valence electrons.

Similarly, the electron configuration for chlorine, Cl, is $1s^2 2s^2 2p^6 3s^2 3p^5$. The nearest smaller noble gas is neon, Ne, with an electron configuration of $1s^2 2s^2 2p$. Therefore, for chlorine, the $1s^2 2s^2 2p$ electrons are the core electrons and the $3s^2 3p^5$ electrons are the valence electrons.

The valence electrons are the only electrons involved in chemical bonding. There are basically two types of bonds formed by valence electrons: ionic [ī-ä′-nik] bonds and covalent bonds. The difference between these two types of chemical bonds has to do with whether the valence electrons that form the chemical bond are shared or not shared between the individual atoms. In a covalent bond the electrons are shared between the two atoms, and in an ionic bond the electrons are not shared.

2.8 IONIC BONDING

2.8.1 Ions

In an ionic bond, the valence electrons are not shared between the individual atoms. This means that the electrons of one atom are either lost to (or gained by) the other atom. When an atom (or molecule) gains or loses an electron, it is called an ion [ī′-ən]. Ionic bonding always occurs between ions. The atoms that most readily form ions are those that have either one or two electrons more than their nearest noble gas, or one or two electrons fewer than their nearest noble gas. The electron configuration for the noble gases is the most *energetically stable* configuration for an atom. This means that all atoms would rather have an electron configuration like that of a noble gas than have fewer or extra electrons. Because of this, atoms will readily give up or gain electrons and become ions to become more like a noble gas.

For example, the alkali metals on the far left-hand column of the periodic table all have only one valence electron. This means that all of these atoms have only one electron more than their nearest noble gas. Because they would rather have an electron configuration like a noble gas, they will easily give up their extra electron to become a positively charged ion. Lithium, sodium, potassium, and the other alkali metals readily form ions, giving up their single valence electron. They are not exactly like noble gases, but they do have the same electron configuration as a noble gas. Because they still have the same number of protons (but one fewer electron), they are all positively charged. That is, they form positive ions called cations [kat'-ī-ənz]. They are illustrated with a small "plus" sign in the upper right-hand corner of their symbol.

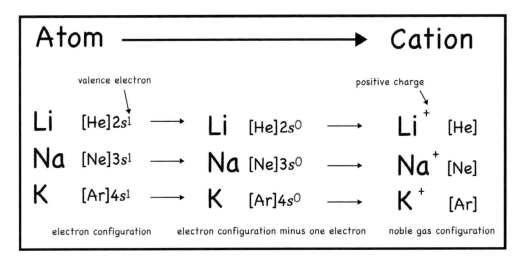

Figure 2.27: The alkali metals lose one electron becoming positively charged ions called cations.

The halogens are on the far right-hand side of the periodic table, and each of these atoms has one fewer electron than the nearest noble gas. In order to have an electron configuration like a noble gas, each of these atoms will readily gain an extra electron to form an ion. Because they have an extra electron, they are negative ions, or anions [a'-nī-ənz], and are illustrated with a small "minus" sign in the upper right-hand corner next to their symbol.

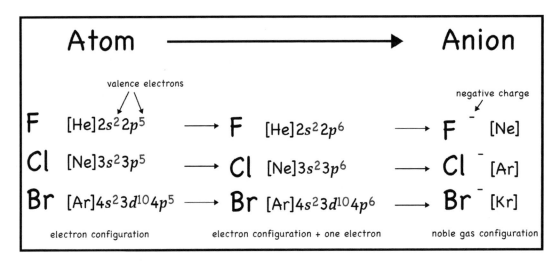

Figure 2.28: The halogens gain one electron becoming negatively charged ions called anions.

2.8.2 Ionic compounds

Because an alkali metal has one more electron than a noble gas and a halogen has one fewer electrons than a noble gas, when an alkali metal meets a halogen, the electron on the alkali metal can jump to the halogen, thus forming an ionic bond. For example, when a lithium atom meets a fluorine atom, the valence electron on the lithium can jump to the fluorine atom creating two ions: a positively charged lithium cation and a negatively charged fluorine anion. Because the lithium ion is positively charged and the flourine ion is negatively charged, they are attracted to each other. They will stick together forming an ionic bond.

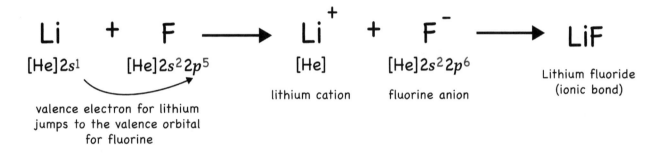

Figure 2.29: Lithium (Li) reacts with fluorine (F) to make lithium fluoride (LiF), a salt.

In the same way, any alkali metal can form an ionic compound with any halogen. As we saw in Section 1.3.5, compounds with halogens and alkali metals are called salts. Table salt, NaCl, is an ionic compound with sodium (an alkali metal) and chlorine (a halogen). Potassium chloride, KCl, is a table salt substitute used by people who need to reduce their sodium intake.

2.8.3 Alkali earth metals

The alkali earth metals, found in the second column along the left-hand side of the periodic table, all have two electrons more than their nearest noble gas. These atoms also form ions and ionic compounds, giving up both of their valence electrons. The ions formed by these atoms have a +2 ("plus two") charge, since they are missing *two* of their electrons.

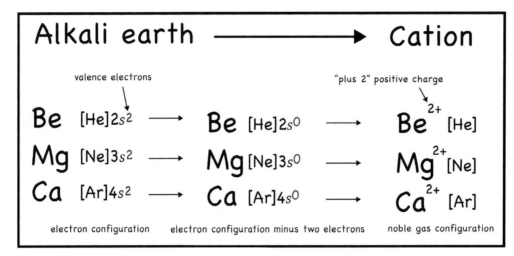

Figure 2.30: The alkali earth metals lose two electrons to become cations with a +2 charge.

They form ionic compounds with the halogens, just like the alkali metals. However, because they are missing two of their electrons, they combine with *two* halogen ions instead of just one. For example, the ionic compound formed by magnesium and chlorine is $MgCl_2$ (one magnesium ion and two chlorine ions). Similarly, barium and calcium form the ionic compounds $BaCl_2$ and $CaCl_2$ with chlorine ions.

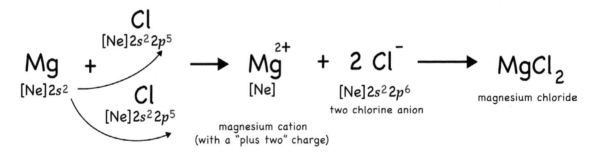

Figure 2.31: Magnesium (Mg) reacts with two chlorine (Cl) ions to make magnesium chloride ($MgCl_2$), a salt.

2.8.4 Hydrogen ions

Perhaps the most important ion of all is the hydrogen ion, H^+. Since hydrogen atoms only have one electron, the hydrogen ion, H^+ has no electrons. Often the H^+ ion is simply called a proton since it has no neutrons and no electrons.

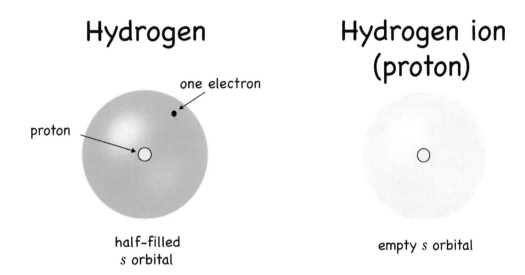

Hydrogen

one electron

proton

half-filled
s orbital

Hydrogen ion (proton)

empty s orbital

Figure 2.32: A hydrogen atom that loses an electron becomes a hydrogen ion, or proton.

Hydrogen ions form ionic compounds, just like the alkali metals. Hydrogen ions combine with the halogens to make hydrogen chloride (HCl), hydrogen bromide (HBr), and so on. These compounds are not salts. Instead, they are acids. Ionic compounds with H^+ often form acids. We will look at acids in more detail in Chapters 4 and 5.

$$H^+ + Cl^- \longrightarrow HCl$$ hydrogen chloride or hydrochloric acid

$$H^+ + Br^- \longrightarrow HBr$$ hydrogen bromide or hydrobromic acid

$$H^+ + F^- \longrightarrow HF$$ hydrogen fluoride or hydrofluoric acid

Figure 2.33: Hydrogen ions react with halogens to make acids.

2.8.5 Ionic compounds often dissolve in water

Ionic compounds are often white, solid, crystalline materials like table salt (NaCl), and are called ionic solids. In an ionic solid, the ions are organized in arrays of alternating cations and anions.

The attractions between the ions are maximized with each cation surrounded by as many anions as possible and each cation surrounded by as many anions as possible. As a result, the bonding forces for ionic solids are very strong.

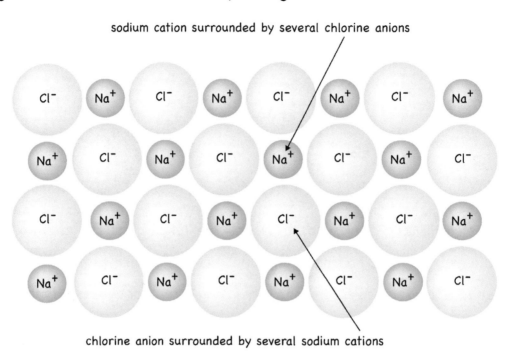

Figure 2.34: Sodium chloride (NaCl) is an ionic solid.

When ionic solids are placed in water, the ions inside the crystal can easily come apart to form free ions. Most ionic solids can easily dissolve in water. The salty taste of ionic compounds in water is caused by the ions they release. Seawater is a very concentrated solution of many different kinds of positive and negative ions. The ability of salty water to conduct electricity is due to the presence of dissolved ions.

2.9 COVALENT BONDING

As we saw in Section 2.6, ionic bonds occur when two atoms achieve the electron configuration of a noble gas by losing or gaining electrons. We saw how Li loses an electron and fluorine gains an electron to form an ionic bond in the compound LiF. But ionic bonding cannot explain how bonds form between two identical atoms, such as H_2, F_2, Cl_2, and N_2. Also, ionic bonding cannot explain how bonds form for many different types of molecules such as methane, CH_4, or ammonia, NH_3. To explain how these molecules bond, we need to understand covalent bonding.

2.9.1 σ bonding

Covalent bonds are formed between atoms that *share* their electrons. Molecules like H_2, F_2, CH_4, and NH_3 are held together by covalent bonds because the atoms in these molecules share their electrons.

To see how covalent bonding works, we will consider the simplest possible case, the bonding between two hydrogen atoms to form a hydrogen molecule, H_2. Each H atom has one electron in a $1s$ orbital with a $1s^1$ electron configuration. When the $1s$ orbitals of the two H atoms come together, they touch and overlap. These overlapping $1s$ orbitals actually merge into one larger orbital that covers both atoms. This larger orbital is called a sigma bonding orbital and is denoted by the symbol "σ."

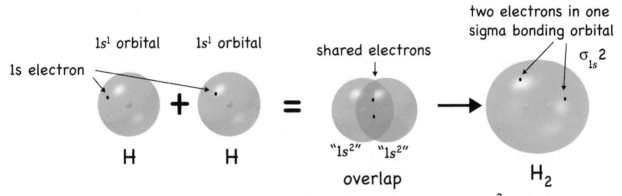

Figure 2.35: A σ_{1s^2} sigma bond forms by the overlap of two $1s^2$ orbitals.

Consequently, the electrons in each orbital are *shared* by both atoms. The two electrons that were originally in the 1s orbitals of the individual H atoms now occupy this one larger σ_{1s} orbital in the H_2 molecule. Each atom has a new $\sigma_{1s}2$ electron configuration, which is like the stable noble gas (helium) electron configuration $1s^2$. The σ_{1s} bonding orbital is an example of a molecular orbital and is responsible for the covalent bonding between the H atoms in the H_2 molecule.

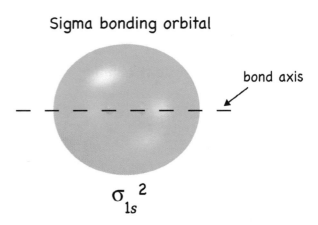

Sigma bonding orbital

bond axis

$\sigma_{1s}{}^2$

Figure 2.36: A sigma bonding orbital.

In general, sigma bonds form whenever two atomic orbitals meet "head on." They form a molecular orbital whose electron density is concentrated along the bond axis (an imaginary line joining the two atoms). A sigma bond is shaped something like a football and forms whenever two *s* orbitals overlap.

For a covalent bond to form, the atomic orbitals cannot be "filled." The individual atoms must have fewer electrons than their nearest noble gas configuration. Helium does not form molecular orbitals because helium has a full 1*s* orbital. Since the 1*s* orbital for helium is already filled, when two helium atoms come together the individual 1*s* orbitals cannot merge into a single bonding orbital because there are too many electrons. Molecular orbitals follow the Pauli principle and can hold only two electrons per orbital, just like atomic orbitals. (See Appendix B.)

The points to remember about covalent bonds are as follows:

• Whenever two atomic orbitals overlap, they merge into a larger molecular orbital.

• If the overlapping orbitals are both half-filled, a covalent bond is formed.

• If the overlapping orbitals are both filled, no bond is formed.

2.9.2 π bonding

We have already seen how sigma bonds are formed when the two 1*s* orbitals of hydrogen combine to form one molecular σ bonding orbital, but what happens when two *p* orbitals combine or when a *p* orbital combines with an *s* orbital? Do they all form sigma bonding orbitals, or are there other kinds of bonding orbitals that can form?

As it turns out, there are *two* basic types of covalent bonding orbitals formed by overlapping atomic orbitals: sigma bonding orbitals and pi [pī] bonding orbitals. Pi bonding orbitals form when two *p* atomic orbitals combine to form a molecular orbital whose electron density is distributed above and below the bond axis. Pi bonds form between the lobes of *p* orbitals or *d* orbitals in a side-by-side fashion. Each pi bonding orbital holds two electrons and is denoted by the symbol "π."

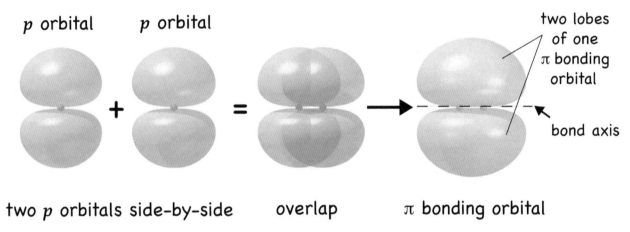

Figure 2.37: Two side-by-side *p* orbitals form a π bonding orbital.

2.10 HYBRID ORBITALS

We have seen how molecular bonding orbitals are formed when valence electrons in atomic orbitals overlap and merge forming both sigma and pi bonds. Sometimes, however, valence electrons form orbitals called hybrid [hī'-brəd] orbitals before they overlap into sigma and pi bonds. For example, beryllium has two valence shell electrons in the 2*s* orbital. On first inspection, it seems that these electrons should not form bonds at all because they are both in a full *s* orbital. However, we also see that there are three empty *p* orbitals. Can these orbitals be used to form bonds? Would beryllium then form three bonds? In fact, the empty *p* orbitals can participate in bonding, but the elements in this column typically form two bonds. Why? These elements usually form two bonds because the *s* orbitals and *p* orbitals for these elements combine to form hybrid orbitals.

A hybrid orbital is a combination of two or more different kinds of orbitals, such as an *s* orbital and a *p* orbital, or a *p* orbital and a *d* orbital. The word *hybrid* comes from the word *hybridia,* which in Latin is the offspring of a tame sow and a wild boar. Hence, a *hybridia* is a mixture of the tame and the wild. A "hybrid orbital" is a mixture of two different types of orbitals.

There are three different types of hybrid orbitals: the *sp* hybrid, [say "es -pee-hybrid"], the *sp²* hybrid, [say "es-pee-two hybrid"], and the *sp³* hybrid [say "es-pee-three-hybrid"]. As their names imply, the *sp* hybrid is made of an *s* orbital and a *p* orbital. The *sp²* hybrid is made of an *s* orbital and *two p* orbitals, and the *sp³* hybrid is made of an *s* orbital and all *three p* orbitals. As we will see, the hybrid orbitals explain the molecular shapes of some molecules.

2.10.1 *sp* hybrid orbitals

When an *s* orbital and a *p* orbital combine, they form *two sp* hybrid orbitals. Note that the *sp* hybrid orbitals have one small lobe and one larger lobe that point in opposite directions.

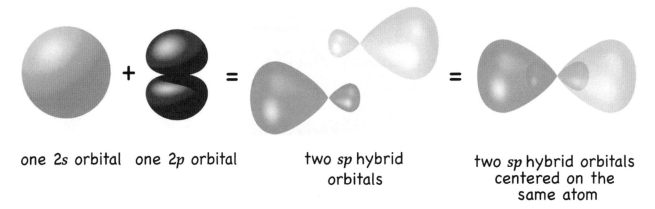

one 2*s* orbital   one 2*p* orbital   two *sp* hybrid   two *sp* hybrid orbitals
                                            orbitals   centered on the
                                                                  same atom

Figure 2.38: One 2*s* and one 2*p* orbital form two *sp* hybrid orbitals.

Hybrid orbitals formed in this way are often used to make linear molecules, such as beryllium hydride, acetylene, and carbon dioxide. For example, beryllium has three empty

2p orbitals. Beryllium uses one of its 2p orbitals to form a hybrid orbital with the 2s orbital in the beryllium hydride molecule. Notice that beryllium hydride is a linear molecule.

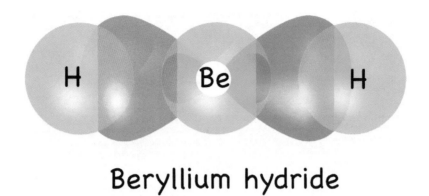

Beryllium hydride

Figure 2.39: Beryllium hydride formed with two *sp* hybrid orbitals.

2.10.2 sp^2 hybrid orbitals

An s orbital and *two p* orbitals can combine to form *three sp^2* hybrid orbitals. Each sp^2 orbital makes an angle of 120° to the others, and all three point to the corners of an equilateral triangle. sp^2 hybrid orbitals are often used to make molecules with a "trigonal planar" geometry (shaped like a triangle), such as borane and formaldehyde.

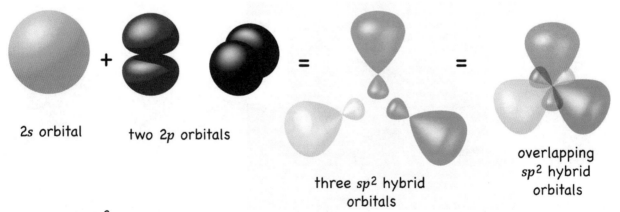

2s orbital two 2p orbitals three sp^2 hybrid orbitals overlapping sp^2 hybrid orbitals

Figure 2.40: sp^2 hybrid orbitals form from an s orbital and two p orbitals. .

For example, boron forms three sp^2 hybrids with its 2s orbital and two of its 2p orbitals when it combines with hydrogen to make borane. Notice that borane is a trigonal planar molecule and that the hydrogens form a triangle around the central boron atom.

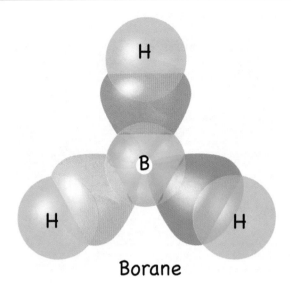

Borane

Figure 2.41: Borane with three sp^2 hybrid orbitals.

2.10.3 sp^3 hybrid orbitals

An *s* orbital and *three p* orbitals combine to form *four sp^3* hybrid orbitals. The four sp^3 hybrid orbitals point to the corners of a regular tetrahedron (a pyramid with triangles on all sides). sp^3 hybrid orbitals are often used to make tetrahedral molecules, which is perhaps the most common shape for the elements, C, N, O, and S.

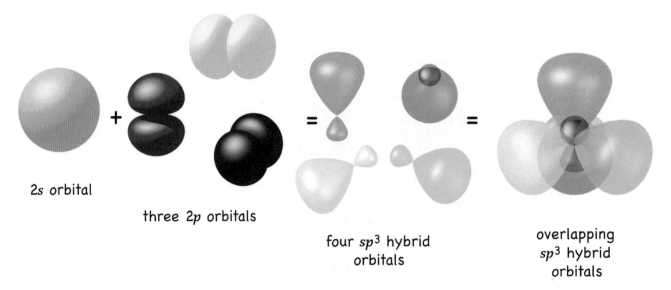

2*s* orbital

three 2*p* orbitals

four sp^3 hybrid orbitals

overlapping sp^3 hybrid orbitals

Figure 2.42: sp^3 hybrid orbitals form from an *s* orbital and three *p* orbitals.

For example, carbon forms four sp^3 hybrid orbitals with its 2s orbital and the three 2p orbitals when it combines with hydrogen to make methane. Notice that methane is a tetrahedral molecule with the four sp^3 hybrid orbitals sticking out in four directions.

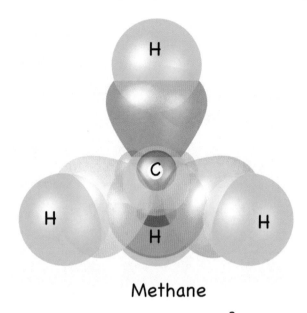

Methane

Figure 2.43: Methane with four sp^3 hybrid orbitals.

(See Appendix A for a full discussion on how to build molecules with covalent bonds.)

2.11 SUMMARY — PART B

- There are two types of bonds formed by valence electrons: ionic bonds and covalent bonds. Ionic bonds do not share electrons; covalent bonds do share electrons.

- When an atom gains or loses an electron it is called an ion. Positively charged ions (atoms that have lost an electron) are called cations, and negatively charged ions (atoms that have gained an electron) are called anions.

- A hydrogen atom that loses an electron is a proton.

- A sigma bonding orbital has the symbol σ and is a molecular orbital of two overlapping atomic orbitals (such as two overlapping s orbitals) in which the electron density lies along the bond axis.

- A pi bonding orbital has the symbol π and is a molecular orbital of two overlapping atomic orbitals oriented side-by-side (such as two side-by-side *p* orbitals) in which the electron density is above and below the bond axis.

- Hybrid orbitals form when two or more different kinds of atomic orbitals combine to form a molecular orbital.

- When an *s* orbital and a *p* orbital combine, they form *two sp* hybrid orbitals.

- When an *s* orbital combines with two *p* orbitals, they form *three sp²* hybrid orbitals.

- When an *s* orbital combines with three *p* orbitals, they form *four sp³* hybrid orbitals.

2.12 STUDY QUESTIONS — PART B

1. When lithium loses an electron, is it an anion or a cation?

2. When sodium loses an electron, is it an anion or a cation?

3. When chlorine gains an electron, is it an anion or a cation?

4. Does fluorine gain or lose an electron in the ionic compound NaF?

5. How many electrons does magnesium lose when it forms an ionic compound with Cl?

6. How many chlorine atoms combine to form an ionic compound with calcium?

7. What kind of bond does an H_2 molecule have?

8. Name the molecular bonding orbital for molecular hydrogen.

9. What kind of molecular orbital is formed by two side-by-side *p* orbitals?

10. List the three types of hybrid orbitals.

CHAPTER 3 CHEMICAL REACTIONS

3.1 CHEMICAL REACTIONS

3.1.1 Introduction

We saw in Chapter 2 how atoms bond with each other through their electrons to form molecules. But what happens to molecules when they meet other atoms or molecules? Do they interact? If so, what happens to their electrons? Do they keep them or give them away? How many molecules or atoms can interact at one time? How many different ways can molecules react?

In Chapter 3, we will study how molecules change their bonds. The processes by which chemical bonds are broken and formed are called chemical reactions. We will look specifically at how chemical bonds are broken and reformed during chemical reactions.

3.1.2 Reactants and products

What are chemical reactions? When we mix baking soda and vinegar, something unusual happens. We observe bubbles and discover that heat is being released. This "something" is evidence of a chemical reaction. A chemical reaction occurs whenever bonds between atoms are created or destroyed. Bonds are being created and destroyed when vinegar reacts with baking soda. We will use the baking soda–vinegar reaction to illustrate many of the most important features of chemical reactions.

In a chemical reaction, the original molecules, called reactants, are converted into new molecules, called products. In the case of baking soda and vinegar, the reactants are the baking soda (sodium bicarbonate [sō'-dē-əm bī-kär'-bə-nāt]) and vinegar (acetic [ə-sē'-tik] acid). The products are carbon dioxide (seen as bubbles), sodium acetate [sō'-dē-əm a'-sə-tāt], and water.

We can write a chemical reaction by showing the reactants on the left-hand side of a chemical equation and the products on the right-hand side. The "arrow" in a chemical equation behaves in the same way an "equals sign" behaves in a mathematical equation.

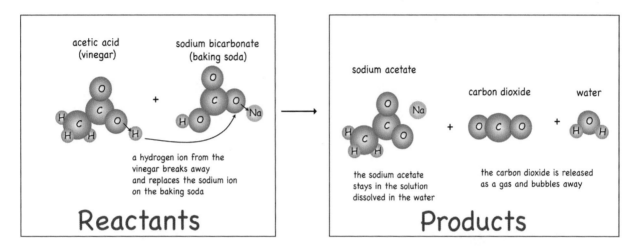

Figure 3.1: The chemical reaction between vinegar and baking soda. The reactants are on the left side of the arrow and the products are on the right side of the arrow.

It is complicated to write out chemical reactions by drawing each individual atom, so chemists use chemical formulas to describe chemical reactions. Using chemical formulas, the chemical reaction for baking soda and vinegar can be written as follows:

| acetic acid | sodium bicarbonate | sodium acetate | carbon dioxide | water |

$$C_2H_4O_2 + NaCO_3H \ \text{-->} \ NaC_2H_3O_2 + CO_2 + H_2O$$

This way of writing a chemical reaction is called a chemical equation. A chemical equation is similar to a mathematical equation (such as 2 + 2 = 4), but it shows what happens to molecules or atoms when they react.

3.1.3 Chemical formulas

In a chemical equation, each molecule is represented by an empirical [im-pir'-i-kəl] formula. An empirical formula is a specific type of chemical formula that shows which atoms are in the molecule and how many of each type are present. The number of each kind of atom is represented by a subscript. For example, acetic acid has 2 carbon atoms, 4 hydrogen atoms, and 2 oxygen atoms. So the molecular formula is $C_2H_4O_2$.

Another kind of chemical formula shows how the atoms are bonded to each other. This is called a structural formula. A structural formula shows how each atom fits together with the other atoms in a molecule. A structural formula contains more information than a molecular formula, since it shows how the atoms are bonded to each other and the number of bonds between each atom. The structural and empirical formulas for acetic acid are written as follows:

Name	Structural formula	Empirical formula

acetic acid

$$\begin{array}{ccc} H & O & \\ | & \| & \\ H-C-C-&O-H \\ | & \\ H \end{array}$$

$C_2H_4O_2$

Notice that one oxygen has a *double bond* to one of the carbon atoms. Also notice that each carbon atom has four bonds (the double bond counts as two), each oxygen has two bonds, and each hydrogen has one bond. All of the atoms follow the rules for bonding as discussed in Chapter 2. See Appendix B for more examples showing the empirical and structural formulas for a variety of molecules.

3.1.4 Stoichiometry

A chemical equation not only shows which molecules are reacting, but also how many molecules of each reactant are involved and how many molecules of each product are produced.

A chemical equation shows the number of each type of reactant and product molecule.

For example, when we write the chemical equation for the reaction between vinegar and baking soda, we see that one molecule of vinegar reacts with one molecule of baking soda to give one molecule of sodium acetate, one molecule of carbon dioxide, and one molecule of water.

$$1 \ C_2H_4O_2 + 1 \ NaCO_3H \ \text{-->} \ 1 \ NaC_2H_3O_2 + 1 \ CO_2 + 1 \ H_2O$$

acetic   sodium   sodium   carbon   water
acid   bicarbonate   acetate   dioxide

This equation shows the stoichiometry [stoi-kē-ä'-mə-trē] of the chemical reaction between vinegar and baking soda. The word *stoichiometry* comes from the Greek word *stoicheion* which means "component," and *metron* which means "measure." Stoichiometry means the "measurements of components" and shows how many molecules of each reactant and product are involved in a chemical reaction. The red "1" in front of each molecule is called the stoichiometric coefficient [stoi-kē-ō-me'-trik kō-ə-fi'-shənt]. The stoichiometric coefficient helps chemists *balance* chemical equations.

3.1.5 Balancing chemical equations

When two or more atoms or molecules combine to form a new molecule, they do so in a precise way. If we look again at the equation for acetic acid and baking soda we discover that the *number of atoms of each element on each side of the equation stays the same.* That is, the number of carbon atoms on the left-hand side (three—with two in acetic [ə-sē'-tik] acid and one in baking soda) equals the number of carbon atoms on the right-hand side (There are three—two in acetate and one in carbon dioxide).

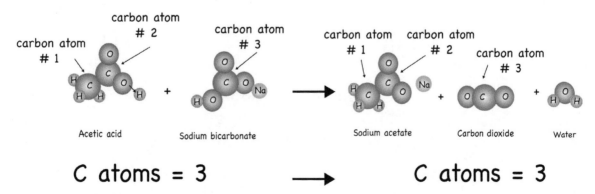

Figure 3.2: There are three carbon atoms on each side of the chemical equation for the reaction between acetic acid (vinegar) and sodium bicarbonate (baking soda).

The same is true for oxygen (5), hydrogen (5), and sodium (1).

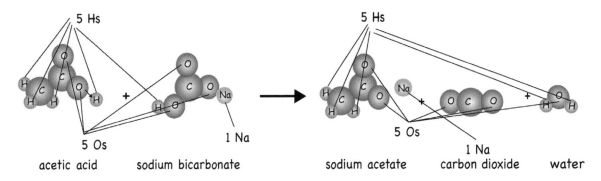

Figure 3.3: There are five oxygen atoms, five hydrogen atoms and one sodium atom on each side of the chemical equation for the reaction between acetic acid (vinegar) and sodium bicarbonate (baking soda).

$$1\ C_2H_4O_2 + 1\ NaCO_3H \dashrightarrow 1\ NaC_2H_3O_2 + 1\ CO_2 + 1\ H_2O$$

The equation for the reaction between vinegar and baking soda, as it is written, is said to be balanced because it obeys the law of conservation of mass. The law of conservation of mass states:

> *In a chemical reaction atoms are neither created nor*
>
> *destroyed, only rearranged to make other molecules.*

A balanced equation shows the conservation of mass by keeping the number of atoms the same on both sides of the equation. In this way, the total mass on the left-hand side of the equation equals the total mass on the right-hand side. So, the rule is as follows:

The number of atoms (for each element) must be equal on both sides of the equation.

But what about the following equation?

$$H_2 + O_2 \dashrightarrow H_2O$$

There are two oxygens on the left-hand side of the equation but only one on the right-hand side, so this equation is unbalanced. We need to find a way to make the number of atoms on the left-hand side of the equation match the number of atoms on the right-hand side.

3.1.6 Using the stoichiometric coefficient

To balance chemical equations, we adjust the stoichiometric coefficients. We could write the chemical equation for water as:

$$(1) \ O_2 + (1) \ H_2 \ \text{-->} \ (1) \ H_2O$$

where the numeric one (1) in front of each molecule is the stoichiometric coefficient. If we were to draw the molecules, the reaction would look like this:

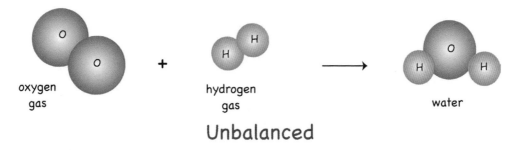

oxygen   +   hydrogen

gas   gas   water

Unbalanced

Figure 3.4: An unbalanced chemical equation for the formation of water.

When we adjust a stoichiometric coeffecient, we multiply all the atoms in a molecule. For example, if we were to place a (2) in front of the H_2 molecule, we would have four hydrogen atoms; if we were to place a (3) in front, we would have six hydrogen atoms; and if we were to place a (4) in front, we would have eight hydrogen atoms and so on.

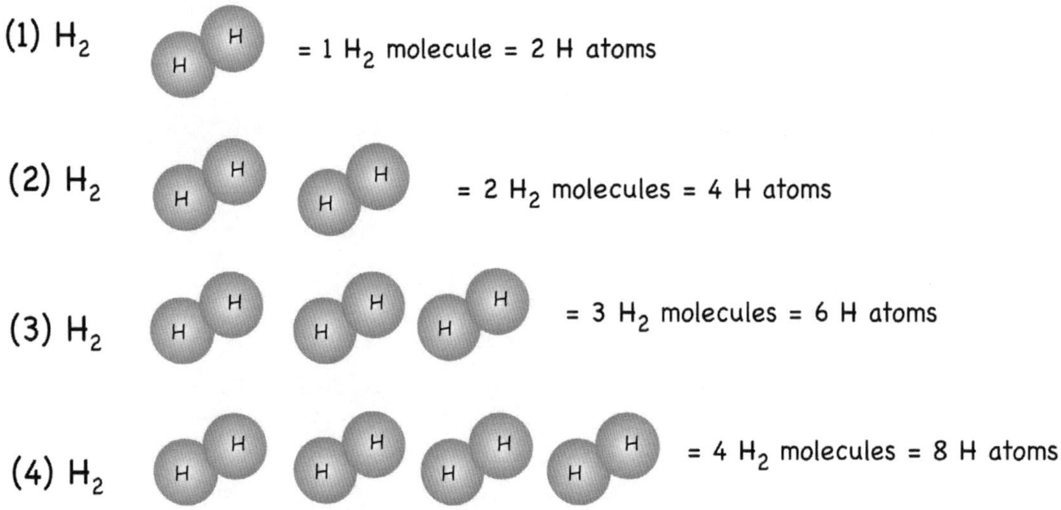

(1) H_2 = 1 H_2 molecule = 2 H atoms

(2) H_2 = 2 H_2 molecules = 4 H atoms

(3) H_2 = 3 H_2 molecules = 6 H atoms

(4) H_2 = 4 H_2 molecules = 8 H atoms

Figure 3.5: The number of atoms in a chemical equation can be adjusted by multiplying a molecule by the stoichiometric coeffecient.

To balance the equation we can change the stoichiometric coefficient in front of one or more of the molecules in the equation. We can use any number we want. One possibility is to multiply the oxygen molecule by 2. This would give us:

$$(1)\ H_2 + (2)\ O_2\ \text{-->}\ (1)\ H_2O$$

However, we can see that the total number of hydrogen atoms and oxygen atoms are not the same on both sides of the equation, and the equation is still unbalanced.

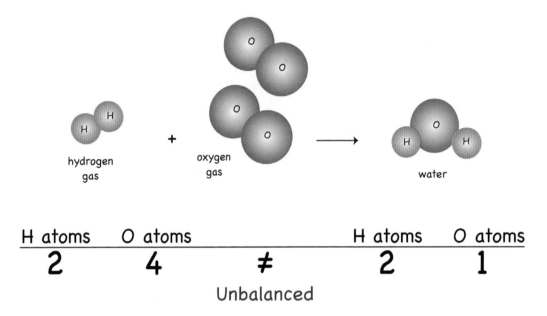

H atoms	O atoms		H atoms	O atoms
2	4	≠	2	1

Unbalanced

Figure 3.6: The stoichiometric coeffecient for oxygen is now 2, but the equation is still unbalanced. There are four oxygen atoms on the left-hand side of the equation and only one oxygen atom on the right-hand side of the equation.

If we multiply the hydrogen molecule by two and the water molecule by two but keep the oxygen molecule multiplied by one, we would get:

$$(2)\ H_2 + (1)\ O_2\ \text{-->}\ (2)\ H_2O$$

We can see that the equation is now balanced with four hydrogen atoms on the left of the equation and four on the right, and two oxygen atoms on the left of the equation and two on the right.

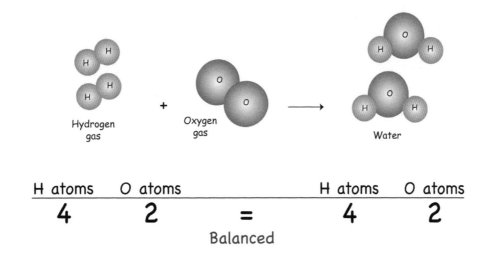

Figure 3.7: The stoichiometric coeffecient for oxygen is (1) and the stoichiometric coeffecient for H is (2). The equation is now balanced with an equal number of oxygen atoms and hydrogen atoms on both sides of the equation.

In order for chemical equations to be meaningful, the reactions must always be balanced. But how do balanced chemical reactions help chemists?

3.2 USING CHEMICAL EQUATIONS

Balanced equations allow chemists to set up a chemical reaction with exactly the right amounts of each chemical. It is like a recipe for "cooking" (reacting) some "ingredients" (reactants) to get a "cake" (products). For example, suppose we wanted to set up a reaction between acetic acid ($C_2H_4O_2$) and sodium bicarbonate ($NaCO_3H$) in such a way that all of the acetic acid and all of the sodium bicarbonate are consumed. How many grams of acetic acid and sodium bicarbonate do we need to mix?

3.2.1 Calculating mass

The chemical equation is a "recipe" for a chemical reaction, but it tells us how many *molecules* react when what we need to know is how many *grams* to mix for the reaction. How do we calculate the mass (number of grams) we need of a product or reactant? We use both the chemical formulas *and* the stoichiometric coefficients to *convert moles to grams* for the reactants and products.

Recall from Chapter 1 that the mass of an element is given in *atomic mass units (amu)*. Also recall from Chapter 1 that a mole of atoms weighs the same (in grams) as its atomic mass (in amu). Therefore, the atomic mass of oxygen is 16 amu, and a mole of oxygen weighs 16 grams. The atomic mass for helium is 4 amu, and a mole of helium atoms weighs 4 grams, and so on. The same is true for molecules. For example, a mole of hydrogen gas, H_2, has mass (in grams) equal to the sum of the atomic masses (in amu) for the individual hydrogen atoms:

1 mole H_2 => 2 X 1 gram (atomic mass for H) = 2 grams

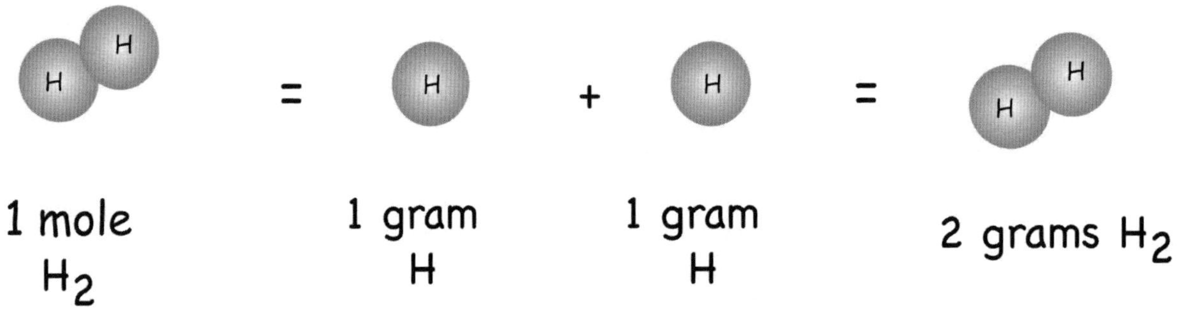

Figure 3.8: 1 mole of hydrogen gas converts to 2 grams of hydrogen gas.

A mole of water molecules has mass (in grams) equal to the sum of the atomic mass for the two hydrogen atoms and the oxygen atom.

1 mole H_2O => 2 X 1 gram (atomic mass for H) + 16 grams (atomic mass for O)

= 18 grams

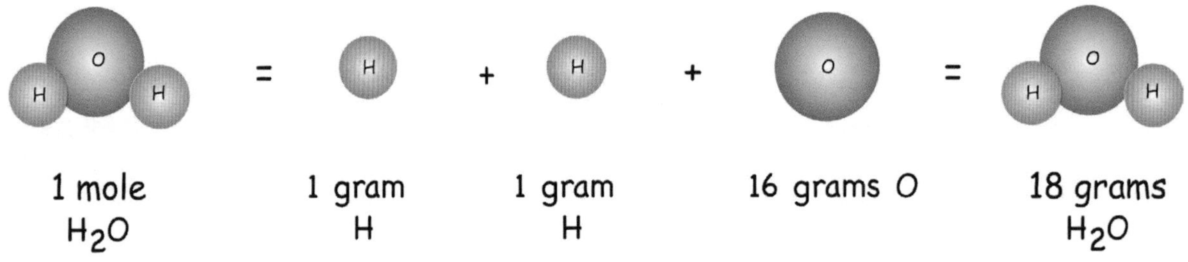

Figure 3.9: 1 mole of water converts to 18 grams of water.

A mole of acetic acid equals the sum of the atomic mass for the two carbon atoms, the four hydrogen atoms, and the two oxygen atoms. So a mole of vinegar weighs:

1 mole $C_2H_4O_2$ => 2 X 12 grams (atomic mass for C) + 4 X 1 gram (atomic mass for H)

+ 2 X 16 gram (atomic mass for O) = 60 grams

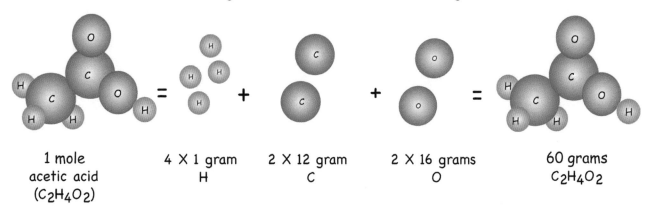

| 1 mole acetic acid ($C_2H_4O_2$) | 4 X 1 gram H | 2 X 12 gram C | 2 X 16 grams O | 60 grams $C_2H_4O_2$ |

Figure 3.10: 1 mole of acetic acid converts to 60 grams of acetic acid.

You can begin to see that if we know how many moles of molecules will react with each other, we can calculate the masses (in grams) that will react with each other.

Let's go back to our question at the beginning of this section, "How many grams of acetic acid and sodium bicarbonate do we need to mix so that all of the reactants are consumed?" According to the balanced chemical equation, one molecule of acetic acid reacts with one molecule of sodium bicarbonate. Therefore, 1 mole of acetic acid molecules will react with 1 mole of sodium bicarbonate molecules. One mole of acetic acid molecules weighs 60 grams and 1 mole of sodium bicarbonate weighs 84 grams.

1 X 23 grams (atomic mass for Na) + 1 X 1 gram (atomic mass for H) + 1 X 12 grams (atomic mass for C) + 3 X 16 grams (atomic mass for O) = 84 grams

Therefore, if we use 60 grams of acetic acid and 84 grams of sodium bicarbonate, they will react completely, with nothing left over.

3.2.2 Combination reaction

We can use balanced chemical reactions to calculate the amount (in grams) of reactants and products for any chemical reaction. For example, in the combination reaction between sodium and chlorine, we find that 2 moles of sodium metal react with 1 mole of chlorine gas to give 2 moles of sodium chloride salt. Recall that a combination reaction occurs when two or more molecules combine to form a single product.

$$2 \text{ Na } + \text{Cl}_2 \text{ --> } 2 \text{ NaCl}$$

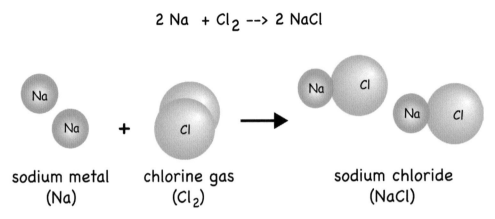

sodium metal   chlorine gas   sodium chloride
    (Na)   (Cl_2)   (NaCl)

Figure 3.11: The combination reaction of sodium metal and chlorine gas to produce sodium chloride.

Sample Problem 3.1

(a) If we started with 2 moles of sodium metal, how many grams of chlorine gas would we need? (b) How many grams of sodium chloride salt will be made?

— —

Answer

We know from the chemical equation that 2 moles of sodium metal react with 1 mole of chlorine gas to make 2 moles of sodium chloride. Since we need 1 mole of chlorine gas, we can calculate how many grams that is:

$$1 \text{ mole } \text{Cl}_2 = 2 \times 35 \text{ grams Cl} = 70 \text{ grams } \text{Cl}_2$$

(a) *We will need 70 grams of Cl$_2$.*

We also know from the chemical equation that we will make 2 moles of sodium chloride. We can calculate the amount of sodium chloride in grams.

2 moles NaCl = (2 X 23 grams Na) + (2 X 35 grams Cl) = 116 grams NaCl

(b) *We will make 116 grams of NaCl.*

So far, we have been converting moles to grams, but it is also possible to convert grams to moles. For example, we can also use chemical equations to calculate how many moles will be made from a given number of grams. Essentially, we do the calculation in the opposite order. Looking at Sample Problem 3.2, we see that grams of reactants can be converted to moles. From this we can calculate how many grams of product the reaction will produce.

Sample Problem 3.2

(a) If we have 92 grams of sodium metal, how many moles of chlorine gas do we need? (b) How many grams of sodium chloride salt will this make?

— —

Answer

First we need to find out how many moles of sodium metal equals 92 grams.

moles Na metal = 92 grams Na metal/23 grams [mass of one mole of Na]

= 4 moles

92 grams Na metal = 4 moles

Next, 1 mole of chlorine gas is needed for every 2 moles of sodium metal. We have 4 moles of sodium metal, so we will need 2 moles of chlorine gas.

2 moles Na metal: 1 mole chlorine gas -->

4 moles Na metal: 2 moles chlorine gas

(a) *We will need 2 moles of chlorine gas for 92 grams of sodium metal.*

Finally, we know that 2 moles of sodium metal give 2 moles of sodium chloride salt. So, if we have 4 moles of sodium metal, we will make 4 moles of sodium chloride salt.

2 moles Na metal: 2 moles sodium chloride salt

4 moles Na metal: 4 moles sodium chloride salt

Now we need to find out how many grams of sodium chloride salt equal 4 moles:

4 moles NaCl = 4 X 1 mole NaCl = 4 X [23 grams Na + 35 grams Cl]

=4 x [58 grams NaCl}

= 232 grams

(b) *We will get 232 grams of sodium chloride salt.*

3.2.3 Decomposition reaction

In the previous examples, we calculated the masses in grams needed for the acid-base reaction between acetic acid and sodium bicarbonate, and for the combination reaction between sodium metal and chlorine gas. However, we can calculate values for any kind of reaction.

For example the decomposition reaction for water is the following:

$$2 \ H_2O \ \text{-->} \ 1 \ O_2 + 2 \ H$$

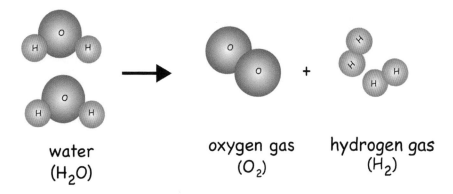

Figure 3.12: The decomposition reaction of water into oxygen gas and hydrogen gas.

In a decomposition reaction one type of reactant molecule breaks apart, or *decomposes*, to form several new molecules as products. In the decomposition reaction for water, we can see from the chemical equation that 2 moles of water will yield 1 mole of oxygen gas and 2 moles of hydrogen gas. From the chemical equation, we can calculate how many moles (or grams) of reactant (or product) we will need.

Practice Problem 3.1

In the decomposition reaction for water, if you have 4 moles of water, how many moles of hydrogen gas will be produced? How many grams?

Answer: 4 moles of H_2 gas, 8 grams.

3.2.4 Displacement reaction

In the displacement reaction between sodium metal and water, sodium hydroxide and hydrogen gas are produced. In a displacement reaction, the atoms from one molecule remove, or *displace*, the atoms from another molecule. We can see from the chemical equation that 2 moles of sodium metal react with 2 moles of water to produce 2 moles of sodium hydroxide and 1 mole of hydrogen gas.

$$2\ Na + 2\ H_2O \rightarrow 2\ NaOH + 1\ H_2$$

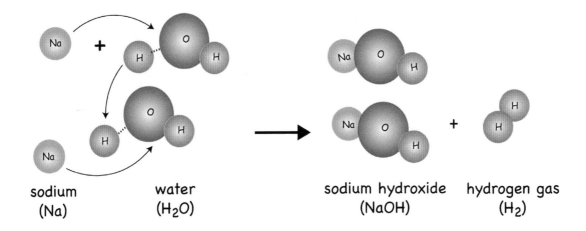

sodium   water   sodium hydroxide   hydrogen gas
(Na)   (H$_2$O)   (NaOH)   (H$_2$)

Figure 3.13: The displacement reaction between sodium metal and water to produce sodium hydroxide and hydrogen gas.

Practice Problem 3.2

In the displacement reaction for sodium and water, if you start with 46 grams of sodium, how many moles of sodium hydroxide will you make?

How many grams?

Answer: 2 moles NaOH, 80 grams.

3.2.5 Exchange reaction

In the exchange reaction between hydrogen chloride and sodium hydroxide, sodium chloride and water are produced. In an exchange reaction, atoms from one molecule trade places, or *exchange*, with the atoms of another molecule. We can see from the chemical equation that 1 mole of hydrogen chloride and 1 mole of sodium hydroxide will give 1 mole of sodium chloride and 1 mole of water.

1 HCl + 1 NaOH --> 1 NaCl + 1 H$_2$O

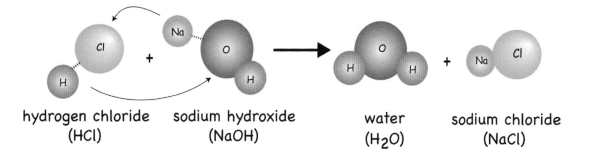

Figure 3.14: The exchange reaction between hydrogen chloride and sodium hydroxide gives water and sodium chloride.

Practice Problem 3.3

In the exchange reaction between hydrogen chloride and sodium hydroxide, if you had 120 grams of sodium hydroxide, how many moles of water would the reaction produce? How many grams?

Answer: 3 moles, 54 grams

3.3 SUMMARY

Here are the main points to remember from this chapter:

• Chemical reactions occur whenever bonds between atoms and molecules are created or destroyed.

• In a chemical reaction, the reactants are converted into products.

• Chemical reactions are written using chemical formulas, and the reaction is represented by a chemical equation.

• In a balanced chemical equation, the number of atoms of each element on the left-hand side equals the number of atoms of each element on the right-hand side

- Chemical reactions obey the law of conservation of mass which says that atoms are neither created nor destroyed.

- Chemical reactions are balanced using stoichiometric coefficients.

- Using balanced chemical equations, we can calculate how much reactant is required and how much product will be produced in a chemical reaction.

3.4 STUDY QUESTIONS

1. Write the molecular formulas for water, vinegar, and baking soda.

2. Write out the balanced equation for the reaction between vinegar and baking soda. Label the reactants and the products.

3. What is the stoichiometric coefficient for O_2 in the following equation?

$$C_6H_{12}O_6 \ + \ 6O_2 \ \text{-->} \ 6CO_2 + 6\,H_2O$$

4. Balance the following equations:

    a. $CO + H_2 \text{-->} CH_4 + H_2O$

    b. $C + O_2 \text{-->} CO_2$

    c. $C_3H_8 + O_2 \text{-->} CO_2 + H_2O$

    d. $Mg + N_2 \text{-->} Mg_3N_2$

5. Is the equation in Problem 3 balanced? Write out a "balance sheet" to show that the equation is balanced (as illustrated in the text).

CHAPTER 4   ACIDS, BASES, AND pH

4.1 ACID–BASE REACTIONS

4.1.1 Introduction

In the first three chapters, we learned about molecules and chemical reactions in general. Now we will focus our attention on a specific class of chemical reactions, called acid–base reactions. An acid–base reaction is a specific kind of exchange reaction that occurs between acids and bases. We have already seen one example of an acid–base reaction with vinegar and baking soda. But what are acids and bases and how do they react?

4.1.2 Acid, bases, and salts

The word *acid* comes from the Latin word *acerbus* or *acidus*, which means "sour or sharp." The Latin word for *vinegar* is *acetum* and is so called because vinegar has a sour or sharp taste. A sharp or sour taste is a property of acids.

Another property of acids is that they react with bases to give salts. In the eighteenth century Guillaume Francois Rouelle, a French chemist, defined chemicals that react with acids to yield salts as a "base for [the salt]." This is where the term *base* comes from. Bases are also called *alkaline.* The term alkali [al'-kə-lī] comes from the Arabic word *al-gili* which means "ashes of saltwort." Saltwort is a bushy plant with prickly leaves found in salt marshes. When it is burned, it produces a crude soda ash. Soda ash is actually sodium carbonate, used for centuries to make soap. A general property of bases is that they are soapy.

Early chemists understood bases as always reacting with acids to produce a salt. The reaction of vinegar (acetic acid) and baking soda (sodium bicarbonate) gives three products: sodium acetate, carbon dioxide, and water.

Saltwort

Figure 4.1: Saltwort produces soda ash (sodium carbonate) when burned.

The acetic acid (vinegar) is the acid, and the sodium bicarbonate (baking soda) is the base. The sodium acetate is the salt.

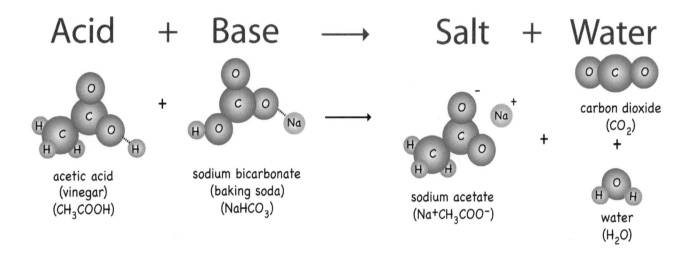

Figure 4.2: The reaction between acetic acid (an acid) and sodium bicarbonate (a base) produces sodium acetate (a salt) and water.

Another acid–base reaction that you should already be familiar with is the reaction between hydrochloric acid and sodium hydroxide. Hydrogen chloride is the acid, sodium hydroxide is the base, and sodium chloride is the salt.

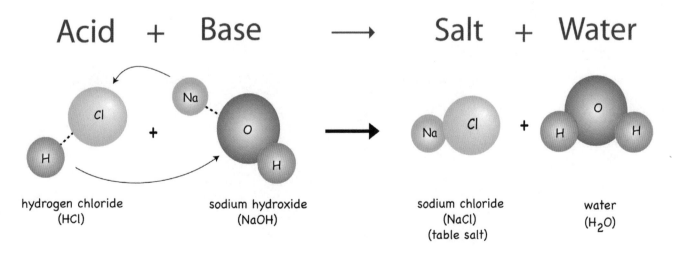

Figure 4.3: The reaction between hydrogen chloride (an acid) and sodium hydroxide (a base) produces sodium chloride (table salt) and water.

Another acid–base reaction is the reaction between hydrogen cyanide and sodium hydroxide. Hydrogen cyanide is the acid, sodium hydroxide is the base, and sodium cyanide is the salt. In this reaction the hydrogen on the hydrogen cyanide molecule changes places with the sodium on the sodium hydroxide, forming sodium cyanide, a salt.

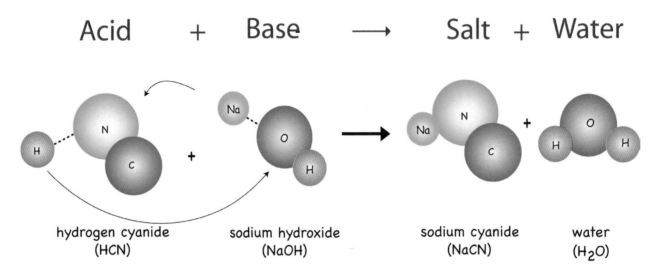

Acid   +   Base   ⟶   Salt + Water

hydrogen cyanide
(HCN)

sodium hydroxide
(NaOH)

sodium cyanide
(NaCN)

water
(H₂O)

Figure 4.4: The reaction between hydrogen cyanide (an acid) and sodium hydroxide (a base) produces sodium cyanide (a salt) and water.

Acid–base reactions are very important and can be found everywhere, even in the foods we eat. For example, oranges and grapefruits contain a mild acid called citric [si'-trik] acid and grapes contain tartaric [tär-tə'-rik] acid. Rhubarb contains malic [ma'-lik] acid and tea contains tannic [tan'-ik] acid. Foods such as beans, bananas, and figs are alkaline, or basic. We also find acids and bases in many of the products we use. For example, we use ammonia (NH_3), a base, to clean our homes, and batteries contain a very powerful acid called sulfuric acid (H_2SO_4).

4.2 ACIDS AND BASES

4.2.1 Arrhenius model

Because acids and bases are so important, chemists have developed several ways of understanding them. What makes acids and bases different from other molecules, and what makes their reactions so special? These were questions that challenged chemists a few hundred years ago. One suggestion came in the early twentieth century from a Swedish chemist named Svante Arrhenius [ə-rē'-nē-əs] (1859-1927). He defined an acid as "any substance that releases a hydrogen ion" (H^+), and a base as "any substance that generates hydroxide ions" (OH^-).

The Arrhenius definitions are still very widely used. Look back over the examples in Section 4.1. All of the acids—acetic acid, hydrogen cyanide, and hydrogen chloride—are Arrhenius acids because all of them give up a hydrogen ion in water.

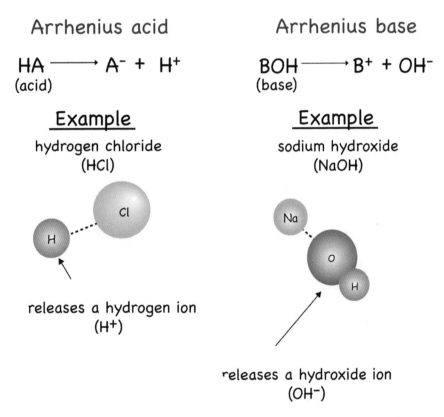

Figure 4.5: Hydrogen chloride is an Arrhenius acid because it releases a proton (H^+), and sodium hydroxide is an Arrhenius base because it releases a hydroxide ion (OH^-).

4.2.2 Monoprotic acids

Acetic acid, hydrocyanic acid, and hydrochloric acid are all Arrhenius acids (see Figure 4.6). If we look carefully at these acids we see that they all release *only one* hydrogen ion. Because these acids release only one hydrogen ion, they are called monoprotic [mä-nō-prō'-tik] acids.

Remember that *mono* comes from the Greek word *monos,* which means "one," and *protic* refers to proton, so a monoprotic acid is one that releases one proton (or hydrogen ion). Table 4.1 shows some common monoprotic acids. Notice that all of these acids release only one hydrogen ion.

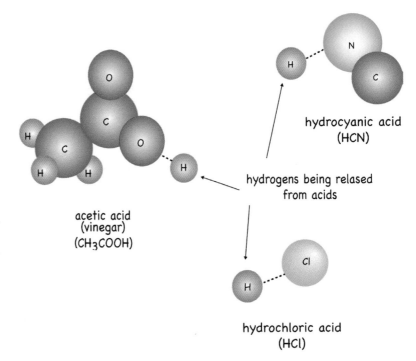

acetic acid
(vinegar)
(CH_3COOH)

hydrocyanic acid
(HCN)

hydrogens being released
from acids

hydrochloric acid
(HCl)

Figure 4.6: Monoprotic acids—acetic acid, hydrocyanic acid, and hydrochloric acid—give off only one proton.

Table 4.1: Common monoprotic acids

Acid	Reaction
chlorous acid	$HClO_2 \dashrightarrow H^+ + ClO_2^-$
nitric acid	$HNO_3 \dashrightarrow H^+ + NO_3^-$
hydrofluoric acid	$HF \dashrightarrow H^+ + F^-$
hypochlorous acid	$HOCl \dashrightarrow H^+ + OCl^-$
hypobromous acid	$HOBr \dashrightarrow H^+ + OBr^-$

4.2.3 Polyprotic acids

There are also acids that release more than one hydrogen atom. These are called polyprotic [pä-lē-prō'-tik] acids. Remember that "poly" comes from the Greek word *polys* which means "many," or more than one, so a polyprotic acid releases more than one proton. Some polyprotic acids are sulfuric acid, carbonic acid, and phosphoric acid. Concentrated sulfuric acid is found in batteries, and small amounts of phosphoric acid are in soda pop.

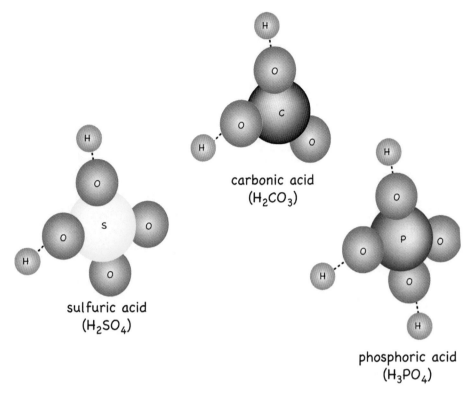

Figure 4.7: Polyprotic acids—sulfuric acid, carbonic acid and phosphoric acid—give off more than one proton.

Polyprotic acids give up their hydrogens one at a time. For example, sulfuric acid gives up one hydrogen to form an intermediate (HSO_4^-), which will then give up its hydrogen to form the final product (SO_4^{2-}).

$$(1) \; H_2SO_4 \; \text{-->} \; H^+ + HSO_4^-$$

$$(2) \; HSO_4^- \; \text{-->} \; H^+ + SO_4^{2-}$$

Reactions of polyprotic acids are often illustrated using two equations as shown. The overall reaction can be written as follows:

$$H_2SO_4 \; \text{-->} \; 2H^+ + SO_4^{2-}$$

Table 4.2 lists some common polyprotic acids.

Table 4.2: Common polyprotic acids

Acid	Reaction
Phosphoric acid (in soda pop)	$H_3PO_4 \dashrightarrow H^+ + H_2PO_4^-$ $H_2PO_4^- \dashrightarrow H^+ + HPO_4^{2-}$ $HPO_4^{2-} \dashrightarrow H^+ + PO_4^{3-}$
Carbonic acid	$H_2CO_3 \dashrightarrow H^+ + HCO_3^-$ $HCO_3^- \dashrightarrow H^+ + CO_3^{2-}$
Ascorbic acid (vitamin C)	$H_2C_6H_6O_6 \dashrightarrow H^+ + HC_6H_6O_6^-$ $HC_6H_6O_6^- \dashrightarrow H^+ + C_6H_6O_6^{2-}$
Sulfuric acid	$H_2SO_4 \dashrightarrow H^+ + HSO_4^-$ $HSO_4^- \dashrightarrow H^+ + SO_4^{2-}$

4.2.4 Arrhenius bases

So far, we have only discussed Arrhenius acids. What about Arrhenius bases? As we mentioned earlier, an Arrhenius base generates hydroxide ions (OH⁻). We saw that sodium hydroxide (NaOH) is an Arrhenius base. Other Arrhenius bases are potassium hydroxide (KOH) and calcium hydroxide (Ca(OH)$_2$) as shown in

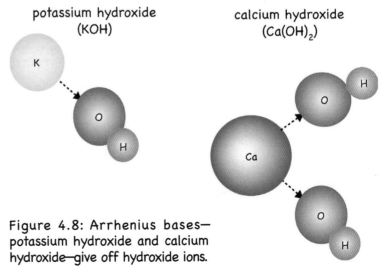

Figure 4.8: Arrhenius bases—potassium hydroxide and calcium hydroxide—give off hydroxide ions.

Figure 4.8. Notice

that in each of these cases, hydroxide ions are released. In the case of calcium hydroxide, two hydroxide ions are released.

Some Arrhenius bases generate hydroxide ions by grabbing an H^+ from a water molecule, leaving an OH^- behind. The most common example is ammonia, (NH_3). In this case NH_3 does not release an OH^- but creates one by taking an H^+ away from water.

$$NH_3 \ + \ H_2O \ ---> \ NH_4^+ \ + \ OH^-$$

Even so, it is counted as an Arrhenius base because OH^- ions are released.

In the Arrhenius model, all of the acid–base reactions produce water. Another way to put it is that the Arrhenius model is limited to describing aqueous [ā'-kwē-əs] solutions. *Aqueous* comes from the Latin word *aqua*, which means "water," so an aqueous solution is a water-based solution. There are other models that describe acid–base reactions that do not occur in water, such as the Brønstead–Lowry model, but since all of the acid–base reactions we will encounter occur in water, we will only use the Arrhenius model.

4.3 CONCENTRATION

We encounter many different acids and bases every day. Some acids and bases are found in the foods we eat, such as phosphoric acid in soda, citric acid in lemons, and potassium hydroxide in cured meats. But other acids and bases, such as those found in cleaning fluids, would be very harmful if swallowed. What is the difference between those acids that are mild enough to eat and those which are harmful?

4.3.1 Concentrated and dilute solutions

All acids and bases are relatively harmless (as acids or bases) when they are dilute, but become harmful when concentrated. The acids and bases in our food and drink are all very dilute. The acids and bases found in cleaners are more concentrated, and the acids and bases found in chemical laboratories or used in industrial processes are very concentrated and can be quite dangerous. What is concentration and how does it affect the toxicity of acids and bases?

In chemistry, concentration for aqueous solutions refers to the number of units (i.e., molecules, moles, or ions) of a substance in a given "volume" of liquid. Concentration is simply the number of "things" in a solution. Solutions that are highly "concentrated" have lots of molecules per unit volume, and solutions that have fewer molecules in them are called "dilute" solutions. We saw from Chapter 3 that a mole is a unit which refers to the number of molecules (ions, atoms, etc.). So, if we say we have so many molecules (moles) in a certain volume (i.e., liters or milliliters), we get a concentration.

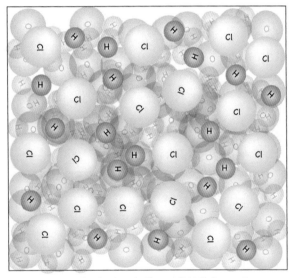

concentrated solution of HCl in water

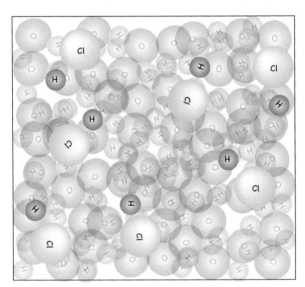

dilute solution of HCl in water

Figure 4.9: A concentrated solution of HCl has more molecules of HCl than a dilute solution of HCl.

4.3.2 Molarity

Chemists refer to concentration in terms of molarity [mō-lər'-i-tē]. Molarity *is moles per liter.* So a 1 M (pronounced "one molar") solution has 1 mole per liter. A 2 M ("two molar") solution has 2 moles per liter, and a 3 M ("three molar") solution has 3 moles per liter, and so on.

Use of terms: The term "molarity" is used as a noun when discussing concentration (e.g. "Find the molarity of this acid solution.") The term "molar" is used as an adjective to describe the concentration of a solution. (e.g."The acid solution is one molar.")

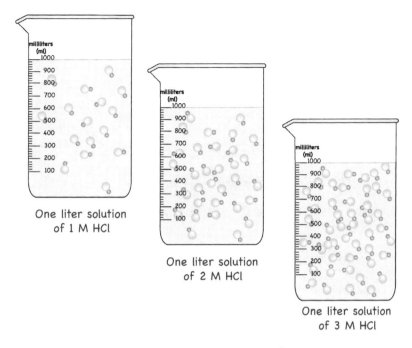

Figure 4.10: As the concentration increases from 1 M to 3 M, the number of HCl molecules increases.

We are not limited to using a liter in every reaction. In fact, we can calculate the molarity of any solution if we know the number of moles and the volume. For example, if we have 1 mole in 1 liter, that would be 1 M. If we have 1 mole in 500 ml (1/2 of a liter), that would be 2 M, and if we had 2 moles in 500 ml (1/2 of a liter) it would be 4 M.

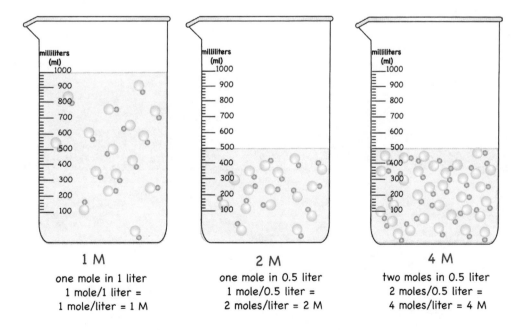

Figure 4.11: To calculate the molarity of a solution take the number of moles and divide by the volume.

4.4 STRENGTH OF ACIDS AND BASES

We encounter many different acids and bases every day. We have seen that some acids are found in the foods we eat, such as phosphoric acid and citric acid, but we also know that there are acids and bases found in cleaning supplies and batteries that would be very harmful if swallowed. How do we tell which acids are mild enough to eat and which are harmful, or which bases we can ingest and which we cannot?

The strength of an acid or a base depends on the concentration of acid or base ions in the solution. For acids, the important chemical species is the hydrogen ion (H^+), so when we speak of *concentrated acid*, we mean a solution with lots of H^+. Similarly for bases, the important chemical species is the hydroxide ion (OH^-), so a *concentrated base* means a solution with lots of hydroxide ions (OH^-).

4.4.1 pH

The strength of an acid or a base can be measured directly using "pH." The pH of a solution indicates how concentrated an acid or a base is. Specifically, pH describes the concentration of H^+ ions in solution. (See Appendix C for a full description of pH.)

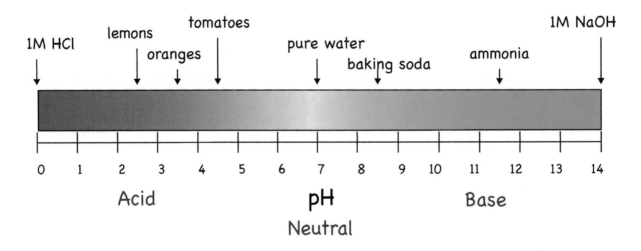

Figure 4.12: pH scale with acids being on the left (in red), bases on the right (in green) and pure water, which is neutral, in the center.

pH is often used as a simple way of indicating how powerful an acid or base solution is. A pH of 7 is "neutral," and is neither an acid nor a base. Solutions with a pH below 7 are acidic, and solutions with a pH above 7 are basic.

Tables 4.3 and 4.4 show how acids and bases with very low concentrations of H^+ or OH^- are common, useful, and usually not dangerous. However, as the concentration increases both acids and bases become very powerful and can instantly destroy skin and clothing.

Table 4.3 Common Acids

Acid solution	H+ concentration (M)	pH	Properties
pure water	0.0000001 (1×10^{-7})	7	too dilute to taste
rain water	0.000001 (1×10^{-6})	6	rain water is slightly acidic because of dissolved CO_2
coffee	0.00001 (1×10^{-5})	5	slightly sour
tomatoes	0.0001 (1×10^{-4})	4	tart
vinegar	0.001 (1×10^{-3})	3	tangy
lemon juice	0.01 (1×10^{-2})	2	very sour; irritates skin after prolonged exposure
gastric juice	0.1 (1×10^{-1})	1	assists in slow digestion of food, irritates skin after brief exposure
muriatic acid	1 (1×10^{0})	0	dissolves hard water stains, burns skin after brief exposure

Sample Problem 4.1

What is the pH of a 0.001 M solution of hydrochloric acid (HCl)?
— —
Answer

The pH of a 0.001 M solution of HCl is 3.

Table 4.4 Common Bases

Base solution	OH⁻ concentration (M)	pH	Properties
pure water	0.0000001 (1×10^{-7})	7	too dilute to taste
baking soda in water	0.000001 (1×10^{-6})	8	slightly bitter
borax	0.00001 (1×10^{-5})	9	used for eye infections
antacid	0.0001 (1×10^{-4})	10	neutralizes stomach acid
dilute potassium hydroxide (KOH), (0.001 M)	0.001 (1×10^{-3})	11	floor cleaner
ammonia window cleaner	0.01 (1×10^{-2})	12	assists detergents and soaps in cleaning glass
KOH (0.1 M)	0.1 (1×10^{-1})	13	cleaner; skin irritant after brief exposure
KOH (1.0 M)	1 (1×10^{0})	14	burns skin on contact

Sample Problem 4.2

What is the pH of a 0.001 M solution of sodium hydroxide (NaOH)?

— —

Answer

The pH of a 0.001 M solution of NaOH is 11.

4.4.2 Strong and weak acids and bases

The concentration of acid or base ions depends both on the number of acid and base molecules in the solution, and on how readily these molecules make acid or base ions (ionize). So far we have considered only strong acids and bases. A strong acid or base breaks up (or ionizes) completely in water. For example, hydrochloric acid, HCl, comes apart completely to make H^+ and Cl^-, leaving no intact HCl molecules in solution.

But some acids and bases only partially break apart. For example, in a 0.1 M solution of acetic acid, only about 1 acetic acid molecule in 100 releases its H$^+$ and becomes ionized. Ninety-nine percent of the acetic acid molecules stay intact! This means that in a 0.1 M acetic acid solution the H$^+$ concentration is only about 0.001 M (pH 3) rather than 0.1 M (pH 1).

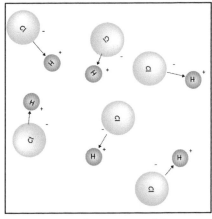 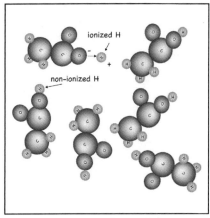

Figure 4.13: Hydrochloric acid is a strong acid and ionizes completely. Acetic acid is a weak acid and does not ionize completely.

a strong acid
hydrochloric acid (HCl)
(0.1M --> pH 1)

a weak acid
acetic acid (CH$_3$COOH)
(0.1M --> pH 3)

Likewise, strong bases will give up their OH$^-$ ions more easily than weak bases. Sodium hydroxide (NaOH), a strong base, breaks up into Na$^+$ and OH$^-$ ions, leaving no intact NaOH molecules in solution. However, barium hydroxide (Ba(OH)$_2$), a weak base, does not ioinize completely.

In a 0.1 M solution of barium hydroxide, the OH$^-$ concentration is more than ten times less than it would be if it were fully ionized, lowering the pH to below 12.

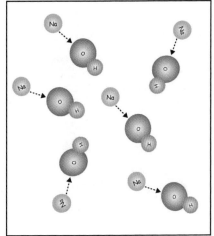 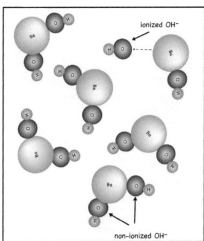

Figure 4.14: Sodium hydroxide is a strong base and ionizes completely. Barium hydroxide is a weak base and does not ionize completely.

a strong base
sodium hydroxide (NaOH)
(0.1M --> pH 13)

a weak base
barium hydroxide Ba(OH)$_2$
(0.1M ---> pH <12)

Sample Problem 4.1

If 0.36 gram of HCl is added to 0.1 liters of water and if all of the HCl comes apart to release H⁺, what will the pH be?

Answer — — — — — — — — — — — — — — — — — —

mol. wt. HCl = (1 gram/mole H + 35 grams/mole Cl) = 36 grams per mole

To find the number of moles in 0.36 grams HCl, divide the amount (0.36 grams) by the molecular weight.

0.36 grams HCl/36 grams per mole = 0.01 moles HCl

To find the concentration, divide the number of moles by the volume (in liters).

0.01 moles HCl/0.1 liters = 0.1 moles per liter, or 0.1 M.

Assume HCl completely dissociates, so there is 0.1 M H⁺ ions in solution.

The pH for a 0.1 M solution of HCl is 1. (See Table 4.3.)

4.5 SUMMARY

Here are the main points to remember from this chapter:

- Acid-base reactions produce salts.

- An Arrhenius acid releases a hydrogen ion, and an Arrhenius base releases a hydroxide ion.

- Monoprotic acids release a single proton.

- Polyprotic acids release more than one proton.

- In chemistry, the concentration of a solution is expressed as molarity which is moles *per liter.*

- The pH of a solution is affected by the concentration of hydrogen ions and by the degree to which the acid or base ionizes. Those acids (or bases) that ionize more readily will be more acidic (or basic) than those that do not ionize as readily, given the same concentration.

- Strong acids and bases ionize completely. Weak acids and bases do not ionize completely.

4.6 STUDY QUESTIONS

1. List three monoprotic acids and write their molecular formulas.

2. List three polyprotic acids and write their molecular formulas.

3. Define an Arrhenius acid and base.

4. Calculate the concentration in molarity for the following:

   a. 5 moles of HCl in 2 liters

   b. 2 moles of NaOH in 1 liter

   c. 0.5 moles of HCl in 1 liter

   d. 36 grams of HCl in 1 liter

5. What is the difference between a strong and a weak acid or base?

6. You have a solution that has a hydrogen ion concentration of 1×10^{-11} mole/liter. What is the pH? Is it an acid or a base?

7. You have a solution that has a hydrogen ion concentration of 1×10^{-1} mole/liter. What is the pH? Is it an acid or a base?

8. What is the hydrogen ion concentration of a solution that has a pH of 6?

9. What is the hydrogen ion concentration of a solution that has a pH of 9?

Challenge

10. The pH of water is 7. What is the hydrogen ion concentration? What is the hydroxyl ion (OH^-) concentration?

CHAPTER 5 ACID-BASE REACTIONS

5.1 ACID-BASE REACTIONS

5.1.1 Introduction

We saw in Chapter 4 that when an acid is added to a base, a salt is produced. In fact, the acidity [ə-sid'-ə-tē] of the acid and the basicity [bā-sis'-ə-tē] of the base no longer exist. The base cancels out the acidity of the acid, and the acid cancels out the basicity of the base. They neutralize [nü'-trə-līz] each other. Thus, an acid-base reaction is commonly called a neutralization reaction.

One practical situation where acid-base neutralization reactions are important is when you use an antacid to cure a stomachache. Stomachaches are often caused by too much stomach acid, so antacids, which are basic, can be used to neturalize acid inside the stomach. Many antacids contain magnesium hydroxide, $Mg(OH)_2$, or aluminum hydroxide, $Al(OH)_3$. Both aluminum hydroxide and magnesium hydroxide are safe to eat because they do not dissolve very much in water, and therefore do not generate high concentrations of OH^- ions.

5.1.2 Neutralization reactions

We can see by looking at the reaction of hydrogen chloride and sodium hydroxide that the acid and the base in this reaction are converted into salt and water. We can also see that one molecule of HCl reacts with one molecule of NaOH.

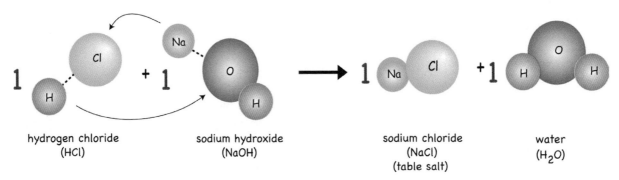

| hydrogen chloride (HCl) | sodium hydroxide (NaOH) | sodium chloride (NaCl) (table salt) | water (H_2O) |

Figure 5.1: One molecule (or mole) of HCl reacts with one molecule (or mole) of NaOH to make one molecule (or mole) of NaCl and one molecule (or mole) of H_2O.

The stoichiometry shows that it takes exactly one acid molecule to neutralize one base molecule and one base molecule to neutralize one acid molecule in this reaction. This is an important property of acid-base reactions. It means that if we wanted to completely neutralize a solution of hydrogen chloride and not leave it acidic or turn it basic, we must know exactly how many molecules of HCl are present and add an equal number of NaOH molecules. If we had two molecules of HCl, we would need two molecules of NaOH. If we had three molecules of HCl, we would need three molecules of NaOH, and so on. If we had one mole of HCl, it would take one mole of NaOH to neutralize it.

We can use the stoichiometry of an acid-base reaction to determine how much acid or how much base to add in order to completely neutralize a solution. For example, suppose we had 1 liter of a 2 M solution of HCl. How much NaOH would we have to add to completely neutralize the HCl?

Knowing the stoichiometry, we see that we would have to add 2 moles of NaOH. This could be one liter of a 2 M solution of NaOH, or two liters of a 1 M solution, or even 500 ml of a 4 M solution. 1 M, 2 M, and 4 M are all different concentrations of the NaOH.

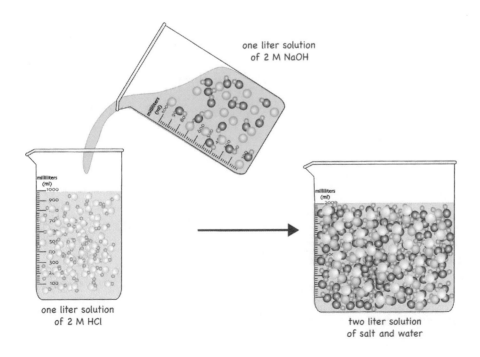

one liter solution
of 2 M NaOH

one liter solution
of 2 M HCl

two liter solution
of salt and water

Figure 5.2: A 1 liter solution of 2 M HCl contains 2 moles of HCl. To completely neutralize the HCl, 2 moles of NaOH are needed. So, a 1 liter solution of 2 M NaOH can be used to completely neutralize the 1 liter solution of 2 M HCl.

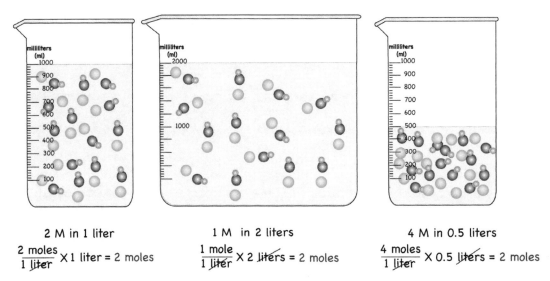

Figure 5.3: All of the solutions—2 M in 1 liter, 1 M in 2 liters, and 4 M in 0.5 liters—contain 2 moles of NaOH.

We can use any concentration of solution or any volume of solution that we like, as long as we use the correct number of moles to neutralize a reaction. So, to neutralize a 2 M solution of HCl, we could use one liter of a 2 M solution of NaOH, or two liters of a 1 M solution of NaOH, or 500 ml of a 4 M solution. All of these have *different concentrations*, but the *same number of moles*.

5.2 TITRATIONS

5.2.1 Introduction

So far, we have only been discussing the concentration of solutions needed to neutralize a known acid, such as 2 M HCl. But what if we don't know the concentration of the acid? How can we know how much base to add?

If the concentration of an acid or base is unknown, but we want to find out what it is, we can titrate [tī'-trāt] the unknown acid or base with a known concentration of acid or base. This is called perfoming a titration [tī-trā'-shən]. The word *titration*, comes from the word *titre* which in old French meant "assay" which is a test of quality. So a titration, is a "test of quality." Titrations are used not only for acid-base reactions, but also for other reactions as well. For example, a medical doctor may use a titration to determine the concentration of protein in a sample of fluid. An industrial worker could use a titration to determine the concentration of metal ions in a solution.

The fundamental idea behind titration is to use a *known* solution to find out the concentration of an *unknown* solution. Before we begin an acid-base titration, we need to have some way to monitor the change in pH. Typically an acid-base indicator [in'-də-kā-tər] is added to the acid (or base) solution before beginning the titration. An acid-base indicator is any substance that will not interfere with the acid-base reaction, but will change color as the pH changes, thereby *indicating* when the titration is complete. The indicator is chosen so that its color changes rapidly right at the point where the acid and base have neutralized each other. A pH meter can also be used during a titration. The pH meter continuously monitors the pH as the titration is performed.

5.2.2 Strong acid titrated with a strong base

Suppose we have an unknown concentration of a strong acid solution (like HCl), and we want to determine its concentration. After we have added an acid-base indicator, we begin the titration by slowly dripping a known concentration of a strong base (like NaOH) into the acid solution. Because we know the concentration of the base (say 0.1 M) and because we measure the volume of solution we've added, we *always* know exactly how many moles of base we've added. For example, if the base concentration is 1.0 mole/liter, and we have dripped in 10.0 ml (which is 0.01 liters), we have added 1.0 mole/liter x 0.01 liters = 0.01 mole of base. (See Appendix D for a full discussion of dimensional analysis.)

When enough base has been added so that all the acid is neutralized, the acid-base indicator will change colors. The color change tells us that the number of moles of base we've added equals the number of moles of acid that we started with. Since we know how many moles of base were added, we now know how many moles of acid we had in our acid solution. For example, if we had an unknown concentration of HCl in a beaker and we added some cabbage dye indicator to it, the color would be pink. If we added NaOH to the beaker, eventually all of the HCl would be neutralized, and the solution would turn green (basic). When the solution turns green, the pH has gone from acidic to basic. This is called the endpoint of the reaction.

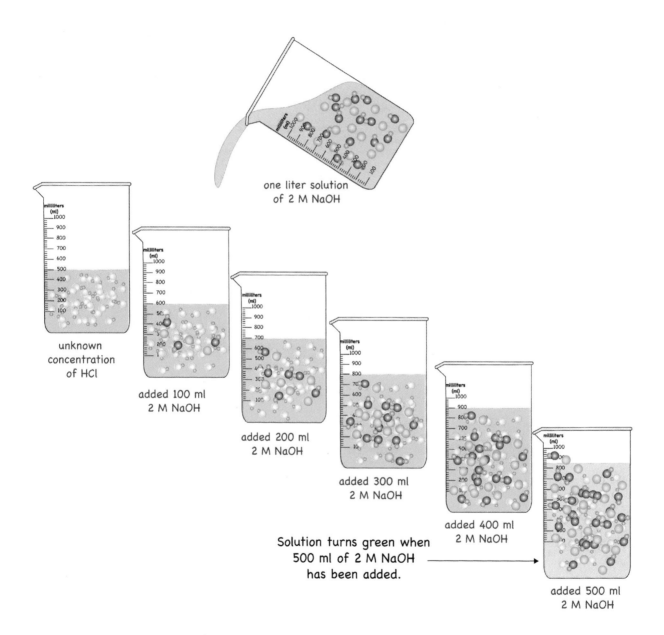

one liter solution
of 2 M NaOH

unknown
concentration
of HCl

added 100 ml
2 M NaOH

added 200 ml
2 M NaOH

added 300 ml
2 M NaOH

added 400 ml
2 M NaOH

Solution turns green when
500 ml of 2 M NaOH
has been added.

added 500 ml
2 M NaOH

Figure 5.4: The titration of an unknown concentration of HCl with a known concentration of NaOH. When the solution changes pH (as indicated by the color change) there has been enough NaOH added to neutralized the HCl. Because we know the concentration of NaOH and the stoichiometry for the reaction, we can calculate the concentration of HCl which was unknown.

If we know the concentration of NaOH and record the amount of NaOH we add to turn the solution green (basic), then we can figure out how much HCl we had in the beaker in the first place (because we know that one molecule of NaOH will neutralize one molecule of HCl). So, if we added 500 ml of a 2 M solution of NaOH, we would have added 1 mole of NaOH. About how much HCl was in the solution? *1 mole, HCl*

$$\frac{2 \text{ moles}}{1 \text{ liter}} \times 0.5 \text{ liter} = 1 \text{ mole}$$

What is the approximate concentration of HCl if we had 1 mole in 500 ml? *2 M.*

$$\frac{1 \text{ mole}}{500 \text{ ml}} \times \frac{1000 \text{ ml}}{1 \text{ liter}} = \frac{(1 \times 1000) \text{ moles}}{(500 \times 1) \text{ liters}} = 2 \text{ M}$$

5.2.3 Graphing titrations

We can see the endpoint of an acid-base reaction most clearly by graphing the titration. To graph the titration, we make a plot of "amount of base added" in "milliliters" vs. "pH" or "color" as shown in Figure 5.5. In the previous example, the titration was taken to the true endpoint. This is the point where the acid and base have been added in equal amounts so that they neutralize each other. Hence, the true endpoint is also called the equivalence [i-kwi'-və-ləns] point—the point where the amount of base added is equivalent to the amount of acid originally present. It is only when the amount of base begins to equal the amount of acid in the solution that the pH or color begins to change rapidly.

At the equivalence point, the amount of acid equals the amount of base. For a strong acid and a strong base, the equivalence point is pH 7, neutral. This is also the steepest and most rapidly changing part of the titration curve. As the very next amount is added, the color of the solution abruptly changes and the endpoint is reached.

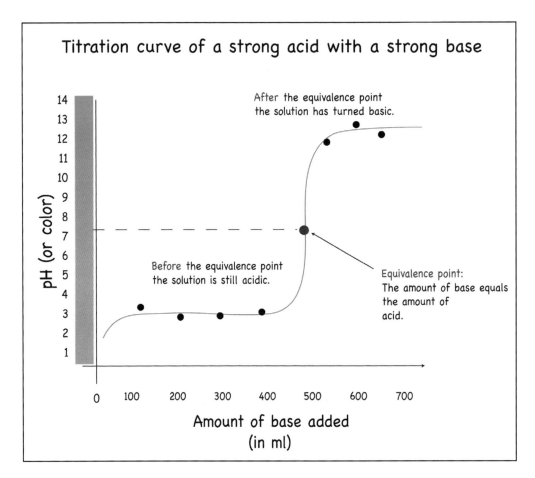

Figure 5.5: A titration curve of a strong acid with a strong base. The equivalence point is where the acid is completely neutralized by the base. For a strong acid and a strong base, the equivalence point has a pH of 7.

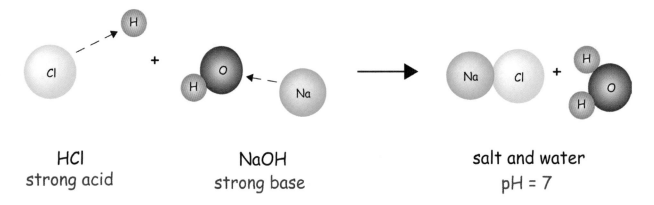

Figure 5.6: The pH is 7 at the equivalence point of a titration of a strong acid with a strong base.

5.2.4 Titrations of weak acids with strong bases

Recall from Chapter 4 that a weak acid or a weak base is an acid or base that does not ionize completely, and therefore most of their molecules do not release H^+ or generate OH^- ions. When a weak acid or a weak base is titrated, the titration curve looks a little different. For example, when formic acid (CHOOH), a weak acid, is titrated with sodium hydroxide, a strong base, the titration curve looks like this:

Figure 5.7: A titration curve of a weak acid with a strong base. The equivalence point is, again, where the acid is completely neutralized by the base, but the pH is higher.

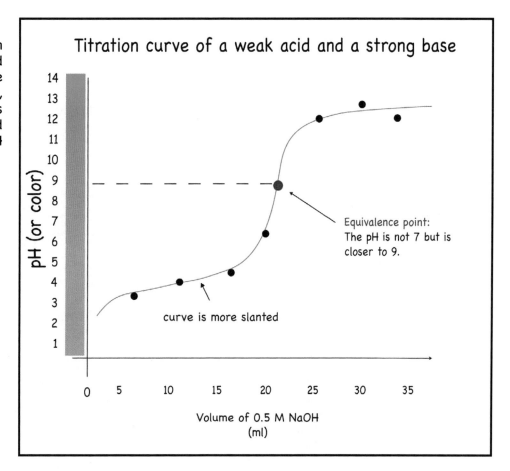

The curve looks very similar to the strong acid case, but the slowly changing part of the curve is more slanted, the pH changes more quickly, and the rapidly changing part is not as steep. Overall, the curve is "smoother" than the strong acid case. Notice that the equivalence point is not pH 7, but is closer to pH 9. The pH at the equivalence point is higher because the ionized acid product ($CHOO^-$) is basic.

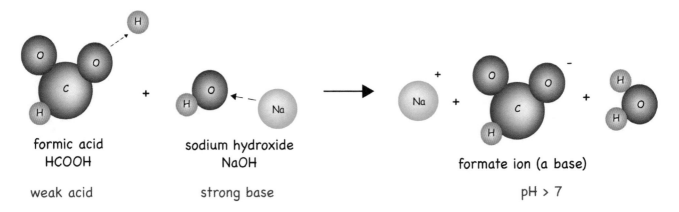

Figure 5.8: The pH is higher than 7 at the equivalence point of a titration of a weak acid with a strong base.

5.2.5 Titrations of strong acids with weak bases

If we look at the titration of a strong acid with a weak base, we find that the pH at the equivalence point is less than 7. For example, the equivalence point for a titration of NH_3 (a weak base) with HCl (a strong acid) is at pH = 5.3.

Figure 5.9: The pH is lower than 7 at the equivalence point of a titration of a strong acid with a weak base.

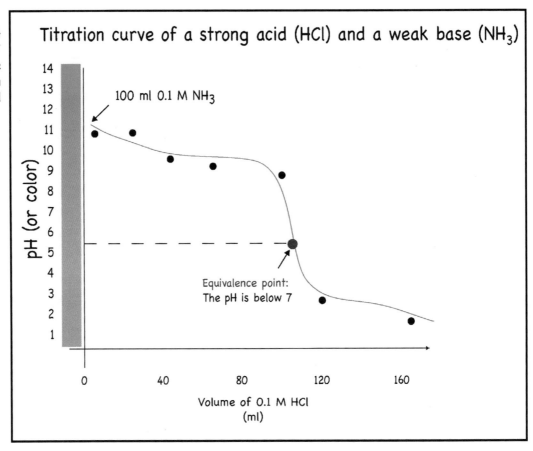

5.2.6 Titrations of polyprotic acids

In all of the previous examples, the acid being titrated is monoprotic—it only has one H^+. All monoprotic acids show similar titration curves that bend upward near the equivalence point and level off again as more base is added. But what about acids that have more than one proton? Do they behave the same way when they are titrated, or do they behave differently?

Polyprotic acids, those acids with more than one proton, have titration curves that are similar to monoprotic acids except they have more "bumps." For a polyprotic acid, each proton reacts in turn as more base is added, so the titration curve has two (or more) rapid rises, and two (or more) equivalence points. For example, the titration curve of sulfurous acid (H_2SO_3) and sodium hydroxide (NaOH) (shown in Figure 5.10) has two "bumps" and two equivalence points as H_2SO_3 releases two H^+ ions.

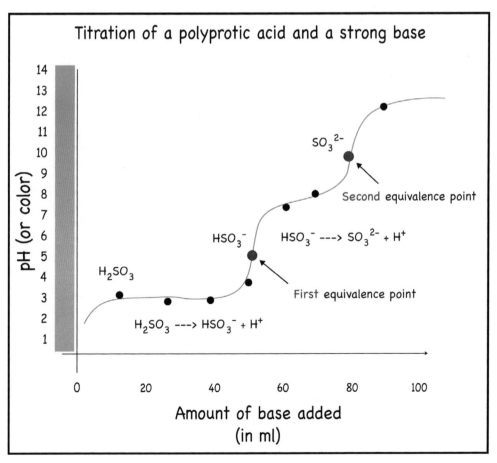

Figure 5.10: A titration curve of a polyprotic acid shows several "bumps," one for each proton being ionized.

The base neutralizes the first H^+ ion released, so we get one equivalence point. Then, as more OH^- is added, the second H^+ ion gets neutralized, and there is a second equivalence point.

5.3 SUMMARY

Here are the main points to remember from this chapter:

- An acid-base reaction neutralizes both the acid and the base.

- It can be determined from the stoichiometry how much acid (or base) is required to completely neutralize a given amount of base (or acid).

- Molarity is defined as "moles per liter."

- A titration can be used to find the unknown concentration of a substance by using a known concentration of some other substance.

- When the endpoint of a neutralization reaction is reached, the reaction is complete and the pH of the solution does not change significantly.

- At the equivalence point during a titration, the number of moles of acid (or base) equals the number of moles of base (or acid).

- The pH = 7 at the equivalence point of a titration of a strong acid and a strong base.

- The pH > 7 at the equivalence point of a titration of a weak acid and a strong base.

- The pH < 7 at the equivalence point of a titration of a strong acid and a weak base.

- Titration curves with polyprotic acids show multiple "bumps", one for each proton that is being ionized.

5.4 STUDY QUESTIONS

1. How many moles of NaOH does it take to neutralize 6 moles of HCl?

2. Give the molarity of the following solutions:

    a. 5 moles in 10 liters

    b. 2 moles in 8 liters

    c. 6 moles in 3 liters

    d. 5 moles in 1 liter

3. You have a 2 M solution of NaOH. You use 100 ml in a titration to reach the equivalence point. How many moles of NaOH did you use?

4. Using the number of moles calculated in problem # 3, how many moles of HCl would you have had in that titration?

5. You do a titration and get the curve shown in the graph to the right.

    What kind of solutions do you have?

    a. strong acid and a strong base

    b. weak acid and a strong base

    c. strong acid and a weak base

    d. polyprotic acid

6. You do a titration and get the following curve.

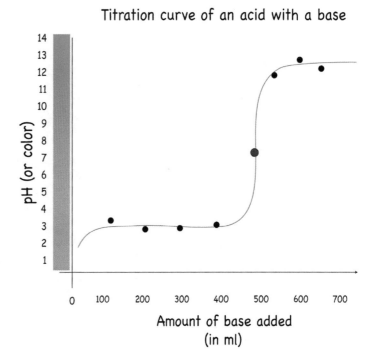

Titration curve of an acid with a base

What kind of solutions do you have?

a. strong acid and a strong base

b. weak acid and a strong base

c. strong acid and a weak base

d. polyprotic acid

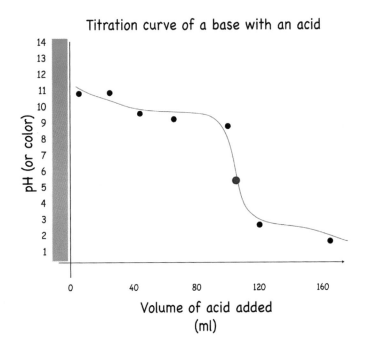

Titration curve of a base with an acid

7. You have 500 ml of a 1 M solution of HCl. Draw the curve for a titration performed using 1 M NaOH. Show the pH at the equivalence point.

8. Draw a general titration curve for H_2SO_4 titrated with NaOH.

9. Draw a general titration curve for H_3PO_4 titrated with NaOH.

10. Draw a general titration curve for NaOH titrated with HCl.

CHAPTER 6　　　MIXTURES

6.1 INTRODUCTION

6.1.1 What is a mixture?

When we look closely at the world around us, we find that almost everything is made of mixtures. A mixture is two or more substances that are physically mixed, but not chemically bonded. For example, the air we breathe is really a mixture of several different gases including oxygen (O_2), nitrogen (N_2), and carbon dioxide (CO_2). Notice that carbon dioxide is not a mixture because the atoms (carbon and oxygen) are bonded chemically. Therefore, it is called a compound. But air *is* a mixture since the oxygen, nitrogen, and carbon dioxide are not chemically combined, only physically mixed together. The water we drink is usually a mixture of water molecules and dissolved ions, such as Na^+, Mg^{2+}, or Ca^{2+}.

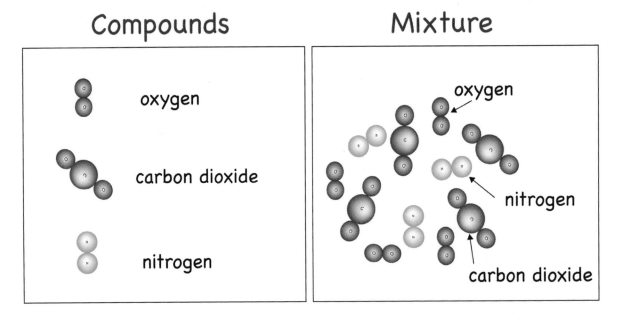

Figure 6.1: A compound, such as oxygen gas, carbon dioxide, or nitrogen, is chemically bonded. Mixtures are not chemically bonded.

6.1.2 Mixture of mixtures

The foods we eat are mixtures. Bread, cheese, lasagna, and even chocolate bars are all mixtures. Looking more closely, we find that mixtures are often mixtures of mixtures.

For example, bread contains yeast, oil, sugar, salt, wheat, and eggs. But each of these items is itself a mixture of molecules or atoms. Yeast is made of carbohydrates and proteins; oil has oleic acid and perhaps linoleic acid; eggs have fats, water, and protein; and wheat has many compounds, including starches, amino acids, and proteins. Most of the things around us are complex mixtures of one kind or another.

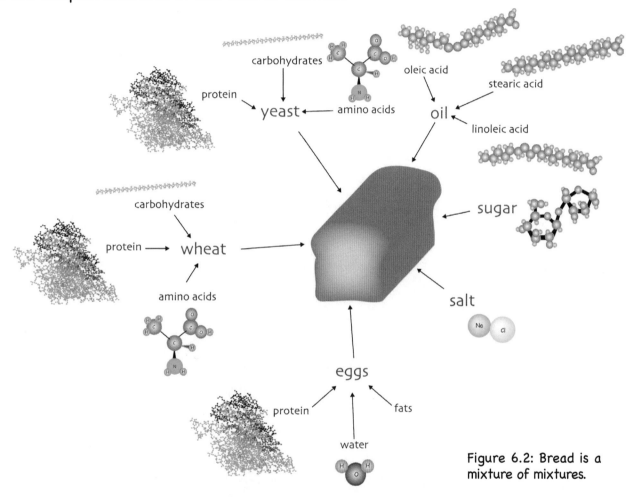

Figure 6.2: Bread is a mixture of mixtures.

6.2 TYPES OF MIXTURES

6.2.1 Homogeneous and heterogeneous

Recall from Chapter 1 that there are two main types of mixtures: homogeneous [hō-mə-jē'-nē-əs] mixtures and heterogeneous [he-tə-rə-jē'-nē-es] mixtures. The word homogeneous means "same kind" and the word heterogeneous means "other kind." Therefore, a homogeneous mixture is a mixture that is the *same* everywhere, and a heterogeneous mixture is a mixture that is *not the same* everywhere. To put it more simply, a homogeneous mixture appears uniform, whereas a heterogeneous mixture is milky or even lumpy.

The main difference between a homogeneous mixture and a heterogeneous mixture is the size of the things that are mixed. In a homogeneous mixture, the molecules are mixed on a molecular level so they are essentially *invisible*. For example, the individual chlorine ions, sodium

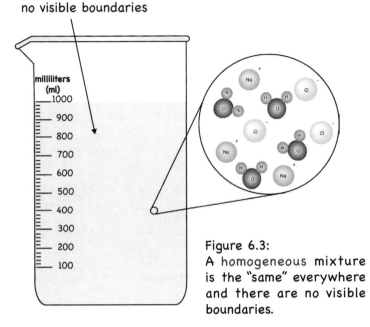

Figure 6.3:
A homogeneous mixture is the "same" everywhere and there are no visible boundaries.

ions, and water molecules in a homogeneous mixture of salt water cannot be seen with our eyes. The molecules are too small. We do not observe a visible boundary between the sodium ions, chloride ions, and water molecules because ions and molecules are on a *molecular scale*.

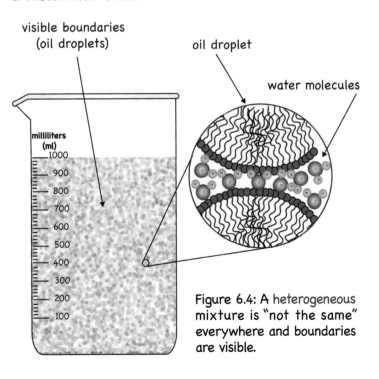

Figure 6.4: A heterogeneous mixture is "not the same" everywhere and boundaries are visible.

On the other hand, a heterogeneous mixture typically has particles that are small, but much larger than those in a homogeneous mixture. They are on a macromolecular [ma-krō-mə-le'-kyə-lər] scale and are often *visible*. For example, salad dressing made of oil and vinegar (and hopefully a touch of garlic) has a *visible* boundary. When the dressing is shaken vigorously, the droplets become very small and the mixture turns milky, but it never becomes clear. Oil and water never mix at the molecular level. Because the atoms and molecules form macromolecular structures (oil droplets), the particles are usually large enough to see with our eyes.

6.2.2 Solutions and colloids

Solutions are a type of homogeneous mixture. We normally think of solutions as liquids, but in fact, the term *solution* can also be applied to both solids and gases. For example, 12 carat gold is a *solid solution* of gold atoms, silver, zinc, and copper atoms mixed together in a solid. Air is a *gaseous solution* of many gases, including oxygen, nitrogen, and carbon dioxide. Soda pop is a *liquid solution* that contains carbon dioxide, water, and phosphoric acid. So a solution can be in any form: solid, liquid, or gas. We will learn more about solutions in the next section.

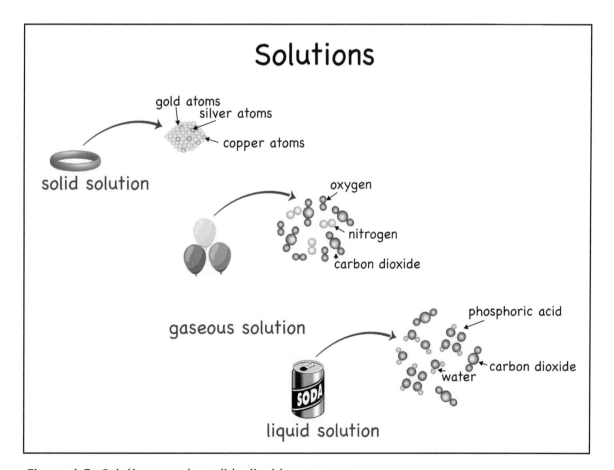

Figure 6.5: Solutions can be solids, liquids, or gases.

Some mixtures might seem like homogeneous solutions, but are, in fact, heterogeneous colloids [kä'-loidz]. Recall that a heterogeneous mixture is characterized by the fact that it often has visible particles. A colloid, however, has particles that are quite difficult to see individually, but are still much larger than individual molecules. For example, milk is a colloid. Milk appears to the unaided eye as a homogeneous mixture since the white color of milk is uniform throughout. However, milk is actually made up of water, protein, and fats. The proteins and fats are gathered into oil-like particles that do not mix homogeneously with the water. So, even though the particles in milk can't be seen, milk is a heterogeneous mixture.

There are different types of colloids. The differences between colloids depend on whether or not the components that are mixed are solids, liquids, or gases. Milk—a type of colloid—

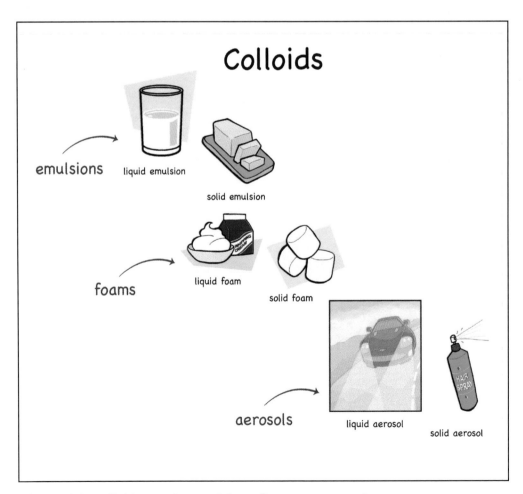

Figure 6.6: Colloids can be emulsions, foams, or aerosols.

is called an emulsion [i-məl'-shən]. An emulsion is a liquid (proteins) mixed into a liquid (water). Butter is also a colloid and is called a solid emulsion. A solid emulsion is a liquid (proteins) mixed into a solid (fats at room temperature). Whipped cream is called a foam. A foam is a gas (air) mixed into a liquid (water and proteins). A marshmallow is a solid foam. A solid foam is a gas (air) mixed into a solid (cooked sugar at room temperature). Hair spray, fog, and smoke are aerosols [ar'-ə-sälz]. Aerosols are either liquids (water—fog) or solids (particles—smoke) mixed into a gas (air).

6.3 SOLUBILITY OF SOLUTIONS

6.3.1 Introduction

What happens when salt or sugar dissolves in water? Why do they form a homogeneous mixture? Why doesn't water dissolve in oil, or oil in water? Why do oil and water form a heterogeneous mixture? If oil does not dissolve in water, what will oil dissolve in?

These questions address the physical property called solubility [säl-yə-bil'-ə-tē]. When a molecule or compound dissolves in something, we say it is soluble [säl'-yə-bəl]. That is, we will get a homogeneous mixture of atoms, molecules, or ions dispersed in each other with no clumping, droplets, or large particles. Solubility is a physical property and not a chemical property, since no chemical reaction takes place. Soluble compounds form homogeneous mixtures, but insoluble compounds form heterogeneous mixtures. This is because the molecules stay in clumps or droplets and do not disperse. But what makes a compound soluble or insoluble?

6.3.2 Solubility and polarity

A solution is usually made up of a small amount of one substance dissolved into a large amount of another substance. The substance that dissolves is called the solute [säl'-yoot], and the substance it dissolves into is called the solvent [säl'-vənt]. The solvent is the most abundant substance. For example, a small amount of salt dissolves in a larger amount of water, so the *salt is the solute* and the *water is the solvent*. The solubility of a solute is the maximum amount of *solute* (in grams or moles) that dissolves in a given volume of *solvent* (in liters or milliliters) at a given temperature. For example, the solubility of NaCl in water is 39.12 g/100 ml at 100°C. This means that, at most, 39.12 grams of salt will dissolve in 100 ml of water at 100°C.

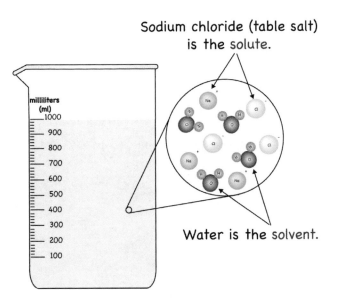

Figure 6.7: Sodium chloride is the solute and water is the solvent in a salt-water mixture.

Perhaps the most important characteristic that determines whether a solute will dissolve in a given solvent is called polarity [pō-lar'-i-tē]. Polarity depends on *both* the electronegativity [i-lek-trō-ne-gə-tiv'-i-tē] of the atoms in a molecule and the shape of the molecule itself.

6.3.3 Polarity and electronegativity

The electronegativity of an atom is the measure of its ability to draw electrons toward it. Figure 6.8 shows the electronegativity of a few atoms. Notice that as the atomic number increases from left to right on the periodic table, the electronegativity also increases. The electronegativities decrease as you move down the periodic table. In Chapter 2, we learned that sodium and chlorine form an ionic bond because sodium loses its valence 3s electron to become Na$^+$, and chlorine gains the electron to become Cl$^-$. Chlorine has *high* electronegativity at 3.0 and sodium has *low* electronegativity at 0.9. This is why chlorine can draw the electron away from sodium and why sodium and chlorine form an ionic bond. The greater the difference in electronegativity, the more ionic is the bond. All ionic bonds

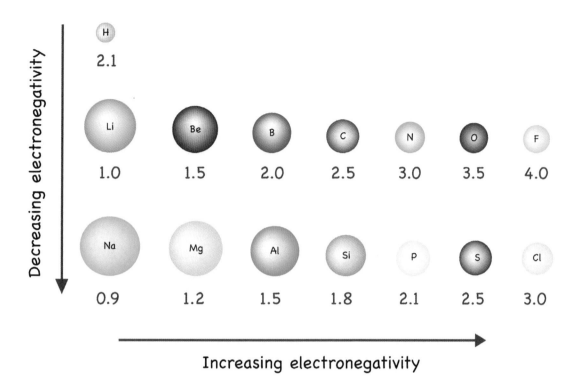

Figure 6.8: The electronegativity increases as you go from left to right on the periodic table and decreases as you go down.

are polar [pō'-lər], meaning that one of the atoms carries a positive charge and the other atom carries a negative charge.

Some covalent bonds are also polar. For example, water has polar bonds. The electronegativity of oxygen is considerably higher than the electronegativity of hydrogen. This means that the oxygen atoms in a water molecule will pull the electrons away from hydrogen. Therefore, the oxygen atom will be negative and the hydrogen atoms will both be positive. The fact that oxygen is more electronegative than hydrogen helps make water polar.

6.3.4 Polarity and shape

For a molecule to be polar, the shape of the molecule matters. Water is a bent molecule with the hydrogens sticking out away from the oxygen at an angle of about 120° (see Figure 6.9). If water were linear—with the hydrogens sticking out on both ends—water would not be polar. This is because the little poles (or dipoles) on each bond cancel each other out in a linear molecule resulting in no overall charge on the molecule. However, because water is not a linear molecule, but bent, the pulling of the electrons toward the oxygen atom causes the water molecule to have a net negative charge around the oxygen and a net positive charge around the hydrogens. This is what is meant by *polar*—it has poles: a positive pole and a negative pole.

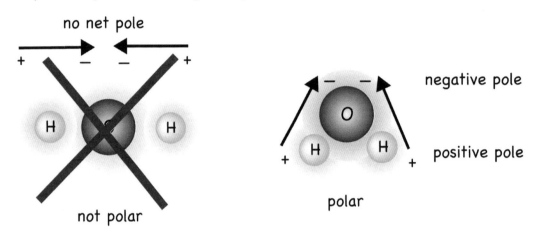

Figure 6.9: Water is a polar molecule because the O—H bonds are approximately at a 120° angle.

6.3.5 Like dissolves like

The rule for solubility is as follows:

> Like dissolves like.

This means that polar and ionic compounds tend to dissolve in polar solvents, and nonpolar (or weakly polar) molecules tend to dissolve in nonpolar (or weakly polar) solvents. Water is a very polar solvent, so only polar (or ionic) molecules dissolve in water. This is why sodium chloride, table salt, dissolves in water. Sodium chloride forms an ionic bond and so readily dissolves in a polar solvent like water (see Figure 6.10). On the other hand, octane, a very nonpolar molecule in gasoline, will not dissolve ionic or polar molecules, but will dissolve nonpolar molecules. Some cleaners use nonpolar solvents to dissolve nonpolar substances such as glue, gum, or grease.

6.3.6 Solubility and temperature

The ability of a solute to dissolve in a given amount of a solvent depends not only on the polarity of molecules in the solvent and the solute, but also on the *temperature* of the solvent. Energy is required for polar molecules, like water, to break weak ionic bonds of molecules, like salt. If energy is added in the form of heat, more solute will be able to dissolve in a given amount of solvent.

For example, about 35 grams of table salt (NaCl) will dissolve in 100 grams of water at room temperature. If you added 39 grams of table salt to 100 grams of water at room temperature, the extra 4 grams of salt would not dissolve no matter how much you stirred or mixed the solution. However, if the water was heated to 100°C, the 39 grams of table salt would dissolve.

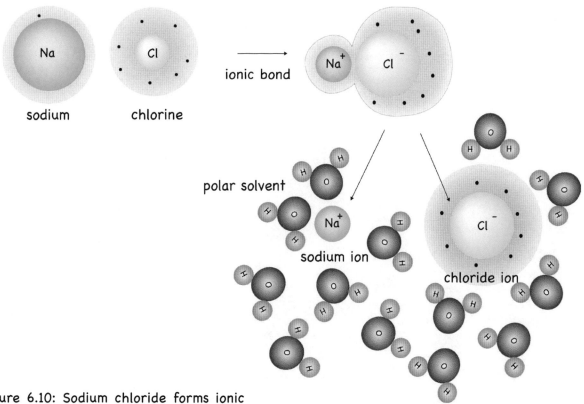

Figure 6.10: Sodium chloride forms ionic bonds that can be easily separated in a polar solvent such as water.

A solution that has less than the amount of solute able to dissolve in a given solvent is called a subsaturated solution. If a solution has the maximum amount of solute dissolved in a solvent, it is called a saturated solution. It is often possible to create a supersaturated solution in which the solution has *more* than the maximum amount of solute dissolved in it. How can that be possible? A supersaturated solution of table salt and water can be made by dissolving 39 grams of table salt in 100 grams of water heated to 100°C. Once all of the salt has dissolved, the solution is then slowly cooled to room temperature. The 39 grams of table salt will remain dissolved in the room temperature water. This is a supersaturated solution. It turns out that a supersaturated solution can be made with a variety of solutes and solvents.

6.4 SURFACTANTS

6.4.1 Introduction

Polar substances are often called hydrophilic [hī-drə-fi'-lik] substances. Hydro comes from the Greek word *hydro* which means "water" and philic comes from the Greek word *philein* which means "loving." So hydrophilic literally means "water loving." Hydrophilic molecules are molecules that "love," and hence dissolve in, water.

Salts, acids and bases, alcohols, and

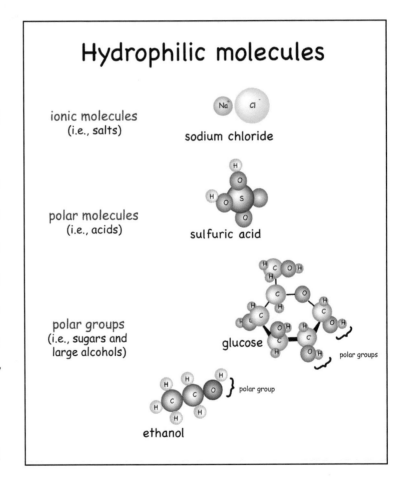

Figure 6.11: Hydrophilic molecules "love water" and can be ionic, polar, or contain polar groups.

sugars are all hydrophilic molecules. They are hydrophilic because they are either ionic, polar, or have one or more polar groups attached to them.

Nonpolar substances are called hydrophobic [hī'-drə-fō'-bik]. Phobic comes from the Greek word *phobos* which means "to fear." So hydrophobic literally means "to fear water." Hydrophobic molecules do not like water, and so they do not dissolve in water.

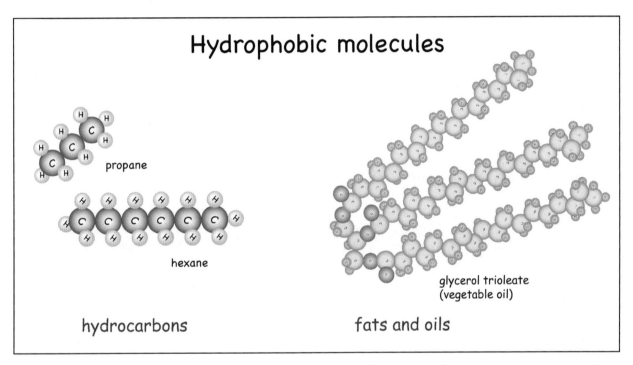

Figure 6.12: Hydrophobic molecules are molecules that "fear water" such as hydrocarbons, fats, and oils.

Oils, fats, and hydrocarbons (like gasoline) are hydrophobic molecules. They are hydrophobic because they are neither polar molecules nor do they have polar groups attached to them.

6.4.2 Soaps

What about molecules that are *both* hydrophilic and hydrophobic? Soaps are molecules that have both a hydrophobic group (tail) and a hydrophilic group (head). Soaps are part of a broader category of molecules called surfactants [sər-fak'-təntz]. Both soaps and detergents are surfactants. Surfactants are used to clean grease, oil, and other hydrophobic molecules from clothing, hands, or other items.

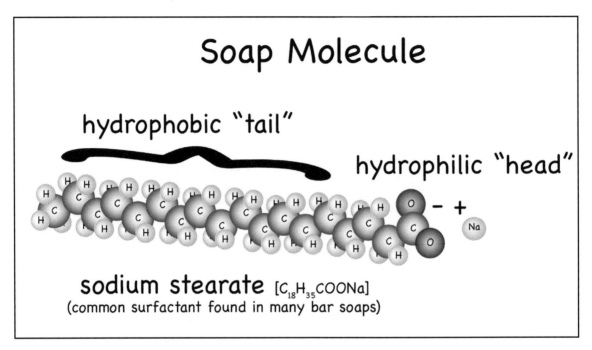

Figure 6.13: A soap molecule with a polar (hydrophilic) head and a nonpolar (hydrophobic) tail.

Surfactants can make even nonpolar, hydrophobic molecules "dissolve" in water. That is why dish soap can clean greasy dishes and hands. Surfactants work by making an emulsion with hydrophobic molecules in the form of a micelle [mī-sel']. For example, when a surfactant meets with both water and oil, it forms a ball with the hydrophobic molecules (oil) surrounded by the surfactant. The surfactant molecules have their greasy tails pointed inward dissolved in the oil, and their polar heads pointed outward dissolved in the water.

Because surfactants have both a hydrophobic tail and a hydrophilic head, they are able to trap hydrophobic molecules in micelles and bring them into an emulsion. Soap solutions are colloids and are milky in appearance.

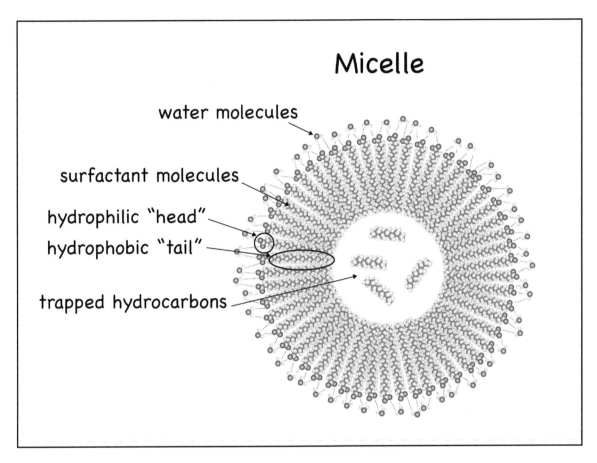

Figure 6.14: A micelle with grease molecules trapped inside the nonpolar ends

6.4.3 Biological membranes

Another place in which surfactant-like molecules are important is in cell membranes. The membranes that surround cells are made of "soap-like" molecules organized into a bilayer [bī'-lā-ər]. The prefix *bi-* comes from the Latin word *bis*, which means "two." A membrane bilayer has "two layers" of molecules stacked on top of each other in opposite directions. The soap-like molecules that make up a membrane bilayer are slightly different than detergent molecules that form micelles.

Membrane bilayer molecules sometimes have two tails and a phosphorus group in the head region. The most abundant membrane molecules are called phospholipids [fəs-fō-lip'-idz].

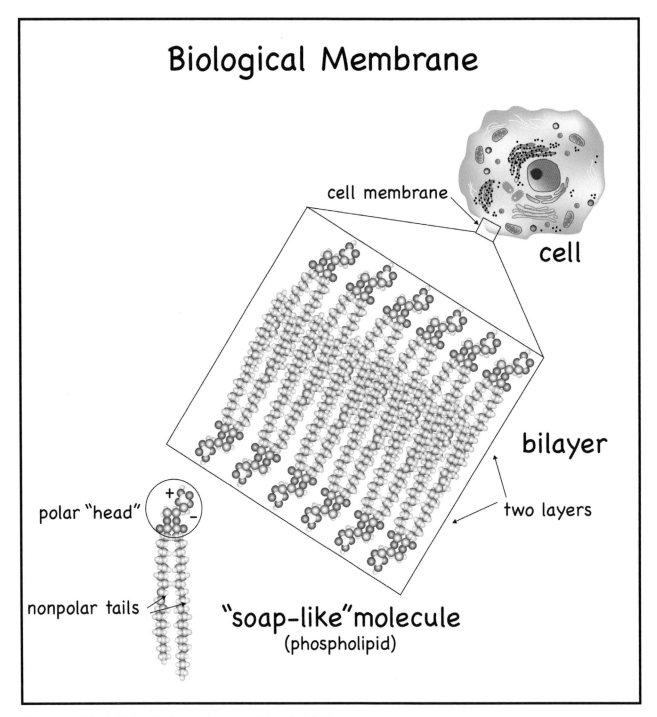

Biological Membrane

cell membrane

cell

bilayer

two layers

polar "head"

nonpolar tails

"soap-like" molecule
(phospholipid)

Figure 6.15: A biological membrane with a lipid bilayer.

6.5 SUMMARY

Here are the main points to remember from this chapter:

- A mixture is a collection of molecules or atoms that are not bonded to each other.

- In a homogeneous solution, the particles are dispersed as individual molecules on a molecular scale.

- In a heterogeneous mixture, the particles are dispersed into clumps or droplets on a macromolecular scale.

- In a colloid, the molecules are gathered into droplets or micelles that are too small to see with our eyes but are still much larger than individual molecules.

- Solutions result from one type of molecule (the solute) dissolving into another type of molecule (the solvent).

- Electronegativity is the measure used to determine how well an atom can draw electrons toward itself.

- Molecules that are polar have atoms of different electronegativities.

- Molecules that are "like" each other dissolve. Polar molecules will dissolve in each other and nonpolar molecules will dissolve in each other. Polar molecules do not dissolve in nonpolar molecules.

- Surfactants are molecules with a polar (or hydrophilic) end and a nonpolar (or hydrophobic) end.

6.6 STUDY QUESTIONS

1.   Describe the difference between a mixture and a compound.

2.   List three mixtures.

3.   List three compounds.

4.   Give an example of a homogeneous solution.

5.   Give an example of a heterogeneous mixture.

6.   List three kinds of solutions.

7.   List three kinds of colloids.

8.   Define *solute* and *solvent*.

9.   Define *electronegativity*.

10. Why is water polar? (Give two reasons.)

CHAPTER 7 SEPARATING MIXTURES

7.1 PRINCIPLES OF SEPARATION

7.1.1 Introduction

Once two items have been mixed, how can they be separated? We know how to separate pebbles and stones, but is it possible to separate smaller items like atoms and molecules?

What chemical or physical techniques could help or hinder separating small items, like atoms or molecules?

The techniques used to separate mixtures depend on the kinds of items that have been mixed. For example, we can hand sort mixtures of large components, such as

pebbles and stones. Hand sorting is a technique used to separate large items, and it is something everyone has done at one time or another (e.g., cleaning your room). But what about a mixture of sand and salt, or salt and sugar? How can these kinds of mixtures be separated? Both sand and salt and salt and sugar are too small to be hand sorted. In addition salt and sugar are both the same color! What about a mixture of two clear liquids, such as water and alcohol? What techniques can be used to separate these kinds of mixtures?

7.1.2 Types of mixtures

The technique used to separate a mixture depends on the chemical and physical properties of the items that are mixed together. Chemical properties are the properties of an atom or molecule that result in chemical reactions. For example, sodium metal will react violently with water, producing hydrogen gas and sodium hydroxide. This is a *chemical property* of sodium metal.

$$2 \text{ Na } (s) + 2 \text{ H}_2\text{O } (l) \dashrightarrow 2 \text{ NaOH } (aq) + \text{H}_2 \text{ } (g) \qquad \text{(see footnote)}$$

Pure substances, like gold or graphite, are separated using chemical methods based on their chemical properties. Physical properties, on the other hand, do not result in chemical reactions, but are properties that make atoms and molecules different without changing them chemically.

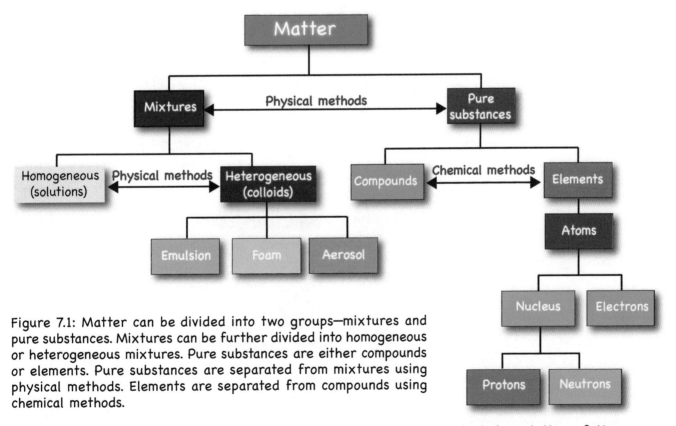

Figure 7.1: Matter can be divided into two groups—mixtures and pure substances. Mixtures can be further divided into homogeneous or heterogeneous mixtures. Pure substances are either compounds or elements. Pure substances are separated from mixtures using physical methods. Elements are separated from compounds using chemical methods.

The abbreviations next to the chemical formulas give the physical description of the molecules; that is, (s) stands for solid, (l) stands for liquid, (aq) stands for aqueous, and (g) stands for gaseous.

In this chapter we will look at ways to separate mixtures using physical properties. Physical properties include color, size, melting point, boiling point, volatility, and solubility. In any mixture, ingredients can have different physical properties and these differences can be used to separate them.

7.1.3 Properties of mixtures

When deciding how to separate a mixture, it is important to consider all of the physical properties of each component in the mixture. The separation technique used will depend on *differences in the physical properties* between the components of a mixture.

For example, consider a mixture of sand and pebbles. A pebble is much larger than a grain of sand, so there is a significant difference in *size*—a physical property. Both sand and pebbles are made from similar materials (*i.e.,* the materials found in rocks and dirt, such as silicon and quartz). Because they are made of similar materials, they are both solids at room temperature, probably have similar boiling and melting points, and are both insoluble in water. All of these physical properties are similar. The only physical property that is not similar is *size*. Therefore, a good way to separate sand and pebbles would be to use a technique that separates mixtures based on physical *size*, such as filtering or sieving.

Sand and Pebbles

Figure 7.2: A mixture of sand and pebbles can be separated according to *size*.

	Physical properties					
	Color	Size	Melting point	Boiling point	Volatility	Solubility
Sand	–	small	–	–	–	–
Pebbles	–	large	–	–	–	–

Now consider a mixture of sand and table salt. The grains of sand and table salt crystals are both similar in size, so they cannot easily be separated using filtering or sieving. However, we know that grains of sand and table salt crystals are not made of the same material. Sand is made mainly of water-insoluble silicon and quartz, but table salt is made of water-soluble sodium chloride. Because sand and table salt have different solubilities in water, they can be separated based on water *solubility*. We could dissolve the salt in water and pour off the water, separating it from the sand.

Sand and table salt

Physical properties					
Color	Size	Melting point	Boiling point	Volatility	Solubility

	Color	Size	Melting point	Boiling point	Volatility	Solubility
Sand	-	-	-	-	-	water-insoluble
Table Salt	-	-	-	-	-	water-soluble

Figure 7.3: A mixture of sand and table salt can be separated according to *solubility*.

Now consider a mixture of alcohol and water. A mixture of alcohol and water is much harder to separate than a mixture of sand and pebbles or sand and salt because both water and alcohol are liquids composed of individual molecules. Because they are both on the molecular scale, they cannot be separated based on size. Also, alcohol is soluble in water, so alcohol cannot be separated from water based on water solubility. To find a suitable way to separate alcohol and water we have to look at their other physical properties. For example, if we compare the boiling points for alcohol and water we see that they are slightly different. Water boils at 100 °C and alcohol boils around 80 °C. Because alcohol boils at a lower temperature, alcohol is more *volatile* than water. We can separate a mixture of alcohol and water using their difference in *volatility*.

Alcohol and water

Physical properties					
Color	Size	Melting point	Boiling point	Volatility	Solubility

	Color	Size	Melting point	Boiling point	Volatility	Solubility
Alcohol	–	–	–	80 °C	lower (than water)	–
Water	–	–	–	100 °C	higher (than alcohol)	–

Figure 7.4: A mixture of water and alcohol can be separated according to *volatility*.

7.2 TECHNIQUES OF SEPARATION

The preceding examples illustrate several circumstances in which techniques of separation based on physical properties are needed. Over time, chemists have developed a number of different methods to separate mixtures based on differences in physical properties. These techniques include filtration, evaporation, distillation, recrystallization, extraction, and chromatography.

7.2.1 Filtration

Filtration [fil-trā'-shən] separates components of a mixture based on the differences in their *physical size*. A mixture of sand and pebbles can be separated using filtration because their physical sizes are different. To separate a mixture by filtration, a filter is used. A filter can be anything from a metal sheet with large holes in it, to a colander, a sieve, or a piece of paper. The holes in a filter are called pores. The pore size of a filter should be selected so that only part of the mixture will go through the pores with the remaining mixture retained by the filter. The pore size will vary depending on the relative sizes of the components of the mixture. For example, a metal sheet with large holes punched through it may be used to separate large rocks or stones from smaller rocks or sand. On the other hand, a mixture of smaller rocks and fine sand needs to be separated with a filter that has a smaller pore size, such as a sieve or wire mesh.

In chemistry, paper filters are commonly used to separate chemical precipitates [pri-sip′-i-tātz] (solids) from the aqueous (i.e., water) portion, of a chemical reaction. Paper filters have microscopic pores that allow water to seep through while retaining the solids. For example, the chemical reaction between silver nitrate and sodium chloride produces a water-insoluble precipitate called silver chloride. To separate the silver chloride from the water, a filter paper is used. A simple filtration apparatus consists of filter paper in a funnel placed on top of a collection flask.

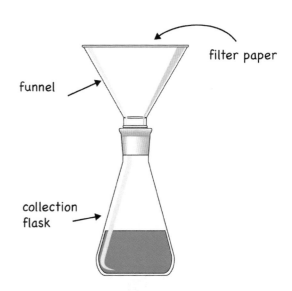

Figure 7.5: A filtration apparatus with filter paper, funnel, and collection flask.

The aqueous silver chloride mixture is poured through the filter paper. The water flows through the paper and is collected in the collection flask at the bottom and the silver chloride precipitate is retained on the filter paper.

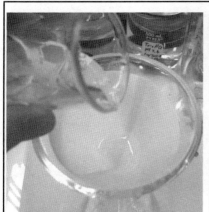

The silver chloride water mixture is poured through the filter paper.

The silver chloride precipitate is separated from the water and stays on the filter paper.

Figure 7.6: The separation of a silver chloride precipitate using filtration.

7.2.2 Evaporation

Evaporation [i-va-pə-rā'-shən] separates components of a mixture based on their differences in volatility [vä-lə-ti'-li-tē] (i.e. their ability to become a gas). Molecules that are volatile have a lower boiling point than molecules that are not volatile. For example, a mixture of water and dissolved salt cannot be separated by filtration or crystallization because both salt and water are similar in size. But because water is *more volatile (i.e., has a lower boiling point)* than salt, a salt–water mixture can be separated using evaporation.

Evaporation is a simple technique that is used in a variety of situations. For example, French chefs use the differences in volatility between alcohol and water to create fine main course dishes or tasty desserts. When alcohol is added to a water mixture of spices or sugars, for example, the mixture is generally heated. Because the alcohol in the mixture is more volatile than the water, it boils off, or evaporates, sooner than water, leaving behind only the added flavoring the dissolved molecules in the alcohol provide.

7.2.3 Distillation

Distillation [dis-tə-lā'-shən] also separates components of a mixture based on their differences in *volatility*. Distillation is performed using a distillation apparatus. A distillation apparatus is able to capture the more volatile component and cools it back to a liquid, thus separating it from the other components in the mixture. For example, at sea level, water boils at 100°C and ethanol (alcohol) boils at 78.5°C. A simple distillation apparatus can be used to separate the alcohol from the water. The alcohol–water mixture is heated until the temperature is between 78.5°C and 100°C. Both alcohol and water vapor are formed. But because alcohol is more volatile than water, there is more alcohol vapor than water vapor that goes up the column of the apparatus. As the vapors rise, they cool and recondense onto the walls of the column, forming a new mixture of water and alcohol that has more alcohol than the original mixture. This new mixture continues to re-evaporate and condense further up the column. Once the vapor mixture reaches the top, it passes through a condenser. The condenser is a long tube that has cold water flowing through it. This water is separated from the alcohol–water vapor mixture by a tube. The condenser is used to cool the vapor mixture back into a liquid. The liquid drips into a collection flask. Most of the water has been separated away from the alcohol-water mixture, leaving the water behind.

Some mixtures, like salt and water or motor oil and gasoline, can be separated nearly completely by distillation because their boiling points are very different. But other mixtures with similar boiling points, like water and alcohol, can only be partially separated. Because water and alcohol have similar boiling points, they also have similar *vapor pressures*. This means that the vapor above a water-alcohol mixture always has both alcohol and water in it. This property is called azeotropy [ā-zē-o'-trō-pē]. Because an alcohol–water mixture is an azeotrope [ə-zē'-ə-trōp], it can never be separated beyond around 80% pure by distillation. This is why the strongest alcoholic drinks are 80% alcohol, or 160 proof.

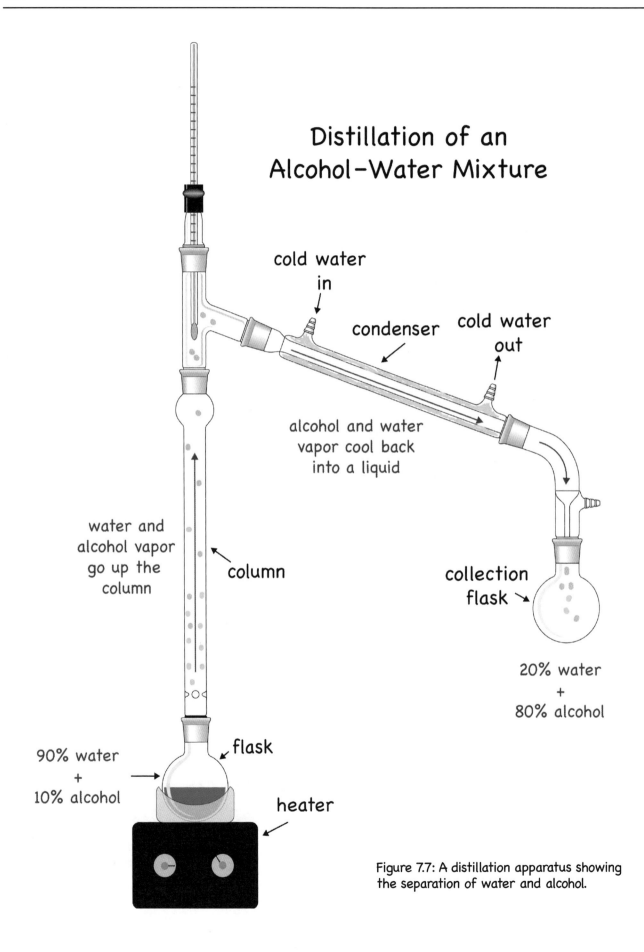

Distillation of an Alcohol–Water Mixture

cold water in

condenser

cold water out

alcohol and water vapor cool back into a liquid

water and alcohol vapor go up the column

column

collection flask

20% water + 80% alcohol

90% water + 10% alcohol

flask

heater

Figure 7.7: A distillation apparatus showing the separation of water and alcohol.

7.2.4 Recrystallization

Recrystallization separates components of a mixture based on their *temperature-dependent solubility*. Recall from Chapter 6 that solubility is the physical property that determines how much of a given *solute* will dissolve in a given amount of *solvent*. Also recall that solubility in aqueous solutions depends on the temperature of the solution.

Imagine that we have a mixture of potassium nitrate (KNO_3) that is contaminated with a small amount of table salt, sodium chloride (NaCl). Both potassium nitrate and sodium chloride are white salts that are soluble in water. We can use their difference in solubility to recrystallize one salt from the other. Because crystals tend to exclude contaminates from cocrystallizing, the salts can be separated.

Imagine that we have 100 grams of KNO_3 and just a few grams of NaCl. If we dissolve the mixture in 100 ml of water and heat the mixture to 60°C we will get a *supersaturated* solution of KNO_3 and an *unsaturated* solution of NaCl. A supersaturated solution will tend to form crystals. When we then take

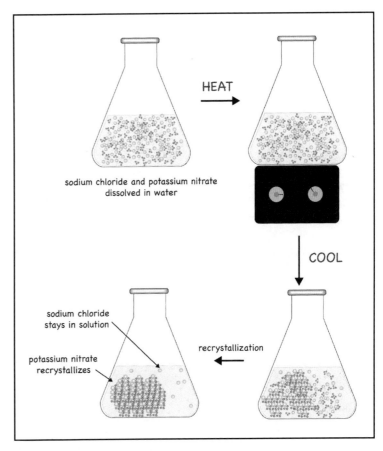

Figure 7.8: A mixture of salts can be separated using recrystallization, where the solution is heated and then recooled.

the mixture and cool it slowly to 0°C the supersaturated solution of KNO_3 will form crystals of pure KNO_3 leaving the NaCl behind in the aqueous solution. The aqueous unsaturated NaCl can be removed, leaving behind the purified KNO_3 crystals.

Recrystallization is used to purify silicon for making microchips. In this case, molten silicon is heated and slowly cooled. As the molten silicon cools, purified silicon crystals form and any impurities are removed because they do not form crystals with the silicon.

7.2.5 Extraction

Extraction [ik-strak'-shən] also separates components of a mixture based on their differences in *solubility.* Extraction is based on the idea that some components of a mixture will be *more* soluble in certain solvents and other components will be *less* soluble in those same solvents. For example, many pigments found in flowers, leaves, or other foods can be purified using extraction. Extraction has been used for centuries to purify dyes from natural products. Before synthetic dyes became popular, extraction of plant and flower pigments provided the main source of coloring for clothing and other textiles.

To extract pigments from a leaf or flower, the leaf or flower is first ground or crushed, and a solvent, such as water or alcohol, is added. Depending on the desired pigment, the mixture might be heated or allowed to sit for several hours. Because the pigments are soluble in the solvent, they separate from the the *insoluble* solid material of the leaf or flower. This is the simplest form of extraction.

7.2.6 Chromatography

Chromatography [krō-mə-tä'-grə-fē] separates components of a mixture using differences in *mobility through a solid.* Recall that the word chromatography comes from the Greek word *chroma*, which means "color" and *graphy*, which means "to write." Chromatography literally means to "write with color."

In general, mixtures are separated by chromatography by first dissolving them in a solvent (called the mobile phase) and then passing the dissolved mixture over a solid (called the stationary phase). As the mixture in the mobile phase passes over the stationary phase, the components in the mixture will migrate differently (depending on their solubility in the mobile phase) over the stationary phase.

There are two main types of chromatography—gas chromatography and liquid chromatography—that differ in the type of *mobile phase* (either liquid, or gas) that is being used. As the name implies, in gas chromatography, the components of the mixture are dissolved in a gas. Gas chromatography is commonly used to separate small molecules that are volatile and can be carried in a gas.

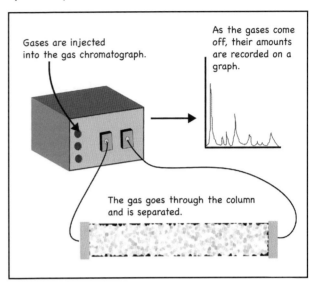

Figure 7.9: Schematic of a gas chromatograph separating gases as they come off the stationary phase (column).

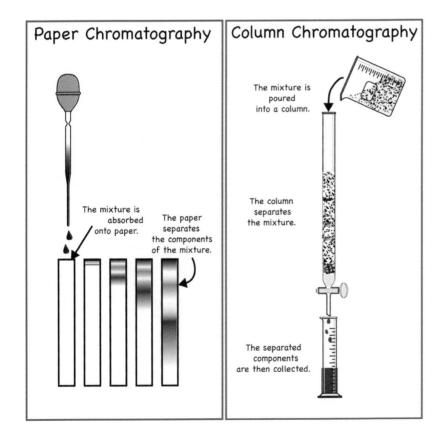

In liquid chromatography, the components of the mixture are dissolved in a liquid. There are two types of liquid chromatography—paper chromatography and column chromatography. Paper

Figure 7.10: Paper chromatography and column chromatography are two types of liquid chromatography.

chromatography utilizes paper as the stationary phase, and in column chromatography the stationary phase is made of silicon beads packed into a column. Liquid chromatography is commonly used to separate larger molecules, such as pigments, proteins, or DNA, which are soluble in a liquid.

7.3 SUMMARY

Here are the main points to remember from this chapter:

- The techniques used to separate mixtures depend on the chemical and physical properties of the components in the mixture.

- Physical properties include color, size, melting point, boiling point, volatility, and solubility.

- Separation techniques depend on the *differences in physical properties* for each component in a mixture.

- Filtration separates components of a mixture based on the differences in their *physical size*.

- Evaporation and distillation separate components of a mixture based on their differences in *volatility*.

- Recrystallization and extraction separate components of a mixture based on their differences in *solubility*.

- Chromatography separates components of a mixture based on their differences in mobility through a solid.

7.4 STUDY QUESTIONS

1. List some of the physical properties of a mixture of sand and pebbles, and describe a good separation technique.

2. List some of the physical properties of a mixture of sand and table salt, and describe a good separation technique.

3. List some of the physical properties of a mixture of alcohol and water, and describe a good separation technique.

4. Table 7.1 describes some of the physical properties for several different compounds.

Table 7.1 Physical Properties of Different Compounds

Name	Boiling Point	Water Soluble	Size	Color
water (H_2O)	100°C	–	liquid	clear
alcohol (CH_3CH_2OH)	78.5°C	yes	liquid	clear
benzene (C_6H_6)	80.1°C	no	liquid	clear
phenol (C_6H_5OH)	181.7°C	no	liquid	clear
copper nuggets (Cu)	2567°C	no	3 mm	metallic
table salt (NaCl)	1413°C	yes	0.5 mm	white crystals
red dye (generic)	–	yes	liquid	red
yellow dye (generic)	–	yes	liquid	yellow
chalk dust ($CaCO_3$)	825°C	no	fine powder	white
egg white (protein)	–	yes	liquid	clear

Using Table 7.1, describe a separation technique for each of the following mixtures, and explain why you think your technique will work:

  a. water and copper nuggets

  b. water and table salt

  c. chalk dust and table salt

  d. benzene and table salt

  e. egg whites and water

  f. red dye and yellow dye

  g. copper nuggets and egg whites

CHALLENGE

You have a mixture of table salt, chalk dust, copper nuggets, and water. How would you separate them?

CHAPTER 8 THE CHEMISTRY OF CARBON

THE CHEMISTRY OF CARBON - PART A

THE CHEMISTRY OF CARBON - PART B

THE CHEMISTRY OF CARBON — PART A

8.1 ORGANIC CHEMISTRY

8.1.1 Introduction

So far we have studied the chemistry of the elements in the periodic table without focusing on any one of them. Organic chemistry singles out just one element for special consideration—*carbon*. The chemistry of carbon is especially important because carbon is the most useful and versatile of all the elements in the periodic table. Carbon can be used to form more kinds of molecules than any other element. Carbon also forms some of the strongest chemical bonds known, and it is the only element that can form very large,

| 6 C |
| Carbon |
| 12.011 |
| $[He]2s^2 2p^2$ |

complex molecules. For these reasons, carbon is essential to all of life as we know it, and understanding the chemistry of carbon will be important if we are to understand the molecules that make up not only our own bodies but also our food.

If we were to make a list of all known molecules (a very, very long list), we would find that the vast majority are based on carbon atoms. Because the chemistry of carbon is so important, the science of chemistry is divided into two main branches: organic chemistry, which deals with carbon-containing molecules; and inorganic chemistry, which deals with everything else.0 With a few exceptions, all molecules that contain carbon are considered to be organic molecules. Table 8.1 shows some common examples of organic molecules.

Carbon dioxide, CO_2; hydrogen cyanide, HCN; graphite; and diamond are not considered by most scientists to be organic substances even though they contain carbon.

Table 8.1 Common Organic Molecules

Name of Molecule	Chemical Formula	Structure
methane	CH_4	
acetylene	C_2H_2	
ethanol	CH_3CH_2OH	
chloroform	$CHCl_3$	
acetic acid	CH_3COOH	
formaldehyde	H_2CO	
glycine	H_2NCH_2COOH	
benzene	C_6H_6	
octane	C_8H_{18}	

There is no limit to the size and complexity of organic molecules. The ones shown in Table 8.1 are often called "small molecules" by organic chemists! There are larger organic molecules found inside living things (proteins, DNA) with thousands or even millions of atoms each. (See Chapter 10.) Organic chemistry is a huge subject. At the college level, it is usually taught as an entire year-long course all by itself. In this chapter, we will only introduce the main ideas and classes of organic molecules. These important ideas include the following concepts:

(1) *isomers* [ī'-sō-mərz]—two molecules with the same atoms, but with different structures;

(2) *functional groups*—special sites on larger molecules at which chemistry can take place and that can be used by organic chemists to build new molecules; and

(3) *parent molecules*—molecules from which other, more complex molecules are built.

8.1.2 Isomers, functional groups, and parent molecules

Whenever two molecules have the same atoms but different structures they are called isomers of each other. Notice that Table 8.3 has two different molecules, n-butane and isobutane, both of which have four carbon atoms. Looking more closely, you can see that both molecules also have 10 hydrogen atoms each, so in fact both are made up of exactly the same number and type of atoms. The difference between them is in their structure— that is, the way in which the atoms are connected to each other. You could take n-butane apart and use the very same atoms to build isobutane, with no extra atoms needed and none left over. Isobutane is an isomer of n-butane. (That's why it's called *iso*butane!)

Isomers are very common in organic chemistry. Because they differ in structure, isomers also differ from each other in their physical and chemical properties, even though they are made up of the same atoms. For example, ethanol, CH_3CH_2OH, and dimethyl ether, CH_3OCH_3, both have two carbons, six hydrogens, and one oxygen, and so are isomers of each other. But ethanol is a liquid at room temperature (it boils at 78°C), and dimethyl ether is a gas (it boils at -23°C). Ethanol is completely soluble without

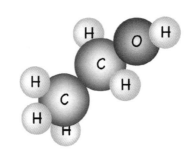

ethanol

liquid at room temperature (boils at 78°C)

high solubility in water

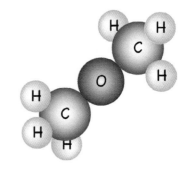

dimethyl ether

gas at room temperature (boils at -23°C)

limited solubility in water

Figure 8.1: Isomers—ethanol and dimethyl ether—have the same number and kind of atoms but different chemical and physical properties.

limit in water, but dimethyl ether has only limited solubility in water. Finally, ethanol takes part in very different kinds of chemical reactions than does dimethyl ether.

So, in organic chemistry it is always necessary to know the *structure* of the molecule; just knowing the number of atoms is not enough. Chemists have worked out two ways to describe the structures of complex molecules. One method is a very complicated system for *naming* organic molecules. The name of the molecule alone can be used to tell how the molecule is built. Sometimes the names become VERY long: The name for the molecule in Figure 8.2 is a rather short one—[4-ethyl-3-methylheptane]. Though naming is often useful, we will not use it in this book. The other method is just to draw the molecule, as in the preceding figures and table. This is much simpler, more straightforward, and is probably more widely used by everyone except the most experienced organic chemists.

The double bond in an alkene, the triple bond in an alkyne, the -OH group on an alcohol, the $-NH_2$ group on an amine, the C=O group of a ketone, the -C=OH group in an aldehyde, and the COOH group of an acid are all *functional groups*. A functional group is a special site on an organic molecule at which chemical reactions occur. Functional groups are used by organic chemists to change molecules and to build new ones. The molecule in Figure 8.2 has two functional groups—a methyl group and an ethyl group. Organic molecules are classified according to their functional groups because the functional groups control both their chemistry and reactions.

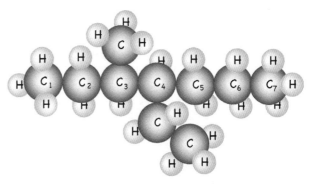

4-ethyl-3-methylheptane

Figure 8.2: The parent molecule is the 7 carbon chain (heptane). There is a methyl functional group on carbon 3 of the parent chain and an ethyl functional group on carbon 4. Hence the name "4-ethyl-3-methylheptane."

A related idea is the concept of a *parent molecule*. A parent molecule is a simple molecule, often an alkane, from which more complex molecules are built. The parent molecule in Figure 8.2 is the 7-carbon chain called heptane. Another example is the alcohol molecule ethanol, CH_3CH_2OH. (See Figure 8.3.) Ethanol is thought of as a simple alkane, ethane, CH_3CH_3, with an -OH group replacing an H atom at one end. Ethane is thought of as the parent molecule from which ethanol is made. Likewise, the alkene molecule ethene, $CH_2=CH_2$, is thought of as coming from ethane, CH_3CH_3, by removing two H atoms (one from each carbon) and creating a double bond between the two carbons. Once again, ethane is thought of as the parent molecule from which ethene is made. In reality, both ethanol and ethene may come from many sources and are rarely made from ethane. (Ethanol usually comes from anaerobic fermentation in yeast, for example). So the concept of a parent

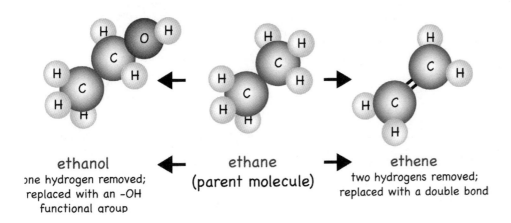

ethanol
one hydrogen removed;
replaced with an -OH
functional group

ethane
(parent molecule)

ethene
two hydrogens removed;
replaced with a double bond

Figure 8.3: The parent molecule for ethene and ethanol is ethane.

molecule is a useful way to *describe* a more complex molecule, although it is usually not the real source of the molecule.

8.1.3 Classes of organic molecules

Because there are so many different kinds of organic molecules, it is useful to classify them into groups, and learn about the groups one at a time. The most common groups of organic molecules are alkanes [al'-kānz], alkenes [al'-kēnz], alkynes [al'-kīnz], aromatics [a-rə-ma'-tiks], alcohols, amines [ə'-mēnz], aldehydes [al'-də-hīdz], acids, ketones [kē'-tōnz], esters [es'-tərz], and amides [ə'-mīdz]. Table 8.2 shows examples of each of these kinds of organic molecules. There are also many other types, but these are sufficient to understand the basics of organic chemistry and most of biology.

Table 8.2 General Groups of Organic Molecules

Name	Description	Structure
Alkanes	molecules that contain only carbon and hydrogen and only single bonds between carbon atoms	(methane)
Alkenes	molecules with one or more double bonds between two carbon atoms	(ethylene)
Alkynes	molecules with one or more triple bonds between two carbon atoms	$H-C\equiv C-H$ (acetylene)
Aromatics	molecules containing a benzene ring See Section 8.2.5.	(benzene)
Alcohols	molecules with an -OH attached to a carbon atom	(methanol)
Amines	molecules with $-NH_2$ attached to a carbon atom	CH_3-C-NH_2 (butylamine)

Aldehydes	molecules with -CH=O	$\underset{\text{CH}_3-\overset{\displaystyle\overset{O}{\|}}{C}-H}{}$ (ethanal)
Acids	molecules with C=OOH	$\underset{\text{CH}_3-\overset{\displaystyle\overset{O}{\|}}{C}-OH}{}$ (acetic acid)
Ketones	molecules with -C=O	$\underset{\text{CH}_3-\overset{\displaystyle\overset{O}{\|}}{C}-CH_3}{}$ (acetone)
Esters	molecules with -C=O-O-	$\underset{\text{CH}_3-\overset{\displaystyle\overset{O}{\|}}{C}-O-CH_2CH_3}{}$ (ethyl acetate)
Amides	molecules with -C=O-NH-	$\underset{\text{CH}_3-\overset{\displaystyle\overset{O}{\|}}{C}-NH_2}{}$ (ethanamide)

It is possible for one molecule to be in more than one group. For example, the molecule $H_2N\text{-}CH_2\text{-}CH_2\text{-}OH$ (called ethanolamine) has both a -OH attached to C, and a $-NH_2$ attached to C, so it is both an alcohol and an amine.

8.2 HYDROCARBONS: ALKANES, ALKENES, ALKYNES, AND AROMATICS

The first four kinds of organic molecules (alkanes, alkenes, alkynes, and aromatics) are all hydrocarbons—that is, they contain only hydrogen and carbon. They are all very nonpolar, flammable, and similar in both appearance and touch (for the solids and liquids).

8.2.1 Alkanes

The simplest organic molecules are the alkanes, with only single bonds, and only carbon and hydrogen. Table 8.3 shows some common examples of alkanes. An alkane can be as long as you like. The shortest is methane, CH_4, with only one carbon atom. Ethane has two carbons, propane has three carbons, and so on up to eicosane with 20 carbons, and polyethylene, which may have hundreds or even thousands of carbons.

Table 8.3 Alkanes

Molecule Name	Structure	Properties	Uses
methane	CH_4	colorless odorless gas	main component of natural gas
ethane	CH_3CH_3	colorless odorless gas	
propane	$CH_3CH_2CH_3$	gas	can be liquefied at high pressure (LP gas used for camp stoves and gas grills)
n-butane	$CH_3CH_2CH_2CH_3$	gas	can be liquefied at low pressure (used in butane lighters)
isobutane	$CH_3CH(CH_3)CH_3$	gas	can be liquefied at low pressure
n-pentane	$CH_3CH_2CH_2CH_2CH_3$	liquid	gasoline-like
n-decane	$CH_3(CH_2)_8CH_3$	liquid	a bit oily
n-eicosane	$CH_3(CH_2)_{18}CH_3$	waxy solid	
polyethylene	$CH_3(CH_2)_nCH_3$	common plastic	(milk bottles, etc.)

The small alkanes are gases, medium ones (from pentane on) are liquids, and the larger ones are solids. All the alkanes are very nonpolar: the liquids are gasoline-like or oily and act as solvents for non-polar substances. The solids are waxes (like paraffin wax) or plastics, with a waxy, greasy feeling to the touch. (This is the way all nonpolar substances feel.) They all burn in air and are often used as fuels (natural gas, LP gas, butane lighters, gasoline, candles, etc.).

8.2.2 Alkenes and alkynes

An alkene is any organic molecule with a carbon-to-carbon double bond, and an alkyne is any molecule with a carbon-to-carbon triple bond. Table 8.4 shows a few common examples (ethylene, butylene, acetylene, etc.). Like the alkanes, the smaller alkenes and alkynes are gases, the medium ones are nonpolar liquids, and the larger ones are waxy solids or plastics. Also like the alkanes, the alkenes and alkynes burn in air. Gasoline is a mixture of many organic molecules, including large amounts of both alkanes and alkenes. Acetylene, the smallest alkyne, burns so hot it is used in welding and cutting torches.

Table 8.4 Alkenes and Alkynes

Alkenes

Name	Structure	Uses
ethene (ethylene)	$H_2C{=}CH_2$	plant hormone that causes ripening of fruit
propene (propylene)	$CH_3{-}CH{=}CH_2$	monomer used to make polypropylene, a common polymer
1-butene (butylene)	$H{-}CH{=}CH{-}CH_2{-}CH_3$	monomer used to make polybutylene, a common polymer
2-butene	$CH_3{-}CH{=}CH{-}CH_3$	

Alkynes

Name	Structure	Uses
ethyne (acetylene)	$H-C\equiv C-H$	used in welding and cutting torches
propyne	$CH_3-C\equiv C-H$	
1-butyne	$H-C\equiv C-C(H)(H)-CH_3$	
2-butyne	$CH_3-C\equiv C-CH_3$	

8.2.3 Reactions of alkenes and alkynes

The double bond in an alkene is much more reactive than the single bonds in alkanes. The triple bond in an alkyne is more reactive still. When an alkene or alkyne reacts, the reaction usually takes place at the double or triple bond even though the molecule may have many single bonds. The characteristic reaction of a double or triple bond is called *addition*. For example, when propylene reacts with hydrochloric acid (HCl), the H and Cl are added to the two carbon atoms that contain the double bond to form chloroalkane.

Recall from Chapter 2 that a double bond consists of a pi bond and a sigma bond. In an addition reaction, the pi bond is destroyed, leaving behind only the single sigma bond.

The two carbon atoms on either side of the old double bond gain two new single bonds to two new atoms. It is also possible to make the reaction go backward and create a double bond instead of destroying one. Then the reaction is called *elimination*:

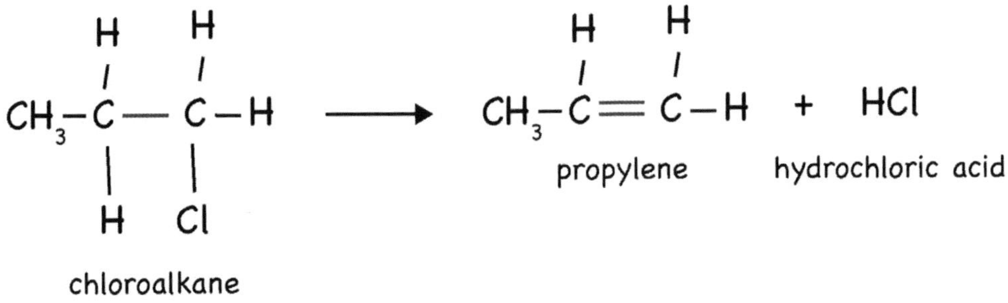

chloroalkane

A triple bond has two pi bonds and one sigma bond, so you can get two addition reactions in a row. First one pi bond is destroyed, leaving a double bond:

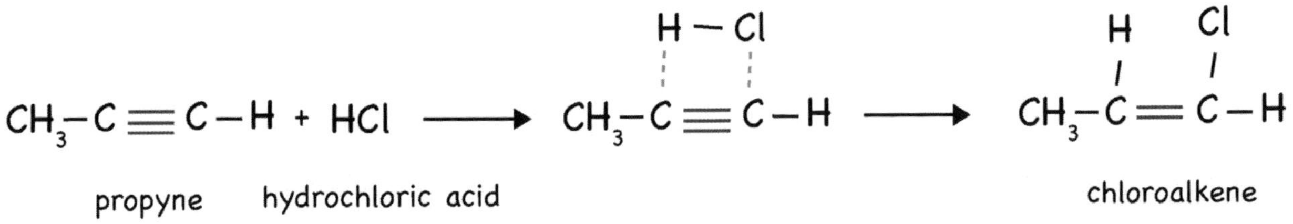

Then the double bond can react to give a single sigma bond:

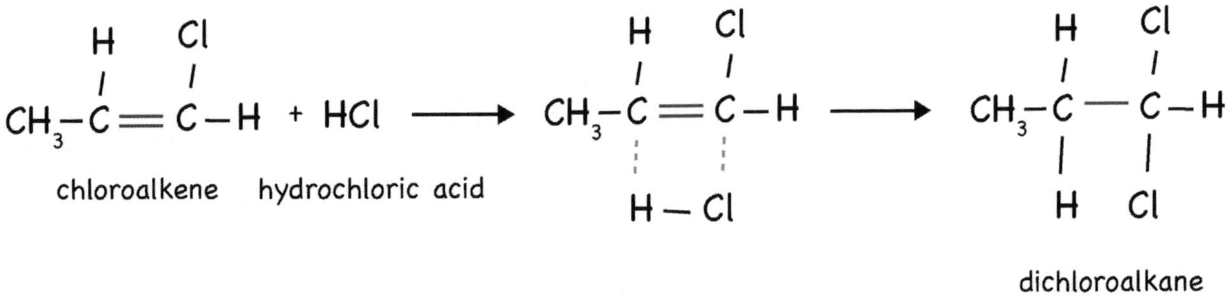

Just like with double bonds, these addition reactions can go backward (in elimination reactions) and make double or triple bonds from molecules with only single bonds.

8.2.4 Functional groups make synthesis possible

Because the double or triple bond is the most reactive part of the molecule, only the double or triple bond is affected, and the rest of the molecule stays the same. This is very useful: It means that we can change one part of the molecule without destroying the rest. Properties like this are the basis for *organic synthesis*, the art of building up new molecules to our own design. Organic synthesis can be used to make organic molecules of all sorts: new plastics, new fibers for clothing, new drugs to cure diseases, and many other things. Organic synthesis is very important for the chemical industry, for medicine, and for chemical research. We will learn more about some of these applications of organic chemistry in the second part of this chapter, and in Chapters 9 and 10.

8.2.5 Aromatics

The last and most complex of the hydrocarbons are the aromatic molecules. (They usually smell good!) There are many different kinds of aromatic molecules, but we will focus on the simplest one, benzene [ben´-zēn].

As you can see in Figure 8.4, benzene is a ring of six carbon atoms and six hydrogens in the shape of a hexagon. There are three double bonds alternating with three single bonds around the ring.

It looks like benzene should be an alkene (because of the double bonds), but since the double and

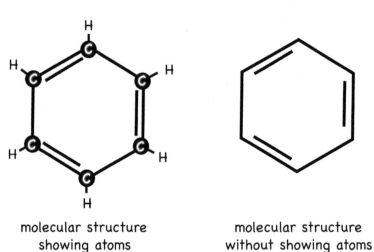

Benzene, C_6H_6

molecular structure
showing atoms

molecular structure
without showing atoms

Figure 8.4: The molecule benzene has six carbon atoms arranged in a hexagon with six hydrogen atoms attached; one to each carbon. There are three double bonds that alternate with three single bonds.

single bonds alternate, the pi bonds merge into a single "pi bonding cloud." The pi bonding cloud looks like two doughnuts, one floating above the ring, the other floating below. Because the pi bonds are all spread out, there aren't any pure double bonds or single

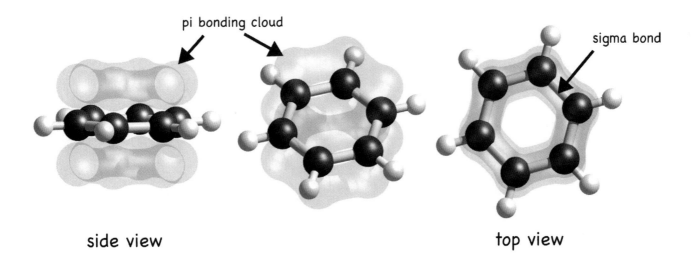

side view   top view

Figure 8.5: The delocalized pi bonding and sigma bonding orbitals for benzene.

bonds. They are said to be delocalized [dē-lō'-kə-līzd]. All six bonds around the ring are the same, and each one is like a bond and a half. If this seems strange, you are right; benzene molecules (and other aromatics) were considered very weird by all chemists until it became possible to understand their bonding using quantum mechanics.

The pi-bonding cloud in benzene is not as reactive as ordinary double bonds, so benzene does not easily undergo addition reactions like alkenes and alkynes do. The characteristic reaction for benzene is a substitution reaction, in which one of its hydrogen atoms gets replaced by something else. (See Figure 8.6.)

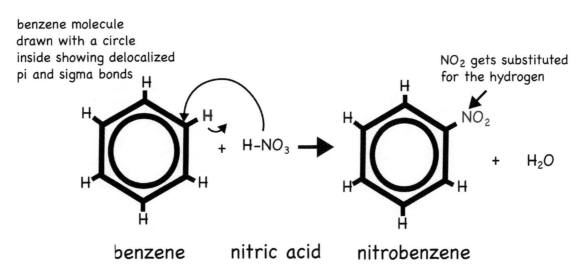

benzene   nitric acid   nitrobenzene

Figure 8.6: Substitution reaction of benzene and nitric acid.

8.3 ALCOHOLS, AMINES, ALDEHYDES, ACIDS, KETONES, ESTERS, AND AMIDES

8.3.1 Alcohols and amines

The simplest organic molecules beyond the hydrocarbons are the alcohols and amines as shown in Table 8.5. An alcohol is any molecule with a -OH group attached to a carbon atom, and an amine is any molecule with a $-NH_2$ group attached to a carbon atom. Both the -OH group and the $-NH_2$ group are very polar, so alcohols and amines are usually polar as well. They tend to dissolve well in water, and the liquid alcohols, especially, can act as solvents for other polar molecules.

Table 8.5 Some Simple Alcohols and Amines

methanol	CH_3OH	methyl alcohol—wood alcohol
ethanol	CH_3CH_2OH	ethyl alcohol—"alcohol" in wine, beer, etc.
1-propanol	$CH_3CH_2CH_2OH$	
2-propanol	$CH_3CH_2CH(OH)CH_3$	isopropyl alcohol—"rubbing alcohol"
1-butanol	$CH_3CH_2CH_2CH_2OH$	
ethylene glycol	$HOCH_2CH_2OH$	antifreeze
glycerol	$HOCH_2CH(OH)CH_2OH$	glycerine
methylamine	CH_3NH_2	
ethylamine	$CH_3CH_2NH_2$	
1-propylamine	$CH_3CH_2CH_2NH_2$	

Both alcohols and amines are very important for living things. All the carbohydrates including sugars, starches, and cellulose, are large alcohols with many -OH (alcohol) groups each. The amino acids from which all proteins are built are amines and acids.

The amines are all quite basic, much like ammonia. When dissolved in water, they generate hydroxyl (OH^-) ions:

$$NH_3 \quad + \quad H_2O \quad \longrightarrow \quad NH_4 \quad + \quad OH^-$$

ammonia   water   ammonium ion   hydroxyl ion

$$CH_3NH_2 \quad + \quad H_2O \quad \longrightarrow \quad CH_3NH_3^+ \quad + \quad OH^-$$

methylamine   water   hydroxyl ion

Amines are often used as bases in the laboratory, and they play a role in controlling pH inside living things.

8.3.2 Aldehydes, acids, and ketones

In our next group, all the molecules have a characteristic feature called a carbonyl [kär′ bə nil], which is a carbon atom that is double bonded to an oxygen. Like alcohols and amines, the carbonyl is polar, so all the molecules in this section are also polar, though not as much so as the alcohols and amines. Depending on what is next to the carbonyl group, the molecule may be an aldehyde, an acid, or a ketone:

- an aldehyde is any molecule with [-C=OH]—that is, it has only an H atom on one side of the carbonyl;

- an acid is any molecule with [-C=OOH]—that is, it has a -OH group next to the carbonyl;

- a ketone is a molecule with carbon atoms on *both* sides, -C-C=O-C-.

Table 8.6 shows simple examples of all three types.

Table 8.6 Aldehydes, Acids, and Ketones

methanal	$$\overset{\displaystyle O}{\underset{\displaystyle H-C-H}{\|}}$$	formaldehyde
ethanal	$$\overset{\displaystyle O}{\underset{\displaystyle CH_3-C-H}{\|}}$$	
octanal	$$CH_3-CH_2CH_2CH_2CH_2CH_2CH_2\overset{\displaystyle O}{\underset{\displaystyle C}{\|}}-OH$$	citrus aroma found in citrus oils
formic acid	$$\overset{\displaystyle O}{\underset{\displaystyle H-C-OH}{\|}}$$	both an acid and an aldehyde
acetic acid	$$\overset{\displaystyle O}{\underset{\displaystyle CH_3-C-OH}{\|}}$$	
glycine	$$\overset{\displaystyle O}{\underset{\displaystyle NH_2-CH_2-C-OH}{\|}}$$	the simplest amino acid (both an acid and an amine)
alanine	$$NH_2-\underset{\displaystyle CH_3}{\overset{\displaystyle O}{\underset{\displaystyle \|}{CH-C}}}-OH$$	the next simplest amino acid
benzoic acid	$$\text{(benzene ring)}-\overset{\displaystyle O}{\underset{\displaystyle C}{\|}}-OH$$	both an aromatic and an acid often used as a preservative in sodas (under the name sodium benzoate—see the label)
propanone	$$\overset{\displaystyle O}{\underset{\displaystyle CH_3-C-CH_3}{\|}}$$	
butanone	$$\overset{\displaystyle O}{\underset{\displaystyle CH_3CH_2-C-CH_3}{\|}}$$	methyl ethyl ketone or MEK, a common solvent
2-pentanone	$$\overset{\displaystyle O}{\underset{\displaystyle CH_3CH_2CH_2-C-CH_3}{\|}}$$	

Aldehydes and ketones often smell nice, and are frequently found in fruit oils and scents. The organic acid group, -COOH, is acidic, of course. When an organic acid is added to water, it releases H^+ ions and so lowers the pH and raises the acidity of the water. For example, for benzoic acid, the reaction is as follows:

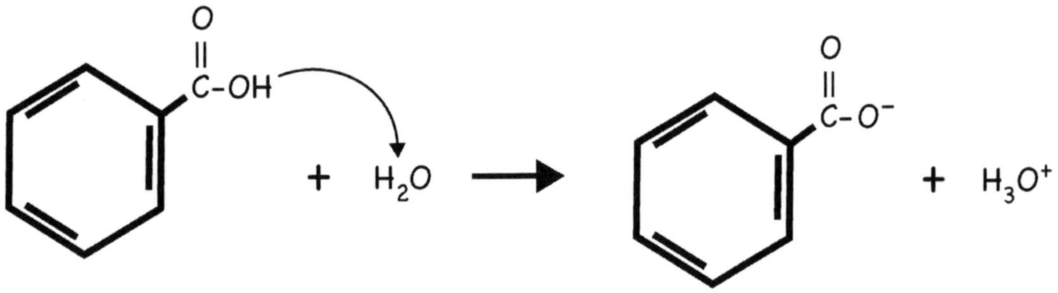

Organic acids are often used inside living cells to control pH. Between the amines and the acids, organic molecules include both bases and acids, so they can be used to control pH over a wide range and in either direction (higher or lower).

8.3.3 Esters and amides

Our last two classes of organic acids—the esters and amides—are a bit more complicated than the earlier classes, but are very important for biology, so we include them here. An ester has a carbonyl, an oxygen next to the carbonyl, and a carbon atom attached to the oxygen. It's like an acid, except instead of a -OH next to the carbonyl, there is a -OR, where R is something organic.

One of the main reasons esters are important is that they provide an easy way to hook two big molecules together.

An ester can be made by reacting an *acid* with an *alcohol*. For example, acetic acid will react with ethanol to make an ester called ethyl acetate.

$$\underset{\text{acetic acid}}{CH_3\text{-}\overset{\overset{\displaystyle O}{\|}}{C}\text{-}OH} + \underset{\text{ethanol}}{CH_3\text{-}CH_2\text{-}OH} \longrightarrow \underset{\substack{\text{ethyl acetate}\\ \text{(an ester)}}}{CH_3\text{-}\overset{\overset{\displaystyle O}{\|}}{C}\text{-}O\text{-}CH_2CH_3} + H_2O$$

In general, the reaction is:

$$R-\overset{\overset{O}{\|}}{C}-OH \; + \; R'OH \;\; \longrightarrow \;\; R-\overset{\overset{O}{\|}}{C}-R' \; + \; H_2O$$

organic acid   alcohol   ester

where R and R' stand for anything organic. Such ester-forming reactions are often used by living cells to make the molecules they need.

In the same way, amides provide a way of linking two molecules together. The only difference is that the reaction is between an acid and an amine, as in:

$$R-\overset{\overset{O}{\|}}{C}-OH \; + \; H_2NR' \;\; \longrightarrow \;\; R-\overset{\overset{O}{\|}}{C}-\underset{\underset{H}{|}}{N}-R' \; + \; H_2O$$

organic acid   amine   amide

where again, R and R' can be anything organic. This reaction is used by cells to link together amino acids to make proteins. For example, glycine and alanine can be linked together to form glycylalanine, a very short peptide with just two amino acids (see Chapter 10):

$$NH_2-\underset{\underset{CH_3}{|}}{CH}-\overset{\overset{O}{\|}}{C}-OH \; + \; H_2N-CH_2-\overset{\overset{O}{\|}}{C}-OH \;\; \longrightarrow \;\; NH_2-\underset{\underset{CH_3}{|}}{CH}-\overset{\overset{O}{\|}}{C}-\underset{\underset{H}{|}}{N}-CH_2-\overset{\overset{O}{\|}}{C}-OH \; + \; H_2O$$

alanine   glycine   glycylalanine

Notice that this new, large molecule still has an amine at one end and an acid at the other end, so we could still add more amino acids to either end to make a larger molecule. In proteins, hundreds of amino acids are hooked together in a long chain using amide linkages.

8.4 SUMMARY — PART A

Here are the main points to remember from this chapter:

• Organic chemistry deals with carbon-containing compounds.

• Isomers are two molecules with the same number and kind of atoms, but with different structures.

• A functional group is a subset of atoms on a molecule that together form a reactive unit.

• A parent molecule is a molecule from which other molecules are built.

• Alkenes, alkynes, alkanes, and aromatics are groups of organic molecules that contain only hydrogen and carbon.

• Benzene has delocalized pi and sigma bonds. *Delocalized* means that the electrons are spread around all six bonds.

8.5 STUDY QUESTIONS — PART A

1. Describe the difference between organic and inorganic chemistry.

2. There are four groups of organic molecules that contain only hydrogen and carbon, called the hydrocarbons. Name these groups and describe the major difference between them. (*Hint*: think about the types of bonds they form.)

3. Draw a benzene molecule.

4. What is the functional group for an acid?

5. What is the functional group for an ester?

THE CHEMISTRY OF CARBON — PART B

8.6 BIOCHEMISTRY

8.6.1 Introduction

So far we have examined a number of different kinds of molecules, from single atoms combining to form small molecules, like water and salt, to multiple atoms combining to form acids or soaps. We have seen that all of these molecules play a role in changing and shaping the world around us, but what about the molecules that are inside our bodies? What kinds of molecules are required for life, and how do they interact with each other?

You have probably noticed that living things require a certain set of molecules for living. For example, we don't need to feed rocks or sand. We put energy into cars in the form of gasoline, but they don't require real nutrients because they are not alive. Once trees have been cut down and made into beds, tables, or chairs, we don't need to give them anything because they are no longer living. However, living things require both the input of additional molecules and a delicate balance of a variety of molecules in order to keep living. Once this balance is disrupted, the living thing ceases to be alive and no longer requires more molecules.

There are many different kinds of molecules that living things require. All living things consume molecules in the form of food, change these molecules into other molecules, and then eliminate molecules that are no longer needed. Some of the molecules that living things require are provided *only* by an outside food source, while some are manufactured right inside the cells! Scientists have discovered that even the smallest living things, like single-celled organisms, contain remarkable machinery to make, store, metabolize, alter, and eliminate molecules of various shapes and sizes.

8.6.2 Nutrients in food

When you eat a banana or a piece of chocolate, your body immediately begins breaking down the molecules inside the food. There are minerals, vitamins, carbohydrates [kär-bō-hī'-drātz], fats, proteins, and other kinds of molecules in the food you eat that your body needs for energy, growth, and the healthy maintenance of the sophisticated molecular machinery inside your body.

8.7 MINERALS

8.7.1 Introduction

The smallest nutrients found in many of the foods we eat are minerals. Minerals are salts or hydrides [hī'-drīdz] of various elements. Minerals are not manufactured inside living things, but are found in the Earth's soil. Plants get their minerals directly from the Earth's soil, and animals get most of their minerals from plants or other animals. Humans require a modest amount of seven different elements

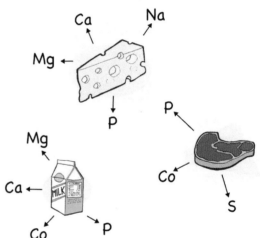

Figure 8.7: Elements such as calcium (Ca), magnesium (Mg), phosphorus, (P), sulfur (S), and cobalt (Co) are found in foods such as cheese, milk, and meat.

found in minerals (calcium, phosphorus, potassium, chlorine, sodium, and magnesium) and trace amounts of several other elements, such as fluorine, cobalt, copper, and iron.

Minerals are not used for fuel, but are used to help maintain many of the systems inside our cells. For example, calcium, magnesium, and phosphorus help strengthen bones and harden teeth; iron is essential for oxygen binding in blood cells; and copper is important for the correct functioning of nerve tissues.

8.7.2 Sources

We get the different minerals we need from a variety of different foods. Calcium and phosphorus are found in milk products, leafy vegetables, and egg yolks. Sodium, potassium, and chlorine are found in table salts, cheese, and dried apricots. Magnesium is found in whole grain cereals and a variety of leafy green vegetables. Iron is found in meat, dried nuts, and molasses; and zinc is found in seafood, nuts, and yeast. Without minerals, our bodies would not function properly. The lack of necessary minerals can result in a variety of diseases or even death.

Table 8.7 Minerals

Mineral	Sources	Uses in body
potassium (K)	avocados, apricots, meats	muscle contraction, making proteins
sodium (Na)	table salt, cheese, cured meats	maintains water balance and cellular pumps
calcium (Ca)	milk, milk products, egg yolk, shellfish	needed for bones and teeth, blood clotting, nerve impulses
chlorine (Cl)	table salt	activates salivary amylase, helps transport CO_2
magnesium (Mg)	milk, dairy products, whole grain cereals, nuts	required for normal muscle and nerve function
sulfur (S)	meat, milk, eggs	found in some proteins, needed for cartilage, bones, and tendons
phosphorus (P)	milk, eggs, meat, fish, nuts, whole grains	needed for bones and teeth, nerve activity, and energy storage
cobalt (Co)	liver, lean meat, fish, milk	needed for vitamin B_{12}
fluorine (Fl)	fluoridated water	tooth structure, prevents dental cavities, and may prevent osteoporosis
copper (Cu)	liver, shellfish, whole grains, and meat	needed for the manufacture of nerve tissues and blood molecules
iodine (I)	iodized salt, shellfish, cod liver oil	needed for making thyroid molecules
manganese (Mn)	nuts, whole grains, fruit	needed for making fats, blood molecules, and carbohydrates
iron (Fe)	meat, liver, nuts, egg yolk, molasses	essential part of blood molecules that bind oxygen

selenium (Se)	seafood, meat, cereal	component of certain proteins
zinc (Zn)	seafood, nuts, yeast, cereal, meat	component of some proteins, required for wound healing, taste, and smell
chromium (Cr)	liver, meat, yeast, cheese, whole grains	component of some proteins and needed for glucose use

8.8 VITAMINS

8.8.1 Introduction

Vitamins are other essential molecules required for the healthy functioning of living things. Humans require a variety of vitamins for growth and good health. Like minerals, vitamins are not used as sources of energy, but instead function as "helper" molecules for several different chemical reactions that occur in the body. As "helper" molecules they are called coenzymes [cō-en′-zīmz]. A coenzyme is a molecule that helps an *enzyme* perform an *enzymatic reaction*. Enzymes are proteins, and we will learn more about proteins in Chapter 10.

8.8.2 Sources

Like minerals, most vitamins are found in the food we eat. However, humans do manufacture two vitamins in their bodies.

Table 8.8 Vitamins

Vitamin	Sources	Uses in body
fat-soluble		
vitamin A	yellow and green vegetables, fish liver oil	needed for normal tooth and bone development, skin
vitamin E	wheat germ, vegetable oil, dark green vegetables	protects cell membranes and prevents hardening of arteries
vitamin D	produced in the skin by ultraviolet light, egg yolk, milk	for normal tooth and bone development, blood clotting
vitamin K	made by bacteria inside the body, also in cabbage, pork liver	needed to form some proteins and for cell function

water-soluble		
vitamin C	fruits, vegetables, tomatoes, potatoes	used in the formation of all connective tissue, helps iron absorption
vitamin B$_1$	liver, fish, eggs, whole grains	needed for making certain sugars
vitamin B$_2$	liver, yeast, egg white, fish	needed for some protein function
vitamin B$_{12}$	liver, meat, dairy foods, eggs	needed for the nervous system, bone marrow, and making DNA
vitamin B$_6$	meat, fish, bananas, sweet potatoes	needed for making DNA and certain proteins
vitamin B$_5$	liver, eggs, yeast, meat	needed to make fats, steroids, and blood molecules

Vitamin D is made in our skin, and vitamin K is made by *E. coli* bacteria that live in our intestines. Because no one food contains all of the vitamins necessary for the healthy maintenance of our bodies, it is important to eat a variety of foods.

Some of the vitamins we need are soluble in water (*water-soluble*), and our bodies absorb these vitamins directly when our digestive tracts uptake water. However, some vitamins are soluble only in fat (*fat-soluble*), and our bodies absorb these vitamins when we intake fats. Vitamin A is an important vitamin that is only soluble in fats, so it is important to eat enough fats for our bodies to uptake vitamin A. Fat-soluble vitamins are stored by our bodies, but water-soluble vitamins are not. Our bodies eliminate excess water-soluble vitamins, but because our bodies store fat-soluble vitamins, it is possible to get too much! For example, too much vitamin A is toxic and can cause nausea, vomiting, or bone and joint pain.

8.9 CARBOHYDRATES

8.9.1 Introduction

Another set of essential molecules for living things are carbohydrates. Carbohydrates are the most abundant class of biological molecules and are found in every living thing. The word carbohydrate comes from the words *carbon* and *hydrate* (meaning "water"), so a carbohydrate is a molecule made of both carbon and water. A general chemical formula for a carbohydrate is $(CH_2O)_n$ where *n* is between 3 and 7.

Carbohydrates are made inside living things through two main biochemical processes: gluconeogenesis [glü-kō-nē-ō-jen'-ə-səs] and photosynthesis [fō-tō-sin'-thə-səs]. Gluconeogenesis comes from the Greek words *glykys,* which means "sweet," *neo,* which means "new," and *gen* which means "birth" or "produce." Gluconeogenesis literally means the "new production of sweet molecules." Gluconeogenesis occurs in the liver and kidneys of humans, and it is the biochemical pathway that makes carbohydrates when no food is consumed (e.g., during a fast). Photosynthesis, on the other hand, is the biochemical process that plants use to convert light energy into food energy, or sugars. The bulk of carbohydrate molecules comes from photosynthesis.

8.9.2 Monosaccharides and oligosaccharides

Carbohydrates are found as small simple sugars and large complex polymers made of chains of simple sugars. The smallest carbohydrates are called monosaccharides [mä-nō-sa'-kə-rīdz]. Mono- is a Greek prefix meaning "one," and saccharide comes from the Greek word *sakcharon,* meaning sugar. A monosaccharide is "one sugar." The smallest monosaccharides have three carbon atoms. These are called trioses [trī-ō'-səs]. Larger simple sugars with four, five, six, and seven carbons are called tetroses [te'-trō-səs], pentoses [pen'-tō-səs], hexoses

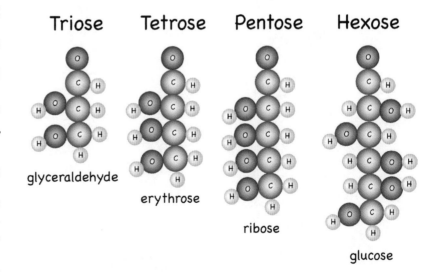

Figure 8.8: Simple sugar carbohydrates. Glyceraldehyde has 3 carbons, erythrose has 4 carbons, ribose has 5 carbons, and glucose has 6 carbons.

[heks'-ō-səs], and heptoses [hep'-tō-səs], respectively. Glucose [glü'-kōs] is a hexose and has six carbon atoms. Ribose [rī'-bōs] is a pentose and has five carbons. Erythrose [i-rith'-rōs] is a tetrose with four carbon atoms, and glyceraldehyde [gli-sə-rə-al'-də-hīd], the simplest sugar, is a triose with only three carbons.

A sugar molecule has two kinds of reactive groups: a carboxyl group on one end and several hydroxyl groups on the other carbons. The carboxyl group can react with any of the hydroxyl group creating a circular molecule. For glucose, it turns out that the carboxyl oxygen reacts best with the second-to-last hydroxyl group on the linear molecule. This creates a six-membered ring called a pyranose. The official name for a circular glucose molecule is glucopyranose [glü-kō-pī'-rə-nōs].

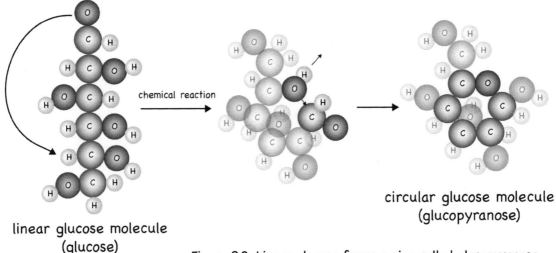

linear glucose molecule
(glucose)

circular glucose molecule
(glucopyranose)

Figure 8.9: Linear glucose forms a ring called glucopyranose.

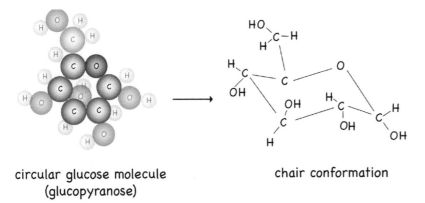

circular glucose molecule
(glucopyranose)

chair conformation

Figure 8.10: Glucopyranose can adopt different conformations.

Glucopyranose can assume different conformations, or shapes, but is typically found in what is known as a chair conformation in which the ends of the ring buckle and fold in opposite directions.

When single sugars are added one to another, larger and more complex carbohydrates are formed. When two monosaccharides are connected, the molecule becomes a disaccharide [dī-sak'-ä-rīd]. (Di- means "two.") Sucrose [sü'-krōs], or table sugar, is a disaccharide of a single fructose and a single glucose.

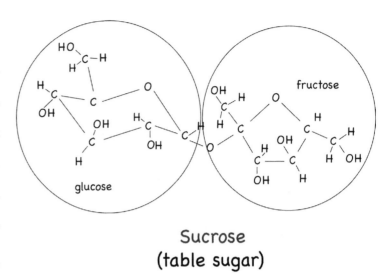

Sucrose
(table sugar)

Figure 8.11: Sucrose—a disaccharide of glucose and fructose

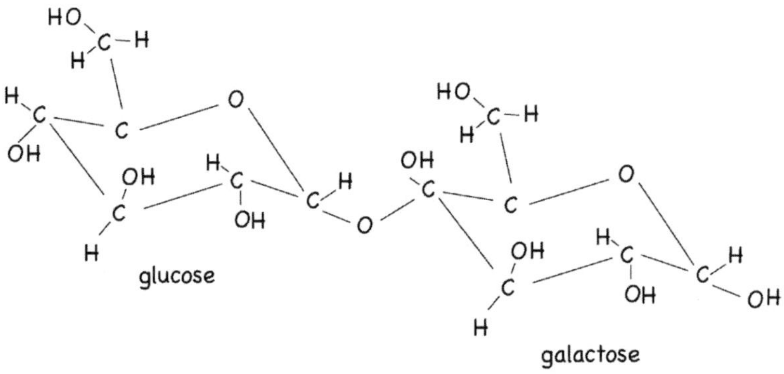

Lactose
(milk sugar)

Figure 8.12: Lactose—a disaccharide of galactose and glucose.

Lactose [lak'-tōs], the sugar found in milk, is made of a glucose and a galactose [gə-lak'-tōs].

The bond formed between the two monosaccharides is called a glycosidic [glī-kō-sid'-ik] bond.

There are two ways a glycosidic bond can form, both of which depend on the orientation of the bonding oxygen. If the oxygen is pointing downward, the bond is called an α-glycosidic [al'-fə-glī-kō-sid'-ik] bond If the oxygen is pointing upward, the bond is called a β-glycosidic bond [bā'-tə glī-kō-sid'-ik].

Glycosidic bonds

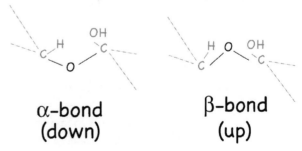

α-bond
(down)

β-bond
(up)

Figure 8.13: Glycosidic bonds can be α (oxygen bond pointing down) or β (oxygen bond pointing up).

When a few more than two saccharides are added together, the molecule is called an oligosaccharide [ä-li-gō-sa'-kə-rīd] (*oligo-* means "few"), and when many saccharides are added together in a long chain, the molecule is called a polysaccharide [*poly-* means "many"].

8.9.3 Polysaccharides

There are two major types of polysaccharides: structural polysaccharides and storage polysaccharides. As the name implies, structural polysaccharides are carbohydrates that are primarily involved in the structural apparatus of plant cells. Storage polysaccharides, on the other hand, are carbohydrates that are used for storing energy. Cellulose and chitin [kī'-tin] are two structural polysaccharides. Cellulose is the primary structural polysaccharide for cell walls in plants. Cellulose is a linear polymer composed of several hundred glucose molecules linked together by a β-glycosidic bond. The long-chain glucose polymers stack on top of each other forming layered plates.

Cellulose

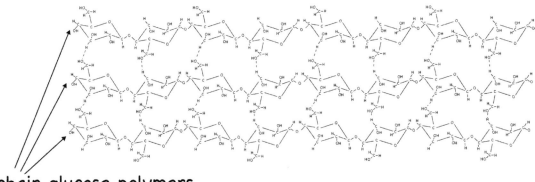

long-chain glucose polymers
(stacking on top of each other)

Figure 8.14: Cellulose is made up of long-chain glucose polymers that stack on top of each other.

Chitin is the main structural polysaccharide found in the exoskeletons of insects, spiders, and crustaceans, and it forms similar stacked layers. Although chitin and cellulose have similar structures, chitin has a different functional group on one of the carbon atoms in its monomer.

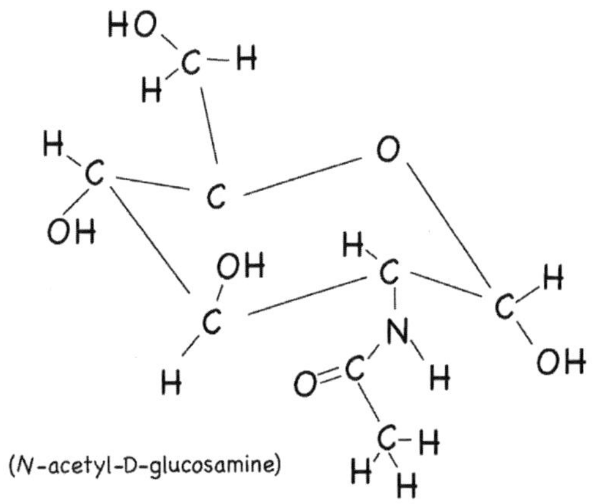

(*N*-acetyl-D-glucosamine)

Figure 8.15: The monomer in chitin.

Starch and glycogen are the primary storage polysaccharides found in plants and animals. Starches are found only in plants, and glycogen is the storage polysaccharide found in animals.

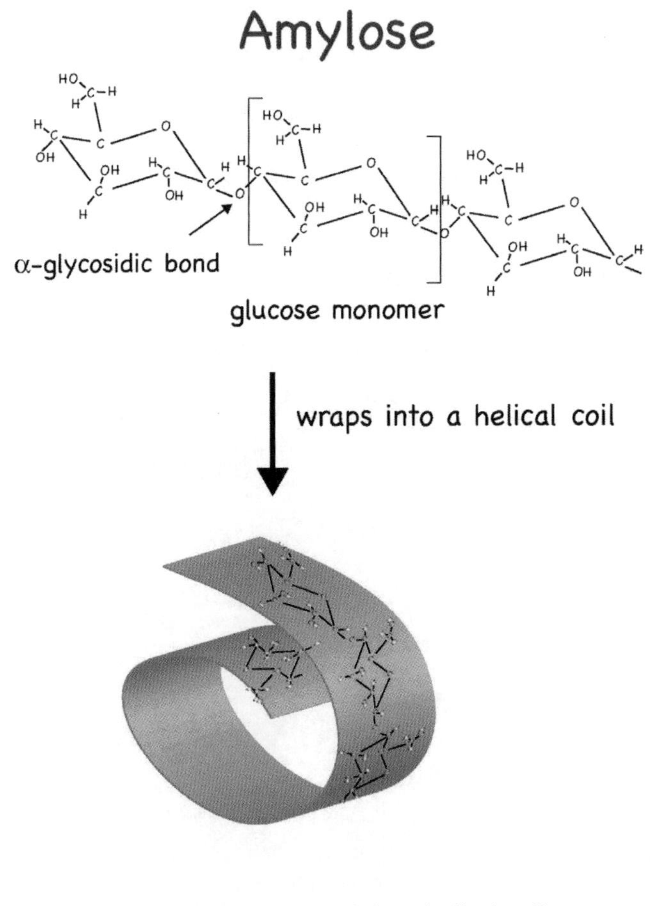

Amylose

α-glycosidic bond

glucose monomer

wraps into a helical coil

Figure 8.16: Amylose wraps into a helical coil.

Starch is composed of two different polysaccharides: amylose [a′-mə-lōs] and amylopectin [a-mə-lō-pek′-tən]. Amylose is a linear polymer of glucose monomers linked together by an α-glycosidic bond.

Amylose forms a spiral coil, or helix [hē′-liks] which looks similar to a Slinky®. It is this unique structure that binds iodine molecules, creating a deep purple color in iodine-stained foods.

Amylopectin is also a polymer of linked glucose monomers hooked together by α-glycosidic bonds. But unlike amylose, amylopectin is branched instead of linear and does not form a helical coil.

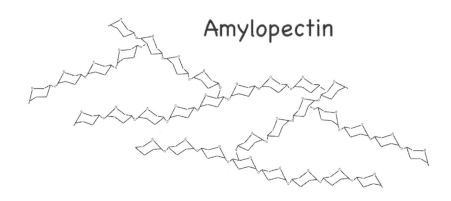

Figure 8.17: Amylopectin is branched.

Glycogen [glī'-kə-jen] is composed of glucose molecules linked by α-glycosidic bonds, similar to amylopectin, but with many more branches. Glycogen is present in nearly all cells, but in humans it is found primarily in liver and skeletal-muscle cells.

8.10 FATS AND LIPIDS

Another important group of nutrients required for the healthy maintenance and function of our bodies is the fats, or lipids. Fats help the body absorb fat-soluble vitamins, are a major source of energy, and are an essential component of cellular membranes.

The most common lipids in living things are made from glycerol [gli'-sər-ôl]. Glycerol is a small three-carbon carbohydrate. Fats are made of a *derivative* of glycerol, called a triglyceride [trī-gli'-ser-īd]. In a triglyceride, the hydroxyl hydrogen has been replaced with a carbon, an oxygen, and an "R" group. The "R" group is any long chain of hydrocarbons.

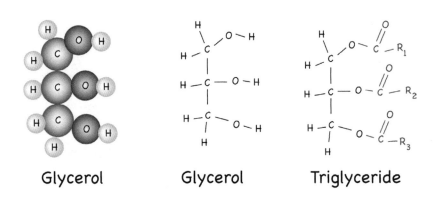

Glycerol   Glycerol   Triglyceride

Figure 8.18: Glycerol—a small three-carbon carbohydrate—is the parent molecule for triglycerides.

Have you ever wondered why animal fat is solid at room temperature, but vegetable oil is liquid at room temperature? Both animal fat and vegetable oil are fats made of a triglyceride and three long chains of hydrocarbons, but animal fat has no double bonds in its hydrocarbon "R" groups, whereas vegetable oils do. If there are no double bonds, the fat is saturated. If it contains double bonds, it is called unsaturated. Saturated fats, such as animal fat, have a higher melting temperature than unsaturated fats. Because animal fats are typically *saturated* and have no double bonds, they are solids at room temperature. Vegetable fats are *unsaturated* (having double bonds) and, having a lower melting temperature than animal fats, are liquids at room temperature.

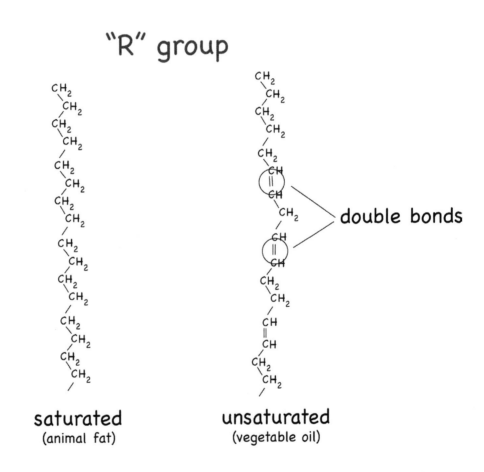

Figure 8.19: The "R" group in animal fat is saturated (has no double bonds). The "R" group in vegetable oil is unsaturated (has double bonds).

8.11 STEROIDS

Finally, another set of important nutrients are called steroids. Steroids are found in both plants and animals and are among the most important natural products produced. Steroids are involved in sex hormones, bile acids, and in the formation of animal membranes.

Cholesterol [kə-les'-tə-rōl] is the most common steroid found in animals. Cholesterol is found in the brain and spinal column tissues of humans and is the major component in animal plasma membranes.

Cholesterol

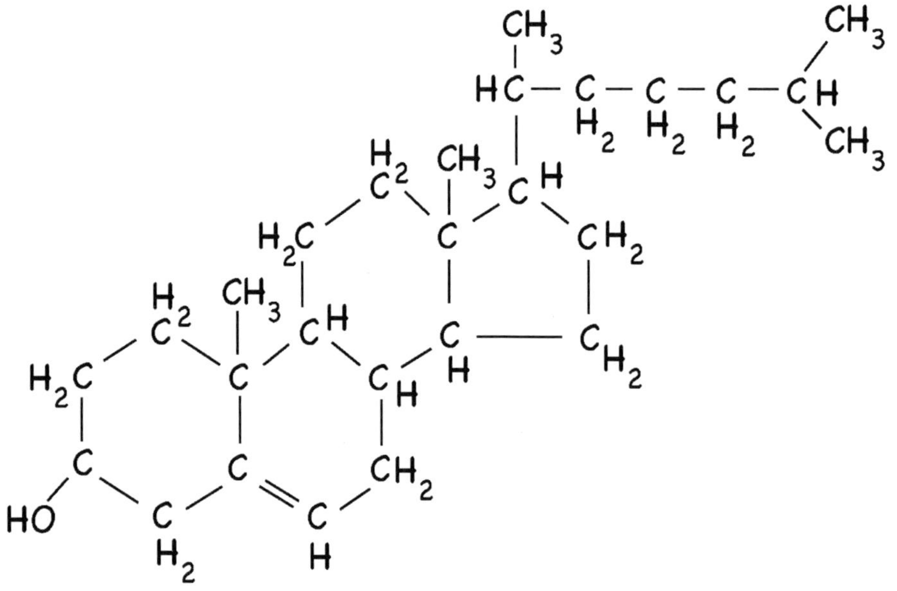

Figure 8.20: Cholesterol is a steroid and is an important molecule for our bodies.

Cholesterol is the primary starting material of steroid hormones, and although there has been significant dietary controversy over cholesterol, it is an important biochemical molecule and vital nutrient for the proper health and maintenance of our bodies.

8.12 SUMMARY — PART B

• Living things require nutrients to stay alive. Humans need many nutrients, such as minerals, vitamins, carbohydrates, fats, and proteins.

• Minerals and vitamins are not used for fuel, but as helper molecules, often called coenzymes.

- Carbohydrates are made of simple sugars or chains of simple sugars, and provide energy for living things.

- A circular six-membered sugar is called a glucopyranose and is typically found in a chair conformation.

- Sugars are linked to each other through glycosidic bonds, which can be "up" (β-glycosidic bond) or "down" (α-glycosidic bond).

- Cellulose and chitin are structural polysaccharides. Cellulose is found in plants, and chitin is found in the exoskeletons of insects and crustaceans. Starch and glycogen are storage polysaccharides found in both plants and animals.

- An unsaturated fat has double bonds, and a saturated fat has no double bonds.

8.13 STUDY QUESTIONS — PART B

1. In your own words, describe the difference between living and nonliving things.

2. List three nutrients we get from food and the foods in which they are found.

3. Through which two biochemical pathways are carbohydrates made?

4. Which two polysaccharides make up glycogen?

5. What is the difference between unsaturated and saturated fats?

CHAPTER 9 POLYMERS

9.1 POLYMERS

9.1.1 Introduction

In Chapter 8 we learned about several molecules—such as polysaccharides—that are long chains of smaller molecules hooked together in a repeating fashion. Molecules with repeating units are called polymers [pä'-lə-mərz]. From Chapter 8, we saw that poly means "many." The word root *mer* comes from the Greek word *meros*, which means "unit," so a polymer is a molecule of "many units."

9.1.2 Polymer uses

Polymers are found everywhere. Both naturally occurring polymers, such as polysaccharides, and man-made polymers, such as plastics or styrofoam, are found in every facet of life. Polymers serve as the primary material for clothing, boats, footballs, roof tiling, garbage bags, and even spaceships. Before the early 1900s only naturally occurring polymers were available. Structural items for housing or carriages were made of wood, and clothing was primarily made of cotton, wool, flax, or silk fibers. Synthetic polymers, in contrast, are man-made molecules that have been developed by organic chemists. The first synthetic polymer, Bakelite, was produced in 1909, followed by rayon in 1911. Today, several hundred synthetic polymers are used in everyday life. Nylon, styrofoam, vinyl, and all plastics are synthetic polymers used for everything from clothing to bottles, paints, and pipes. In this chapter, we focus on synthetic polymers. Biological polymers, like proteins and DNA, are the focus of Chapter 10.

rubber

polyethylene

polyester

nylon

9.2 POLYMER STRUCTURE

9.2.1 Monomers

It was once believed that polymers were simply colloidal aggregates of smaller molecules, but in the 1950s polymers were discovered to be composed of a sequence of repeating units linked together by covalent bonds. The individual units of a polymer are called monomers. Monomers can be anything from simple double-bonded hydrocarbons (alkenes), to more complex molecules containing ring structures. When the repeating monomer units are all identical, the polymer is called a homopolymer. For example, polyethylene is a homopolymer made from a simple alkene, ethylene (also called ethene). The double bond in ethene is the *functional group* that allows the monomers to be hooked together. Polyethylene, polyamide (nylon), polystyrene (styrofoam) and polyvinyl chloride (PVC) are all homopolymers made of a single repeating monomer unit.

ethylene monomer

$$\cdots - \underset{\overset{|}{H}}{\overset{\overset{H}{|}}{C}} - \underset{\overset{|}{H}}{\overset{\overset{H}{|}}{C}} - \underset{\overset{|}{H}}{\overset{\overset{H}{|}}{C}} - \underset{\overset{|}{H}}{\overset{\overset{H}{|}}{C}} - \underset{\overset{|}{H}}{\overset{\overset{H}{|}}{C}} - \boxed{\underset{\overset{|}{H}}{\overset{\overset{H}{|}}{C}} - \underset{\overset{|}{H}}{\overset{\overset{H}{|}}{C}}} - \underset{\overset{|}{H}}{\overset{\overset{H}{|}}{C}} - \underset{\overset{|}{H}}{\overset{\overset{H}{|}}{C}} - \underset{\overset{|}{H}}{\overset{\overset{H}{|}}{C}} - \cdots$$

Polyethylene

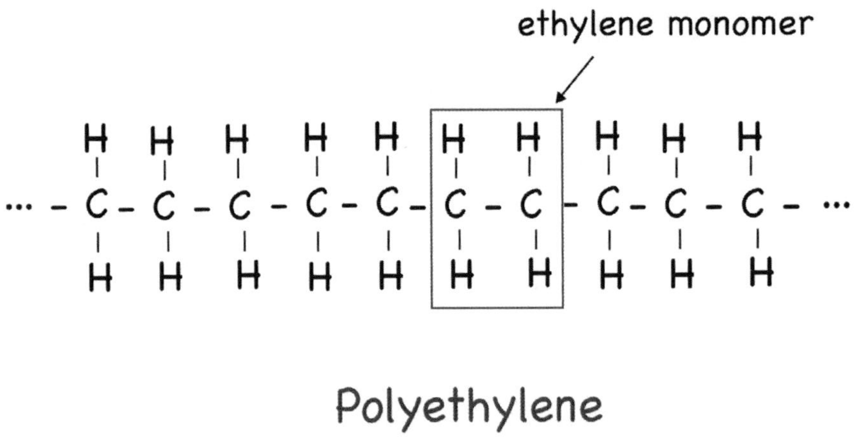

Figure 9.1: Polyethylene is a polymer made of ethylene monomers.

If more than one type of monomer is used, the polymer is called a copolymer. For example KEVLAR® [kev'-lär]—a very strong polymer used for bulletproof vests—is made from two complex monomers: one with two acid functional groups and one with two amino groups.

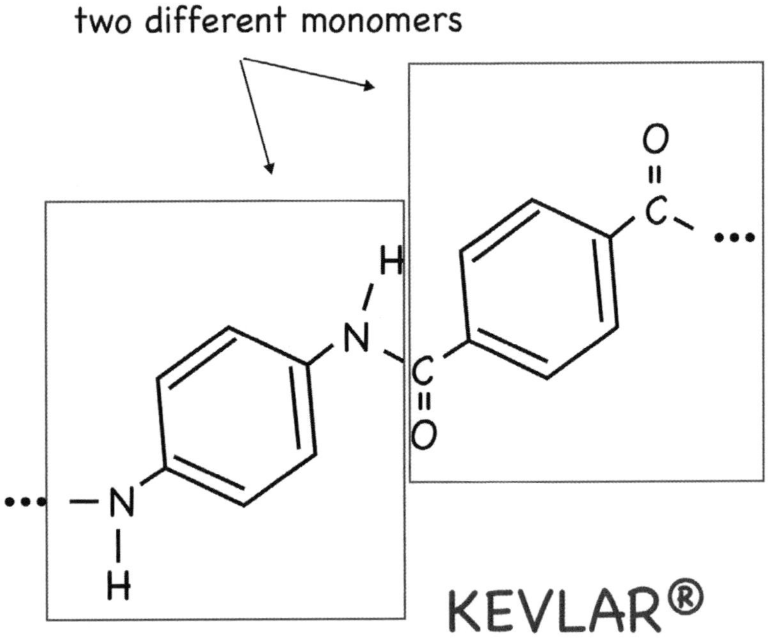

two different monomers

KEVLAR®

Figure 9.2: KEVLAR® is a copolymer composed of two different monomers.

Copolymers can have random repeats, or nonrandom repeats with a variety of different combinations. Most polymers are neither completely random or non-random, but a mixture of both.

9.2.2 Linear or branched

Polymers can be linear or branched. In a linear polymer every monomer unit is connected to the next monomer unit, one after another, end to end. Polyethylene is an example of a linear polymer. Linear polymers vary in length and can have several thousand monomer units linked together. Linear polymers, however, do not stay as a stretched out chain of monomer units, but instead roll up into a random coil. As the name implies, a random coil is a random folding of the long-chain polymer into a more compact ball. The degree to which a polymer will coil depends on several factors, including the type of monomer units in the polymer and the number of single and double bonds covalently linking the monomer units together.

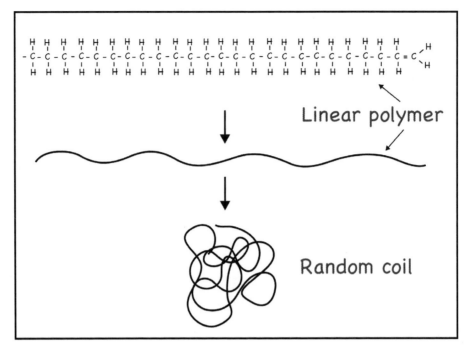

Figure 9.3: Linear polymers fold up and form random coils.

Polymers can also be branched, with chains that are connected to each other in the middle. They can be slightly branched, with only a few branches coming off of the polymer backbone, or highly branched, with many branches connecting additional chains of monomers to the polymer backbone. In fact, polymers can be so extensively branched that there is no backbone at all. Dendrimers are extensively branched polymers that grow with a constantly increasing number of branches. Dendrimers are used as films and fibers because they have excellent surface properties.

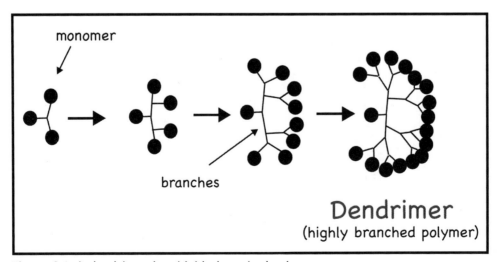

Figure 9.4: A dendrimer is a highly branched polymer.

9.2.3 Cross-links

Polymer molecules can also be connected to each other through cross-links. A cross-link is a covalent bond between any two polymer chains. Cross-links can form as the polymer is built up, or polymerized, or they can be added later by additional chemical reactions. (See Section 9.3.2.) Cross-linking occurs primarily through double bonds or *functional groups* on the monomers, such as alcohols (-OH groups attached to carbon), carbonyl groups, and C=O.

9.3 POLYMER PROPERTIES AND REACTIONS

9.3.1 Polymer structure

The physical properties of a polymer (its hardness, stretchiness, melting temperature, etc.) are largely determined by the structure of the polymer and the way in which the polymer chains pack with each other in a solid. As we have already seen, polymers can be made of a single type of monomer or composed of two or more monomers, forming a copolymer. We also saw how polymers can be linear or branched. These characteristics help determine the physical properties of the polymer (i.e., the melting or boiling point, the viscosity, the hardness or softness, and whether or not the polymer is brittle or elastic).

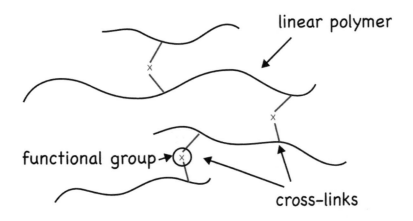

Figure 9.5: Cross-links connect linear polymer chains together.

Thermoplastics are the category of polymers people think of when they hear the word *plastic*. Polyethylene and polystyrene are thermoplastics. Thermoplastics are hard at room temperature, but soften when heated. Because thermoplastics soften when heated, they can be easily molded into a variety of shapes and structures. Football helmets, computer keyboards, and hula hoops are made of thermoplastics.

Synthetic fibers such as nylon or Dacron® have structural properties that are different from those of thermoplastics. Because the monomers of nylon and Dacron® are different from those of thermoplastics, they can be drawn out into long, thin fibers. Polymer fibers of nylon and Dacron® can be quite strong because of these long polymer chains.

Elastomers [i-las'-tə-mərz] are polymers that have the ability to stretch and spring back to their original shape. Natural rubber is an elastomer.

9.3.2 Polymer addition reactions

Polymers are built by hooking monomers together in chemical reactions. This can be done using many different reactions, but we will consider only two: addition reactions and condensation reactions.

Addition reactions link together molecules using double bonds as the functional group. The simplest addition polymer is polyethylene, made by hooking together molecules of ethene (which is commonly called ethylene).

The addition reaction starts with the formation of a free radical. A free radical is just a "dangling bond"—an unbonded electron that is very reactive. Chemists often put special *free radical initiators* into their reactions to create free radicals and get the reaction started. When the free radical on one molecule encounters the double bond on another ethene molecule, it "steals" one of the two electrons in the pi bond of the ethene. This causes a new carbon–carbon bond to be formed, linking the two molecules together. But one of the electrons in the pi bond is still left over, so it becomes a new free radical.

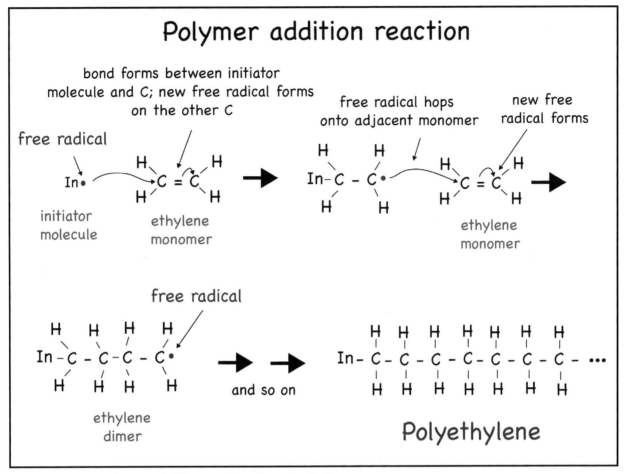

Figure 9.6: The polymer addition reaction for polyethylene.

There is now a new, bigger molecule with four carbons, but it still has a reactive free radical on one end. Now another ethene can encounter the free radical, bond to the growing chain, and form a six-carbon molecule with a free radical on *its* end. In this way, we can go on adding new units to the chain, two carbons at a time, until it is thousands of carbons long.

9.3.3 Termination, branching, cross-linking

In real life, no chemical reaction happens perfectly. Side reactions may destroy the active free radical and thus stop the polymer chain from growing. This is called chain termination. Also, in the reaction vessel, many polymer chains can get started and grow at the same time. If the free radical on one growing chain hits the middle of a second chain, the polymers can become branched or cross-linked.

By controlling temperature and pressure and by using certain chemical additives, chemists can control how these side reactions happen to some extent. This allows us to make many different forms of polyethylene: some with short chains, some with long chains, some with no branches, some with many branches, some with no cross-links, and some with many cross-links.

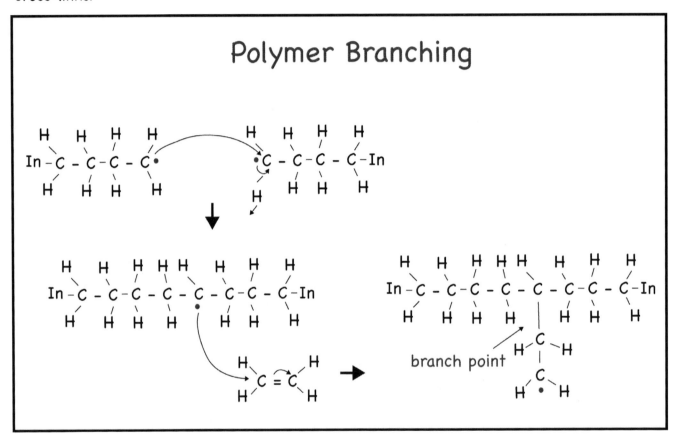

Figure 9.7: Polymer branching can occur when unwanted side reactions occur.

The size, branching, and cross-linking of a polymer greatly affect its properties, as we saw earlier. The chemists who synthesize polymers can make polyethylene hard or soft, rubbery or brittle, easily melted or hard to melt, by adjusting these properties.

9.3.4 Polyethylene is all around you

Polyethylene is one of the most common plastics in use today. If you look at the bottom of any plastic bottle, you will likely find a little triangle with the letters "HDPE" or "LDPE." These letters stand for "high density polyethylene" or "low density polyethylene."

These are just two types of the many forms of polyethylene. High density polyethylene is made from long, unbranched chains that pack well together. This makes HDPE quite hard and tough. It is used for bottles and other items that need to be strong or are meant to be used for a long time. Low density polyethylene is made from branched

polyethylene chains that do not pack together as well. Thus, it is softer and more easily degraded. It is used for disposable items, like lunch bags, that do not need to be very strong and are meant to be used only once.

9.3.5 Other addition polymers

Polyethylene is far from the only polymer made using addition reactions. Table 9.1 shows several other monomer molecules with double bonds that can be chained together to form polymers.

Most of these monomers form polymers with side chains—that is, with something that dangles off the main backbone of the polymer. Side chains greatly affect the properties of the polymer. For example, polyvinyl alcohol has -OH side chains. This means that unlike polyethylene, which is extremely nonpolar and insoluble, polyvinyl alcohol is very polar and dissolves easily in water. It can even be eaten, so it is used as a thickener in foods!

Table 9.1: Common Polymers and Their Uses

Monomer Name	Structure (monomer in red)	Polymer Name	Common Uses
ethene (ethylene)		polyethylene	bags, films, toys, computer keyboards
vinyl chloride		polyvinyl chloride	PVC pipes, raincoats
vinyl alcohol		polyvinyl alcohol	coatings, "slime"
styrene		polystyrene	foam insulation, drinking cups
methyl methacrylate		Lucite®	Plexiglas™, clear plastic sheets, contact lenses
tetrafluoro ethylene		polytetrafluoro ethylene (PTFE) Teflon®	nonstick coatings, watertight seals

9.3.6 Forming polymers by condensation reactions

In Chapter 8, we learned that esters can be made by hooking together an *acid* and an *alcohol*:

$$\underset{\text{acetic acid}}{CH_3-\overset{\overset{\displaystyle O}{\|}}{C}-OH} \quad + \quad \underset{\text{ethanol}}{CH_3-CH_2-OH} \quad \longrightarrow \quad \underset{\substack{\text{ethyl acetate} \\ \text{(an ester)}}}{CH_3-\overset{\overset{\displaystyle O}{\|}}{C}-O-CH_2CH_3} \quad + \quad H_2O$$

Similarly, we can form amides by linking an *acid* and an *amine*:

$$\underset{\text{organic acid}}{R-\overset{\overset{\displaystyle O}{\|}}{C}-OH} \quad + \quad \underset{\text{amine}}{H_2NR`} \quad \longrightarrow \quad \underset{\text{amide}}{R-\overset{\overset{\displaystyle O}{\|}}{C}-\underset{\underset{\displaystyle H}{|}}{N}-R'} \quad + \quad H_2O$$

Both of these reactions are condensation reactions. A condensation reaction is a chemical reaction in which two monomers combine to form a new molecule, giving off a by-product such as water. This type of reaction is very useful for chaining monomer units together into long-chain polymers called condensation polymers.

One of the first and still one of the most important of the condensation polymers is nylon-6,6 (see Figure 9.8). Nylon is a polyamide [pä-lē-a'-mīd], which means it is linked together with amide linkages. It is made with two monomers—one is a double acid, and the other is a double amine. One of the acid groups and one of the amine groups can react to form an amide linkage.

Now the molecule has two monomers but still has an acid at one end and an amide at the other, so it can go on adding new monomers. Each additional monomer makes the chain six carbons and one nitrogen longer. It is possible to grow very long chains in this way.

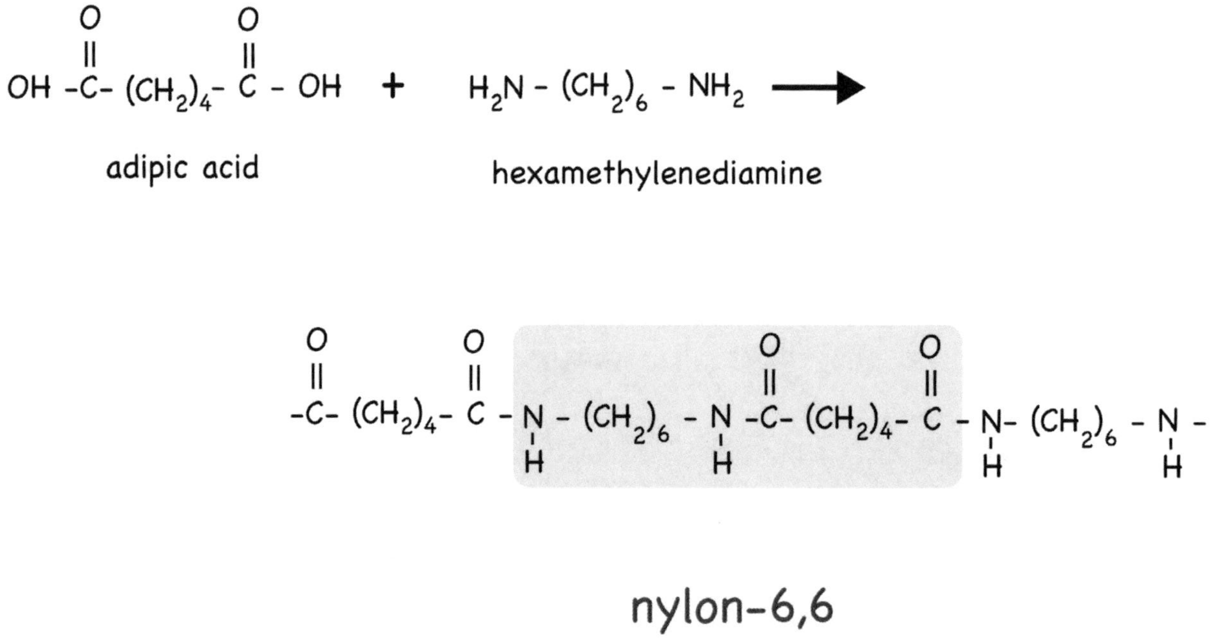

$$OH-\overset{\overset{O}{\|}}{C}-(CH_2)_4-\overset{\overset{O}{\|}}{C}-OH \quad + \quad H_2N-(CH_2)_6-NH_2 \longrightarrow$$

adipic acid   hexamethylenediamine

$$-\overset{\overset{O}{\|}}{C}-(CH_2)_4-\overset{\overset{O}{\|}}{C}-\underset{\overset{|}{H}}{N}-(CH_2)_6-\underset{\overset{|}{H}}{N}-\overset{\overset{O}{\|}}{C}-(CH_2)_4-\overset{\overset{O}{\|}}{C}-\underset{\overset{|}{H}}{N}-(CH_2)_6-\underset{\overset{|}{H}}{N}-$$

nylon-6,6

Figure 9.8: The formation of nylon-6,6 is a condensation reaction between two monomers.

Another common class of condensation polymers is the polyesters, formed by hooking monomers together with ester linkages. For example, a very widely used polyester, known by the trade name Dacron®, is made from a double acid monomer and a double alcohol monomer. Similar to nylon-6,6 in Figure 9.8, the new two-monomer molecule forming the polyester still has functional groups at both ends, and so can keep on growing:

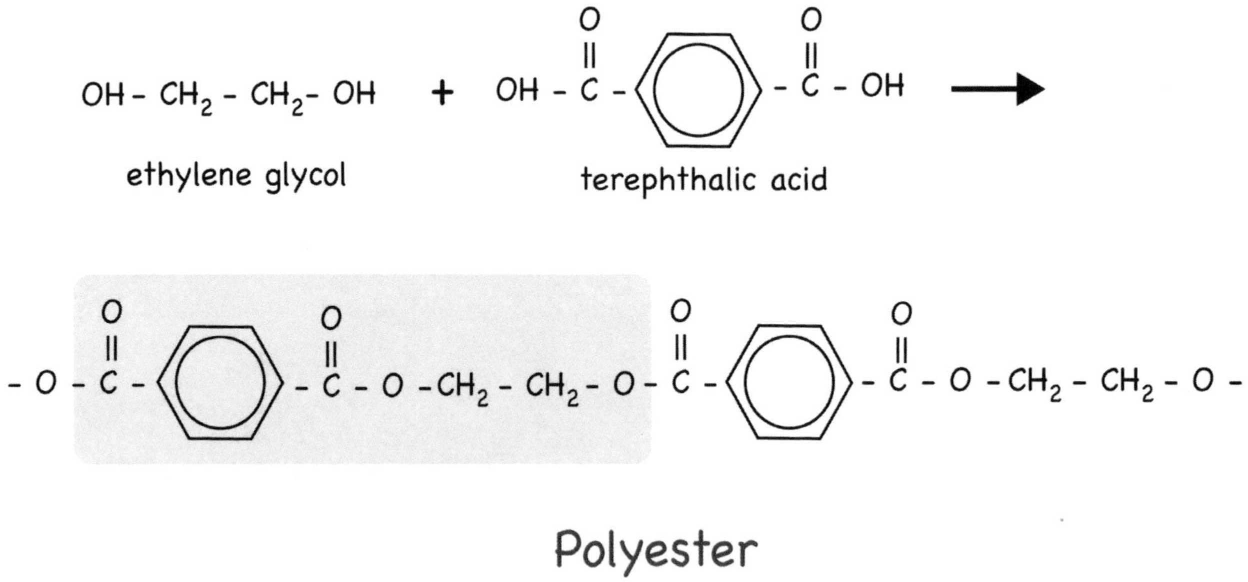

$$OH-CH_2-CH_2-OH \quad + \quad OH-\overset{\overset{O}{\|}}{C}-\langle\bigcirc\rangle-\overset{\overset{O}{\|}}{C}-OH \longrightarrow$$

ethylene glycol   terephthalic acid

$$-O-\overset{\overset{O}{\|}}{C}-\langle\bigcirc\rangle-\overset{\overset{O}{\|}}{C}-O-CH_2-CH_2-O-\overset{\overset{O}{\|}}{C}-\langle\bigcirc\rangle-\overset{\overset{O}{\|}}{C}-O-CH_2-CH_2-O-$$

Polyester

Figure 9.9: The formation of Dacron® is a condensation reaction between two monomers.

The monomers for condensation reactions may have two alcohols, or two amines, in which case they must be paired with a monomer that has two acids. Or a monomer may have one acid and one alcohol so that ester linkages can be formed "tip to tail." In this case, only one kind of monomer is needed. Alternatively, a monomer may have one acid and one amine, so that amide linkages can be formed "tip to tail." The most important example of this case is the amino acids.

When amino acids form a long chain of amide linkages, the resulting polymer is called a protein. As we will see in the next chapter, proteins are the main molecular machines that make all of life possible.

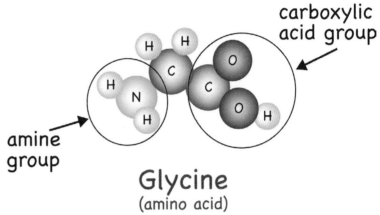

carboxylic acid group

amine group

Glycine
(amino acid)

Synthetic polymers have made it possible for us to improve the overall quality of life for many people. Without synthetic polymers, we would not have been able to cure certain medical conditions, travel at the speed of sound, or fly to the moon.

9.4 SUMMARY

Here are the main points to remember from this chapter:

- A polymer is a molecule of "many units."

- Polymers can contain one type of monomer, or can be composed of two or more different monomer units.

- Polymers can be linear or branched or contain cross-links.

- Polymers, such as polyethylene, can be formed by addition reactions, or they can be formed by condensation reactions, as is Dacron®.

- A monomer can have two reactive groups, such as amino acids, that allow "tip-to-tail" polymer formation.

9.5 STUDY QUESTIONS

1. Give an example of a homopolymer.

2. Give an example of a copolymer.

3. What determines the physical properties of a polymer?

4. Give the name of a thermoplastic.

5. Give the name of a synthetic fiber.

6. Give the name of an elastomer.

7. What is a "free radical?"

8. How are free radicals used in polymer formation?

9. What do "HDPE" and "LDPE" stand for and what is the difference between the two?

10. What is the difference between a condensation reaction and an addition reaction?

CHAPTER 10 BIOLOGICAL POLYMERS

10.1 INTRODUCTION

We discovered in Chapter 9 that chains of repeating units are called polymers. We found that polymers have different properties, determined by the type of monomer unit(s) that make up the polymer and by how the polymer chain interacts with itself or other polymer chains in the form of crosslinks. We found that polymers can be synthetic (made by man) or occur in living things. We will now look at two very important biological polymers found in living things. These are amino acid polymers and nucleic acid polymers.

10.1.1 Polymers in living things

We now know that living things are composed of a system of highly organized and specialized molecules. We discovered in Chapter 8 that there are a variety of small molecules required for the healthy maintenance of our bodies. We saw how vitamins, fats, and steroids are all part of the intricate system that keeps our bodies healthy. We also saw that our bodies require carbohydrates for energy. Recall that carbohydrates can be either single sugar molecules, or many thousand sugar molecules hooked together in the form of starches or cellulose. Starches and cellulose are types of biological polymers. In fact, there are many types of biological polymers that are important for the overall function of biological cells. Two such polymers are amino [ə-mē′-nō] acid polymers, called proteins, and nucleic [nü-klā′-ik] acid polymers, called either DNA or RNA. These two types of polymers are specifically designed to carry out a number of different and very important functions inside the cell. These polymers are found in all living things, and without them, living things would not exist.

10.1.2 Living cells are like tiny computers

It is not much of an exaggeration to say that all living things are made of biological polymers, especially proteins and DNA. Although there are lots of molecules inside living things, proteins, DNA, and RNA are the main machinery and information molecules. A simple analogy might help us understand how proteins, DNA, and RNA function inside cells. A computer has hardware (wires, screens, keyboards, circuits, logic chips, memory, etc.) and also software (computer programs) that controls the hardware. The hardware is the only thing that actually *does* something. The keyboard and the mouse transmit information from you to the computer; the screen transmits information from the computer back to you; the memory and logic circuits allow the computer to process information; the internet board allows you to send and receive signals from the Web; the speakers play music, and so on. All of this is hardware. On the other hand, stored in the computer's memory are programs that control everything the hardware does. The programs are just patterns of 1's and 0's—they are not made of atoms like the hardware. But these patterns nonetheless determine whether the computer displays your latest homework assignment on the screen, connects you to the Web, or plays a CD over the speakers. If you had the right hardware, you could design a program that would calculate the surface area of the moon or one that would launch, fly, and land a space probe or aircraft on Mars.

Inside cells, proteins are machines that play the main role of the hardware. They make it possible for the cell to do something, like swim, crawl, divide, or convert sugar into energy. The DNA is like the memory. It stores the instructions and control programs that tell the proteins and other machines what to do. By programming the DNA correctly, you could tell the cell's hardware to go hunting for

food, to build an outboard motor to make the cell swim, to attack and eat a foreign cell, to divide and form two new cells, or to continue dividing to build a fish, a frog, or a puppy.

10.1.3 Biological machinery

The core of any biological organism is the central genetic machinery. The central genetic machinery is the system of DNA, RNA, and proteins that uses the genetic information in the DNA to create new protein machines. It has four main parts: the DNA itself, which contains all the instructions for making a protein; a protein called RNA polymerase [pə lim' ə rās], which makes a temporary copy of the DNA called messenger RNA (or mRNA for short); and a very large RNA–protein complex called a ribosome [rī'-bə-sōm], which uses the mRNA to make a new protein.

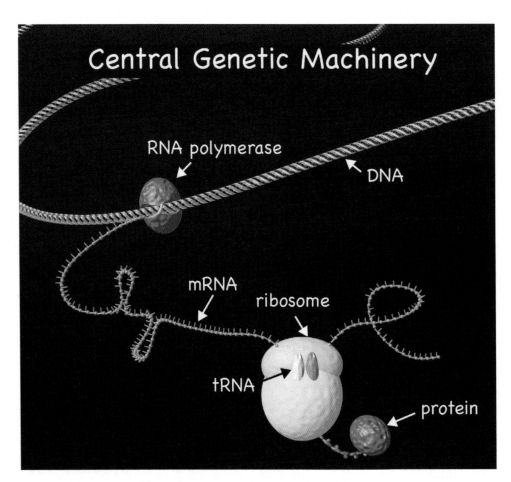

Figure 10.1: The central genetic machinery consists of RNA polymerase, DNA, mRNA, the ribosome, and tRNA working together to make protein.

There are a number of other, smaller parts as well, but these are the main ones. In the next few sections, we will learn more about what proteins are and how the genetic system builds them.

10.2 AMINO ACID POLYMERS: PROTEINS

There are many different kinds of proteins, each one performing a different job inside the cell. Many proteins carry out chemical reactions that help synthesize organic molecules even more efficiently than an organic chemist in the lab! For example, RNA polymerase is a protein that makes the messenger RNA, which is then used by the ribosome to make new protein. (See Figure 10.2) Also, every time a cell divides,

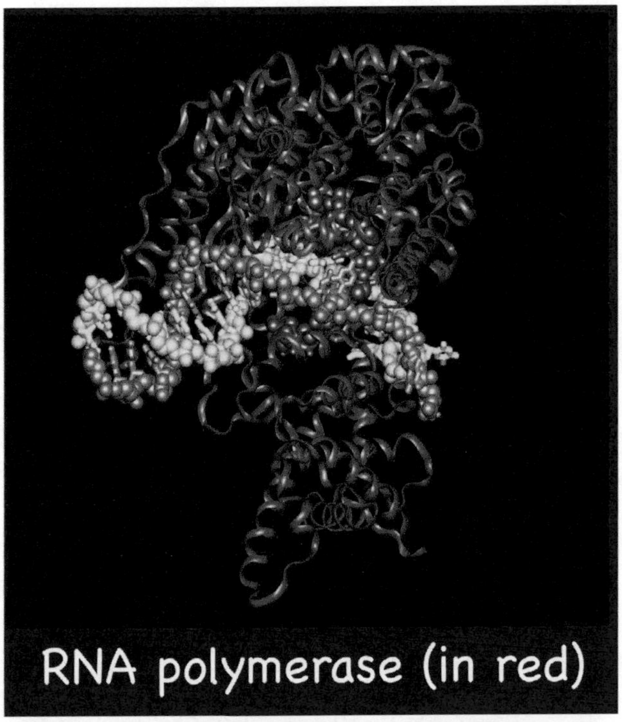

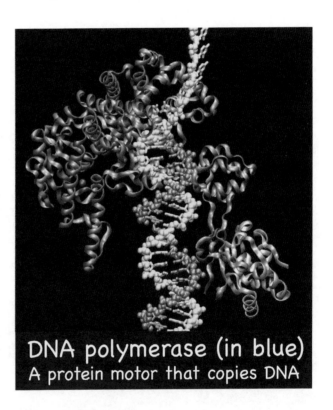

Figure 10.2: RNA polymerase is a protein motor that makes RNA. [Crystal structure by Yin, Y.W., Steitz, T. A., "The Structural Mechanism of Translocation and Helicase Activity in T7 RNA Polymerase," Cell (Cambridge, MA v116 pp. 393–404, 2004 (Protein Data Bank ID 1S76). Illustration by D. J. Keller]

it needs to make a new copy of its DNA. So a protein called a DNA polymerase makes the copy for the new cell. Some proteins

Figure 10.3: DNA polymerase is a protein motor that makes DNA. [Crystal structure by Doublie, S., Tabor, S., Long, A.M., Richardson, C.C., Ellenberger, T. "Crystal structure of a bacteriophage T7 DNA replication complex at 2.2 Å resolution," Nature v391 pp. 251-258, 1998 (Protein Data Bank ID 1C57). Illustration by D. J. Keller]

can cut other proteins, DNA, or RNA, and some molecules pump chemicals from inside the cell to outside the cell. Other proteins are part of large and complex protein assemblies, such as those found in bacterial flagella, which spin propellers so cells can swim. Still

others, like kinesin [kī'-nē-sən], are tiny motors that move molecules from one place to another. Protein motors are everywhere inside every cell doing all of the work that keeps cells living.

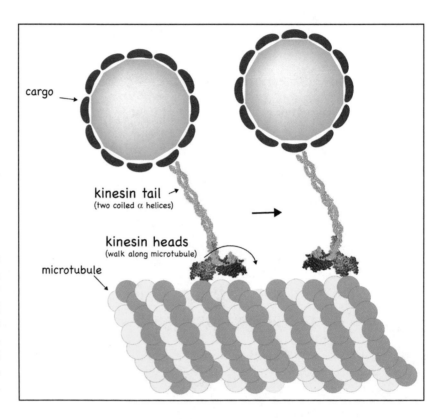

Figure 10.4: Kinesin is a protein motor that moves "cargo" through the cell. It performs this task by "walking" (with the heads) along microtubules. [Kinesin head crystal structure by Kikkawa, M., Sablin, E. P., Okada, Y., Yajima, H., Fletterick, R. J., and Hirokawa, N., "Switch-based Mechanism of Kinesin Motors," Nature v411 pp. 439–445, 2001 (Protein Data Bank ID 1IA0. Illustration by R.W. Keller]

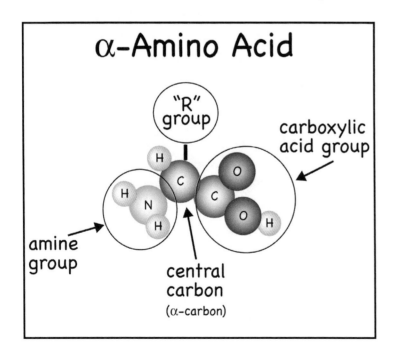

Figure 10.5: An amino acid has two functional groups—a carboxylic acid group and an amine group—attached to a central carbon atom called the α-carbon.

10.2.1 Amino acids

From a chemical point of view, proteins are polymers composed of amino [ə-mē'-nō] acids. There are 20 "standard" amino acids found in living things. All of the amino acids, except for proline, have a central carbon attached to two functional groups: a carboxylic [kär bäk si' lik] acid group and an amine group. The central carbon atom is called the α [al'-fə] carbon. Because they have both an amine and an acid attached to the α-carbon, they are called α-amino acids.

There is also a third group attached to the α-carbon called the "R" group. The "R" stands for different types of atoms or functional groups. For example, the "R" group in glycine [glī'-sēn] is simply a hydrogen atom, and the "R" group in alanine [a'-lə-nēn] is a methyl group.

When we say that there are 20 different amino acids, we mean that there are 20 different R groups. All amino acids have the same "backbone"

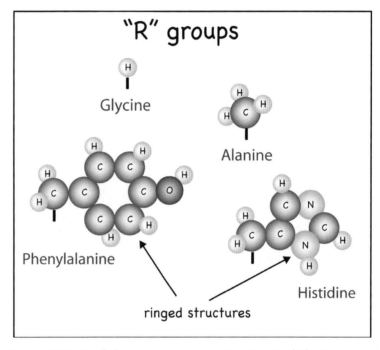

Figure 10.6: The "R" groups can be simple—like the "H" of glycine, or more complex—like the benzene ring of phenylalanine.

consisting of the amine group, the α-carbon, and the acid group, but they have different "R" groups. In principle the "R" group could be anything organic, but only these 20 "R" groups are actually used by living things.

Each of these "R" groups give amino acids different properties. For example, some amino acids such as glutamic [glü-ta'-mik] acid and aspartic [ə-spär'-tik] acid, are acidic. Amino acids can also be basic, such as arginine [är'-jə-nēn] and lysine [lī'-sēn]. The amino acids alanine, leucine [lü'-sēn], and valine [va'-lēn] are *hydrophobic* and do not interact with water. The amino acids asparagine [ə-sper'-ə-jēn] and glutamine [glü'-tə-mēn] contain an amide functional group which is polar, and so these amino acids are *hydrophilic* and interact with water. The "R" group can also be a ringed structure. For example, the "R" group in phenylalanine [fen-əl-al'-ə-nēn] has a six-membered benzene ring. Phenylalanine is thus an aromatic molecule in addition to being an amino acid. The "R" group for histidine [his'-tə-dēn] has a five-membered ring called imidazole [i-mə-da'-zōl]. As we will see in the next few sections, the different properties of the "R" groups control the shapes of proteins and make it possible for proteins to do their jobs.

10.2.2 Peptide bonds

Proteins are polymers made of amino acids. Most proteins are at least a few hundred amino acids long, and some of the largest proteins are thousands of amino acids long. Proteins are more complicated than the synthetic polymers we learned about in Chapter 9, because instead of one or two monomer types, proteins combine up to 20 different types of amino acid monomers in a single polymer chain.

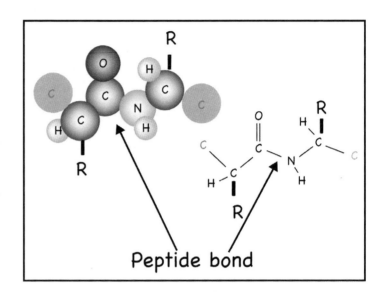

Figure 10.7: A peptide bond is an amide linkage just like those in the synthetic polymers nylon and KEVLAR®.

Amino acids are linked to each other with a peptide bond. A peptide bond is just another name for an amide linkage, exactly like the amide linkages in synthetic polymers such as nylon or KEVLAR®. Amino acids get hooked together by a condensation reaction between the acid group at one end of an amino acid and the amine group at the other end of an adjacent amino acid as shown in Figure 10.8.

Notice that after the reaction the new two-amino-acid molecule still has an amine group at one end and an acid group at the other. This means that more amino acids can be added to either end.

The ribosome [rī'-bə-sōm] (see Figure 10.26) is the molecular machine that hooks amino acids together. It facilitates or *catalyzes* the formation of the peptide bonds between amino acids. Though it is chemically possible to add amino acids to either end of a

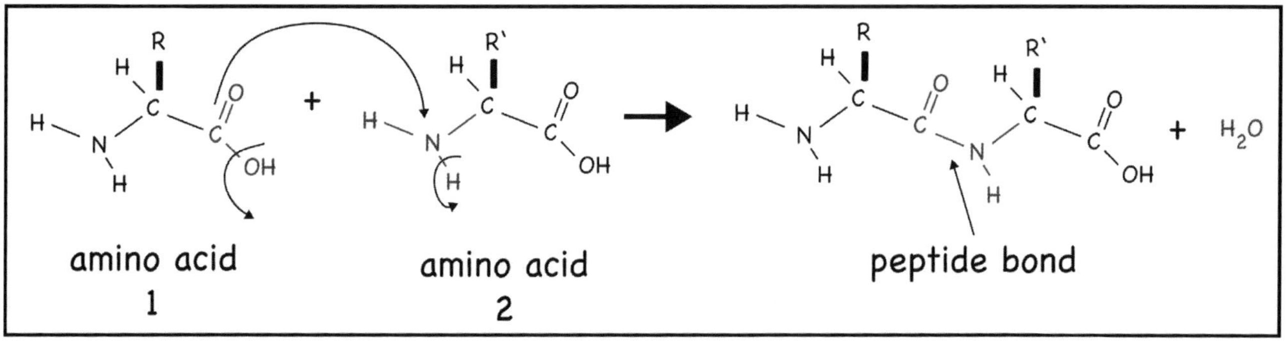

Figure 10.8: In this example, the peptide bond is formed by a condensation reaction between the acid group on "amino acid 1" and the amine group on "amino acid 2."

growing protein, ribosomes always add new amino acids to the end with the *acid group*, never to the end with the amino group. Any number of amino acids can be linked in any order: Alanine–alanine–alanine–alanine is a possible protein, but so is arginine–glycine–glutamic acid–phenylalanine–alanine.

10.2.3 Protein primary structure

This is the most important thing to remember about proteins:

The order of the amino acids in a protein chain determines
what kind of machine the protein becomes.

Because each protein has a different order of amino acids, one protein can become part of a rotary motor, another a pump for sodium ions, and another an RNA polymerase. Having one or more amino acid monomers out of sequence can destroy the protein's function. The order, or sequence, of amino acids in a polymer is called the primary structure. A short hypothetical protein sequence could be arginine–glycine–glutamic acid–phenylalanine–alanine. Connecting these amino acids with peptide bonds would give us the hypothetical protein shown in Figure 10.9.

One end of the protein has an amino group and the other end has an acid group, also called a carboxyl group. By convention, the end of the protein with the amino group is called the N-terminus, and the other end, with the carboxyl group, is called the

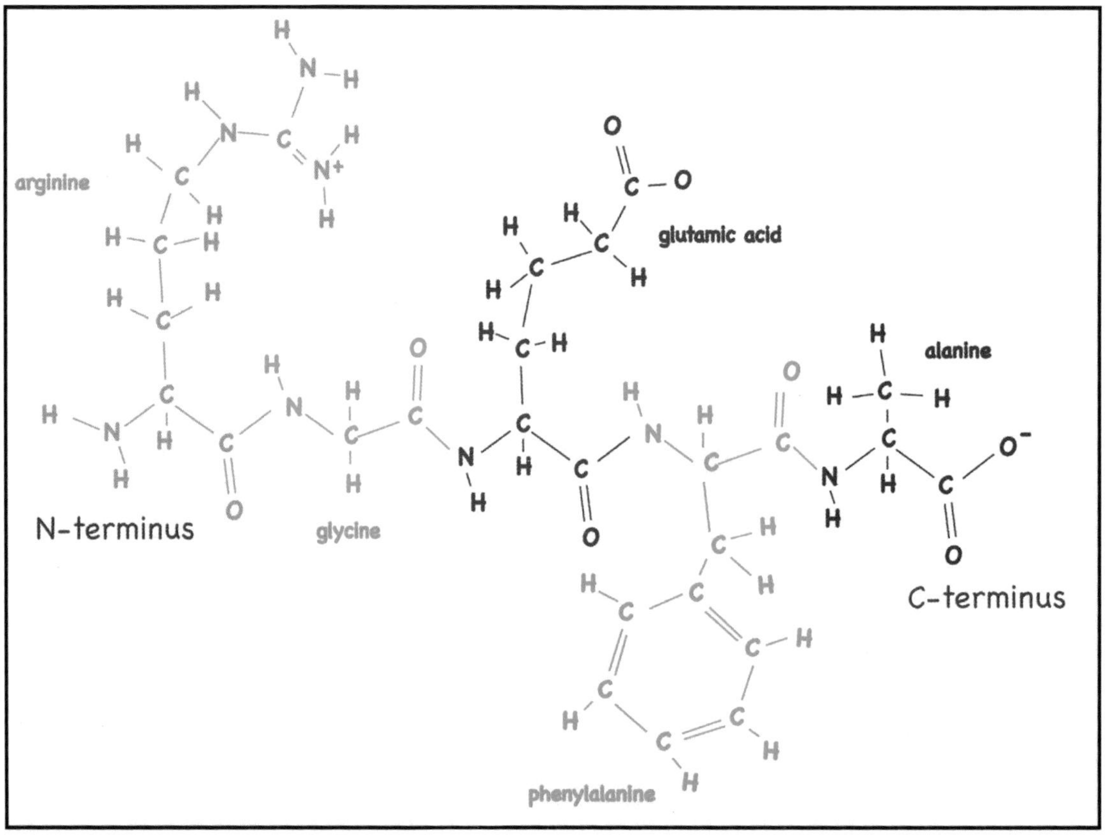

Figure 10.9: The polypeptide chain arginine–glycine–glutamic acid–phenylalanine–alanine forms a hypothetical protein and can be written as Arg Gly Glu Phe Ala or RGEFA.

C-terminus. Since protein sequences can be quite long, instead of writing out the entire name of the amino acids, scientists use abbreviations. Biochemists use two types of abbreviations: a three-letter abbreviation or a single-letter abbreviation. For example, arginine is given the three-letter abbreviation arg and glycine is given the three-letter abbreviation gly. Using three letter abbreviations, the polypeptide-chain sequence becomes arg-gly-glu-phe-ala, which is much easier to write. In the single-letter abbreviations, arginine is R and glycine is G. The sequence now becomes RGEFA. The single-letter abbreviations are shorter to write, but require that you remember the single-letter abbreviations (see Appendix E), which can be harder to remember. Biochemists use the three-letter abbreviations when the sequence is short and the single-letter abbreviations when it is very long.

10.2.4 Protein secondary structure

Once the amino acids are connected together into a long chain, the protein folds up into a compact shape. The sequence of amino acids, or primary structure, determines what shape the protein folds into. The shape of the protein determines what kind of machine the protein will become.

When a protein begins to fold, it first organizes into its secondary structure. There are two basic kinds of secondary structures, called helices [hē'-lə-sēz] and pleated sheets.

Helices are formed when a chain of amino acids, called a polypeptide [pä-lē-pep'-tīd] backbone, twists into a cylindrical coil, much like wrapping a ribbon around a tube. (See Figure 10.10) Notice that a ribbon can be coiled in two directions—left or right. The same is true of protein helices. They can be either right-handed or left-handed. The helices in proteins are right-handed and are called α-helices (alpha helices).

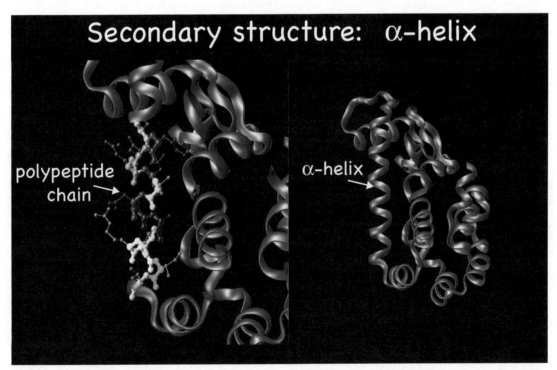

Figure 10.10: The α-helix is a secondary structure where the amino acids wrap around each other into a coil. All proteins have right-handed α-helicies. [The secondary structure of a section of T4 lysozyme—a protein that breaks cell walls. Crystal structure by Faber, H. R., Matthews, B. W. "A mutant T4 lysozyme displays five different crystal conformations." *Nature* v348 pp. 263–266, 1990 (Protein Data Bank ID 256L). Illustration by D. J. Keller]

Another pattern that proteins form is called a β-pleated sheet (beta pleated sheet). In a pleated sheet, the polypeptide backbones line up next to each other in a sheet-like structure. (See Figure 10.11)

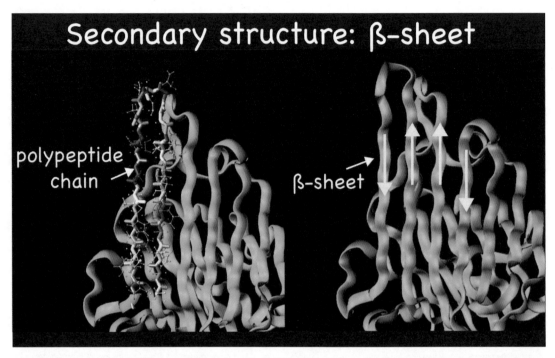

Figure 10.11: The β-sheet is a secondary structure where the polypeptides align in a sheetlike fashion. [The secondary structure of a section of concavalin—a protein that breaks cell walls. Crystal structure by Habash, J., Raftery, J., Nuttall, R., Price, H. J., Wilkinson, C., Kalb, A. J., Helliwell, J. R. "Direct determination of the positions of the deuterium atoms of the bound water in concavalin A by neutron Laue crystallography" *Acta Crystallograhphy*, Section D v56 pp. 541–550, 2000 (Protein Data Bank ID 1C57). Illustration by D. J. Keller]

10.2.5 Protein tertiary structure

Once the polypeptide backbone folds into one or more secondary structures, the protein further folds into what is called the tertiary structure. The tertiary structure determines the overall shape of the protein and is critical for protein function. A protein with the correct primary and secondary structure but an incorrectly folded tertiary structure will not function properly in the cell.

The secondary structures of a protein fold together to form larger three-dimensional tertiary structures, such as domains and barrels. These structures can function alone or together with other proteins.

Protein domains are clusters of 100–200 amino acid monomers folded into a compact unit. These clusters can contain all of the secondary structures, such as helices and pleated sheets. Protein domains often have specialized functions and hence behave as independent parts of the overall protein machine. For example, there are several protein domains for DNA polymerase (see Figure 10.12) called the palm, thumb, and fingers. The thumb domain and the fingers domain hold a piece of DNA in place, and the palm houses the chemical activity for making new DNA. The fingers open and close adding new nucleotides to the newly formed ssDNA (single-stranded DNA).

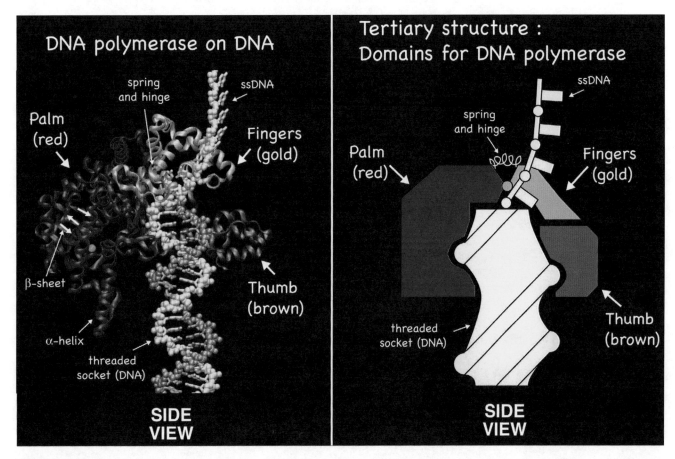

Figure 10.12: The tertiary structure for DNA polymerase consists of several domains performing different functions. The thumb domain and the fingers domain hold the DNA, and the palm domain is where the chemical activity takes place. [Illustration by D. J. Keller]

Barrels are formed primarily by pleated sheets. The pleated sheets line up side by side forming a barrel-shaped structure. The pleated sheets are typically oriented in opposite directions and connected to each other by turns. (See Figure 10.13.)

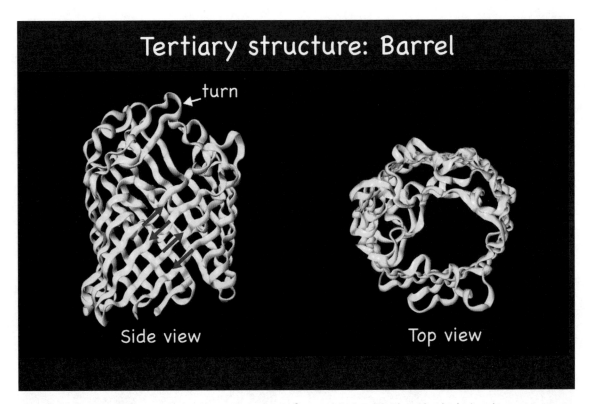

Figure 10.13: Barrels are a tertiary structure formed primarily by pleated sheets. [A single barrel of OmpF protein—a protein found in the bacterial outer membrane. Crystal structure by Phale, P. S., Philippsen, A., Kiefhaber, T., Koebnik, R., Phale, V. P., Schirmer, T., and Rosenbusch, J. P. "Stability of trimeric OmpF porin: the contributions of the latching loop L2," *Biochemistry,* v37 pp. 15663–15670, 1998 (Protein Data Bank ID IBT9). Illustration by D. J. Keller]

10.2.6 Protein quaternary structure

Once a protein has folded into its tertiary structure, it is complete. However, it often happens that two proteins work together to make a single machine. The combination of two or more protein chains functioning together is called quaternary structure. The quaternary structure is yet another level of protein structure complexity. For example, a proteosome [prō′-tē-ō-sōm] (see Figure 10.14) is a large and complex molecular machine that breaks down proteins. It is composed of many protein chains which are arranged into four rings (called α and β) that are stacked, one on top of another. The two β rings are in the center of the proteosome and contain areas (called proteolytic [prō-tē-ə-li′-tik] sites) that break apart or degrade proteins.

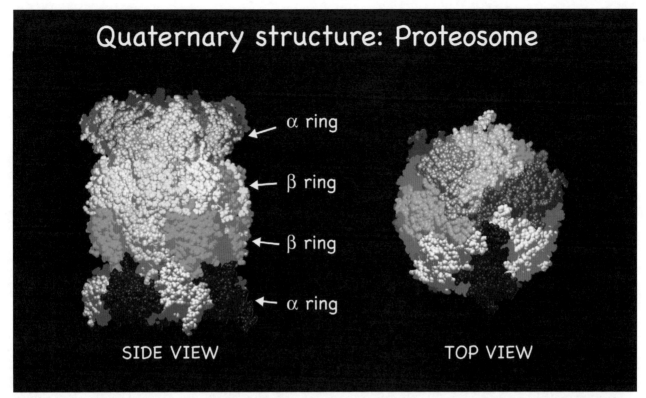

Figure 10.14: The quaternary structure of a proteosome consists of several protein chains arranged in four rings. [The 20S proteosome—a protein machine used to break down other proteins. Crystal structure by Groll, M., Kim, K. B., Kairies, N., Crews, C., "Crystal structure of epoxomicin," *Biochemistry,* v37 pp. 15663–15670, 1998 (Protein Data Bank ID IBT9). Illustration by D. J. Keller]

10.3 NUCLEIC ACID POLYMERS

Proteins do most of the actual work inside cells, but DNA and RNA carry the genetic information. DNA and RNA contain the instructions that tell the cell how to grow, when to divide, which proteins to make, how many proteins to make, and when to die. DNA is like the disk drive of a computer—it stores the permanent copy of all the software for the cell. RNA is like the computer's memory chip—it stores temporary copies of instructions from the DNA. Together, DNA and RNA tell the ribosomes which proteins to make and how to make them.

What is the difference between RNA and DNA? And why are DNA and RNA, rather than proteins, used to store information? The answers to both of these questions lie in the *chemical structures* of DNA and RNA. As we will see, DNA and RNA are very similar to each other, and both have structures that are especially well suited to the task of storing information.

10.3.1 DNA

In 1953, Francis Crick and James Watson determined the structure of DNA using X-ray crystallography [kri-stə-lä'-grə-fē], a technique that allows an image of large molecules to be reconstructed using the scattering of radiation. The discovery of the structure of DNA marks the birth of modern molecular biology. Before this time very little was known about how cells live or what makes them die. But today we know quite a bit about cellular function and activity.

The three letters "D-N-A" stand for deoxyribonucleic [dē-äk'-si-rī-bō-nü-klā-ik] acid. Like a protein, DNA is a polymer made of several different kinds of monomers, and the sequence of these monomers is what allows DNA to do its job. But there are only four different kinds of monomers (instead of the 20 amino acids in proteins), and they are more complicated than amino acids.

The monomer unit for DNA is called a nucleotide [nü'-klē-ə-tīd]. A nucleotide has three main parts: a nucleic [nü-klā'-ik] acid base; a five-membered sugar ring, called a ribose [rī'-bōs] (the "ribo" part of deoxy*ribo*nucleic acid); and a phosphate [fäs'-fāt] group (which is acidic, like phosphoric acid, and is the acid part of deoxyribonucleic acid). The

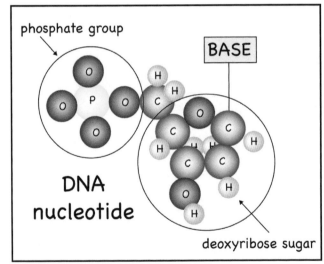

Figure 10.15: DNA nucleotide with a phosphate group, a base, and a deoxyribose sugar.

sugar group on DNA is deoxygenated [dē-äk'-si-jen-ā-təd], which means that it is missing a -OH group on one of its carbon atoms. This is the reason that DNA is called *deoxy*ribonucleic acid.

The nucleotides are connected to each other by a bond between the hydroxyl group on the ribose sugar of one nucleotide and the phosphate group of the adjacent nucleotide.

This type of bond is called a phosphodiester [fəs-fō-dī-es'-ter] bond. It is a link between an alcohol (the –OH on the sugar) and an acid (the phosphate group), so it is like the esters we learned about in Chapters 8 and 9. That is why it's called a phosphod*iester* bond. The chemical reactions that link the nucleotides together are condensation reactions much like the ester linking reactions that create Dacron® (Chapter 9). The DNA polymer thus has a "backbone" formed from sugars and phosphate groups, called the sugar-phosphate backbone. The bases stick out from the sugars like side groups.

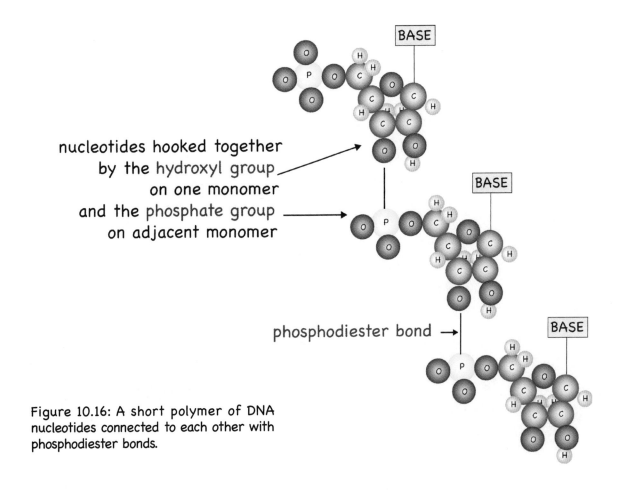

nucleotides hooked together by the hydroxyl group on one monomer

and the phosphate group on adjacent monomer

phosphodiester bond →

Figure 10.16: A short polymer of DNA nucleotides connected to each other with phosphodiester bonds.

10.3.2 Genetic words and the sequence of DNA

Nucleotides all have the same sugar (deoxyribose) and the same phosphate group, but there are four different kinds of nucleic acid bases: adenine [a'-də-nēn] (A), thymine [thī'-mēn] (T), guanine [gwä'-nēn] (G), and cytosine [sī'-tə-sēn] (C). Both adenine (A) and guanine (G) have two rings fused with each other. This type of base is called a purine [pyur'-ēn]. Thymine (T) and cytosine (C) both have single rings and are called pyrimidines [pī-ri'-mə-dēnz].

The sequence of bases along the DNA can therefore be written as a sequence of letters. For example, the letters AATCGCAT stand for adenine-adenine—thymine—cytosine—guanine—cytosine—adenine—thymine.

Each of these bases is one letter of the genetic code. *The sequence of bases along the DNA chain is exactly like words on a page or like*

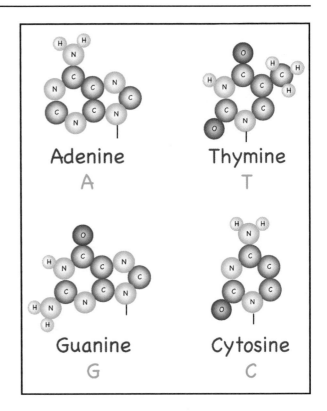

Figure 10.17: The four DNA bases—adenine, thymine, guanine, and cytosine.

the 1's and 0's in a computer memory. They spell out the genetic information that a cell needs to make proteins and to control its network of machines. To be precise, the sequence of bases in the DNA does mainly two things. First, some parts of the DNA code for proteins and are called genes.

| A | T | C | A | T | C |

DNA strand
written as a
sequence of bases
(DNA sequence)

Figure 10.18:
The sequence of DNA bases is written
as a sequence of letters—ATCATC.

Inside a gene *each set of three bases is a code word for an amino acid in a protein*. The DNA sequence[1] AAA–TTT–CCC codes for the amino acids phenylalanine-lysine-glycine; the DNA sequence AGA–TGA–ACC–CTT codes for serine-threonine-tryptophan-glutamic acid and so on. So, the genetic letters in the DNA spell out the sequence of amino acids in a protein, which determines what sort of machine the protein folds into. Section 10.5 tells more about how this actually happens.

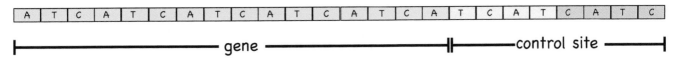

Figure 10.19: A DNA sequence can have genes that code for proteins, or control sites that regulate aspects of the cell.

Second, some parts of the DNA serve as control sites. Rather like a computer program, these special sites determine what type and how much of each protein is made. By controlling the proteins, the control sites also control everything else, such as when the cell divides, whether the cell swims after food, whether the cell attempts to engulf food, and so on.

10.3.3 Hydrogen bonds and molecular recognition

DNA bases stick to each other. The sticking is caused by weak bonds called hydrogen bonds. A hydrogen bond is a very weak chemical bond that forms when a hydrogen atom is bridged between two electron-loving atoms, such as oxygen and nitrogen. In the nucleic acid bases, hydrogen bonds form between a nitrogen on one base and an oxygen on the other. Hydrogen bonding can happen in several different ways between the bases, but the most favorable ways—with the strongest hydrogen bonds—are when an A sticks edge-on to a T and when a G sticks edge-on to a C.

---

[1]The DNA letters must first be converted to RNA letters, so a DNA "AAA" is an RNA "UUU," which is the RNA codon for phenylalanine. (See Sections 10.4 and 10.5.)

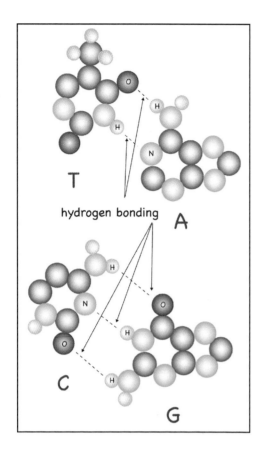

Figure 10.20: The bases "recognize" each other and stick together through hydrogen bonding.

Sticking between the bases of DNA is a form of molecular [mə-le'-kyə-lər] recognition—an A *recognizes* a T and vice versa, and a G *recognizes* a C and vice versa—by the strength of the hydrogen bonding between them. *This molecular recognition is extremely important. It allows the information in DNA to be copied and is the main reason why DNA and RNA are good at storing and transmitting information.*

10.3.4 The double helix

The full DNA polymer usually contains two DNA chains and is called double-stranded DNA, or dsDNA for short. Since it has two DNA chains, it has two copies of the genetic information. The two chains are twisted around each other with the nucleic acid bases in the middle. The bases on one strand stick edge to edge to the bases on the other strand by means of their hydrogen bonds. So the whole structure is like a ladder that has been twisted, with the bases like the rungs of the ladder and the sugar-phosphate backbone like the rails.

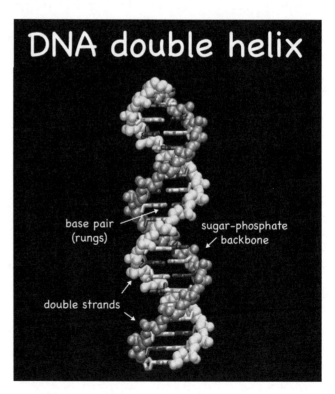

Figure 10.21: A DNA double helix is two chains of nucleic acid polymers wrapped around each other. [Illustration by D. J. Keller]

The stuck-together bases in the middle of the double helix are called base pairs. An A base on one strand is always paired with a T base on the other strand. Likewise, a G base is always paired with a C base. So the "rungs" in the ladder are always A–T or G–C. In this way it is always possible to tell, from looking at one strand, what the sequence is on the other strand.

The double helix structure of DNA is important for its function, which is the safe storage and accurate transmission of genetic information. That is, DNA has to be able to safely store and express the correct codes that the cell needs to make proteins, metabolize nutrients, grow, and divide. The code is found in the bases which are tucked safely inside the double helical coil. Here, they are not easily removed or degraded. In this way, DNA is able to protect the important information that the cell needs to live.

10.4 RNA

The letters "R-N-A" stand for ribonucleic acid. RNA is made from nucleotides with a ribose sugar, a phosphate group, and a nucleic acid base, just like DNA, but with two important differences. First, RNA contains two hydroxyl groups on its ribose sugar and is not "deoxygenated,"

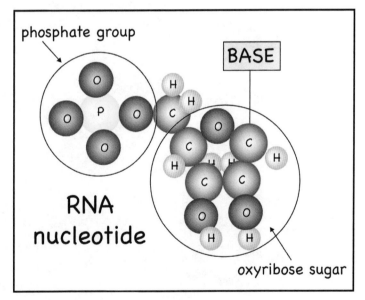

Figure 10.22: An RNA nucleotide is composed of an oxygenated ribose sugar, a phosphate group, and a base.

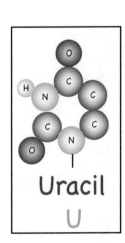

Figure 10.23: Uracil replaces thymine in RNA.

like DNA. This is why RNA is called "ribonucleic acid" instead of "deoxyribonucleic acid." Second, RNA does not have a thymine (T) base, but instead uses a base called uracil (U) [ü'-rə-sil] in place of thymine. These two small differences make RNA a significantly different molecule than DNA. The base pairing in RNA is the same as in DNA, except A forms hydrogen bonds (and hence base pairs) with U instead of with T.

RNA is usually found in complex structures, rather than in a double helix like DNA. RNA can fold back on itself, base pairing in certain regions. Because of this, RNA has many different functions inside cells. The ribosome—the machine that makes proteins—is mostly made of RNA. Another important class of molecules is the transfer RNAs (tRNA)—smaller RNA molecules that play an important role in the synthesis of new proteins.

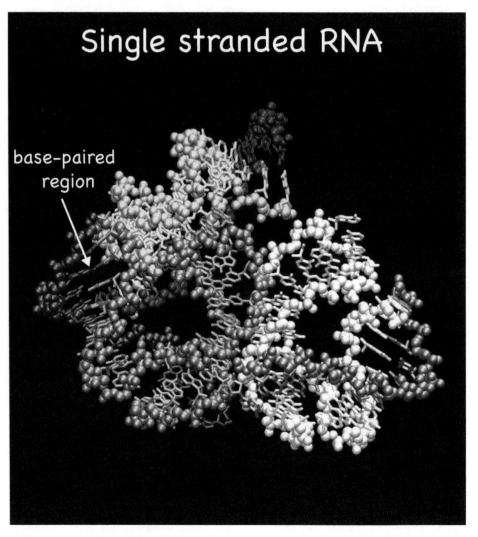

Figure 10.24: Single stranded RNA. [A "hammerhead ribozyme." Crystal structure by Pley, H. W., Flaherty, K. M., and McKay, D. B., "Three-dimensional structure of a hammerhead ribozyme" *Nature,* v372 pp. 68-74, 1994 (Protein Data Bank ID 1HMH). Illustration by D. J. Keller]

But perhaps the most important form of RNA is messenger RNA (mRNA)—the temporary copy of a gene that tells the ribosome which amino acids to use when constructing a protein. Now that we know the basics about DNA, RNA, and proteins, we are ready to learn how they work together to use genetic information to make new proteins.

10.5 BUILDING BIOLOGICAL MACHINES

Cells need new proteins all the time. Whenever a cell has a big job to do—dividing, crawling, hunting for food—it must make a host of new protein machines to carry out the job. At the beginning of the chapter, we briefly described the central genetic machinery, which consists of the DNA, an RNA polymerase, a messenger RNA, and the ribosome (plus numerous other parts). To make new proteins, cells send orders, (like "Make protein X!") to the central genetic machinery. (You may wonder, "How does a cell send an order to its own DNA?" That is an excellent question, but too complicated for us here! For now we will just accept that it can.)

The genetic letters in the DNA carry the code for the amino acids in the protein that is to be made, so the DNA contains the basic *plan* for the protein. The genetic code itself is found in Appendix F. Using Appendix F you can "read" the genetic information in the DNA. At first glance, the sequence of letters in a strand of DNA looks random and meaningless, however it is really a series of three-letter codons [kō'-dänz]. Most of the codons are for amino acids, but some are also "start" and "stop" codons. As we saw earlier, a hypothetical DNA molecule with the sequence AGA–TGA–ACC–CTT codes for the amino acids serine–threonine–tryptophan–glutamic acid. How does this DNA sequence get copied and used to make a new protein?

Making a new protein begins when an RNA polymerase binds to the DNA. This first step in making a new protein is called transcription. The job of the RNA polymerase is to copy (or transcribe) the DNA to make a piece of RNA with a complementary sequence to the DNA. In this way, the instructions for the protein have been transferred to the

RNA. A complementary sequence means that the RNA copy of the DNA is made with *complementary* base pairs for RNA.

So, the A nucleic acid residues in the DNA are U nucleic acid residues in the RNA. The T nucleic acid residues in the DNA are A nucleic acid residues in the RNA. The G nucleic acid residues are C nucleic acid residues in the RNA, and the C nucleic acid residues in the DNA are G nucleic acid residues in the RNA.

The RNA polymerase will only bind at special control sites on the DNA called promoters (a sequence like GAGGCTATATATTCCCCAGGGCTCAGCCAGTGTCTGTAACA), so every gene must have a promoter in front of it. After the RNA polymerase binds, it begins to crawl along the DNA. As it crawls, it unwinds the DNA double helix, exposing the genetic letters inside. Then it copies each DNA letter by adding a new RNA monomer to a growing chain of RNA. This is the messenger RNA (mRNA) mentioned earlier.

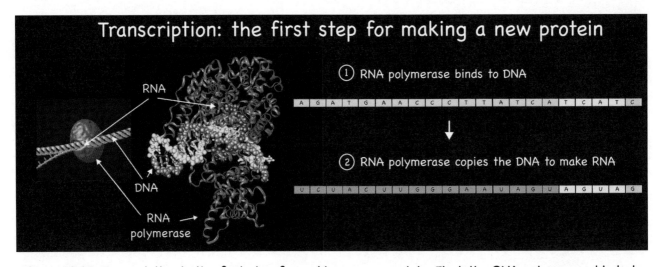

Figure 10.25: Transcription is the first step for making a new protein. First the RNA polymerase binds to DNA and then it copies the DNA to make a *complementary* strand of mRNA. (Illustration by R.W. Keller and D.J. Keller.)

Once the DNA has been accurately copied into a messenger RNA molecule, it can be used to make a protein. This process is called translation. The messenger RNA carrying the DNA code binds to a ribosome. Unlike the DNA, the RNA copy is not a double helix, so the bases of the RNA are exposed and can easily be read by the ribosome.

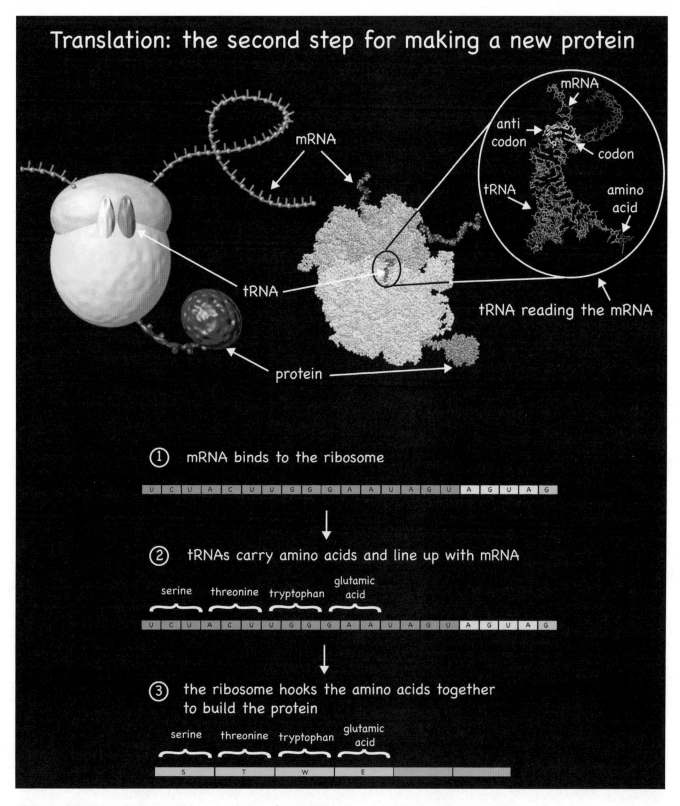

Figure 10.26: Translation is the second step for making a new protein. Ribosome structure from Jenner, L., Romby, P., Rees, B., Schulze-Briese, C., Springer, M., Ehresmann, C., Eshresmann, B., Moras, D., Yusupova, G., Yusupov, M. "Translational operator of mRNA on the ribosome: hw repressor proteins exclude ribosome binding" *Science*, v308 pp. 120–123, 2005 (Protein Data Bank ID 1YL4). Illustration by R.W. Keller and D.J. Keller]

The ribosome reads (or translates) the mRNA three letters at a time with the help of transfer RNA molecules, or tRNAs for short. Transfer RNAs are like little plugs, each with an amino acid on its end. The "plug" end of each tRNA has a set of three bases, called an anticodon, that must match the codon on the mRNA.

The mRNA molecule binds to the inside of the ribosome. Once it is securely fastened, tRNA molecules carrying the amino acids for each new amino acid align with the three-letter codons on the mRNA. For each tRNA, the ribosome links the amino acid it is carrying into the growing chain of amino acids that make up the new protein. As the protein chain grows, it folds into its proper shape (secondary structure, tertiary structure, and, with other proteins, quaternary structure) and becomes a new protein machine.

10.6 SUMMARY

- Two important polymers found in living systems are amino acid polymers, called proteins, and nucleic acid polymers, called DNA or RNA.

- Amino acids are linked by peptide bonds between the carboxyl group on one amino acid and the amino group on the adjacent amino acid.

- The order, or sequence, of amino acids determines the primary structure of proteins.

- The secondary structure of a protein is the way that the polypeptide folds into coils and sheets.

- The tertiary structure of a protein is the way that the coils and sheets of the secondary structure fold into a complex three-dimensional shape.

- The structure of a protein is necessary for its function.

- DNA (deoxyribonucleic acid) and RNA (ribonucleic acid) are the two biological polymers that carry, store, and transmit information inside cells for growth, reproduction, and metabolism.

- DNA molecules are chains of DNA nucleotides linked by a sugar-phosphate backbone. Each DNA nucleotide is built from a sugar (deoxyribose), a phosphate group, and a base (adenine, A; guanine, G; cytosine, C; thymine, T).

- RNA molecules are chains of RNA nucleotides linked by a sugar-phosphate backbone. Each RNA nucleotide is built from a sugar (ribose), a phosphate group, and a base (adenine A; guanine, G; cytosine, C; uracil, U).

- The genetic information in DNA or RNA is given by the base pair sequence of the four bases, which is A,T,C and G in DNA, and A, U, C, and G in RNA.

- The genetic code is composed of three-letter combinations, called codons. Each codon codes for either an amino acid or for a "start" or "stop" signal.

- DNA is a double helix formed from two chains of DNA monomers twisted around each other like a twisted ladder with the bases base paired across the middle. The structure of DNA allows the genetic information to be safely stored.

- RNA polymerase is a protein that "reads" the DNA in order to make a temporary copy of its genetic information out of RNA. The temporary copy is called messenger RNA, or mRNA.

- Proteins are made by a protein machine called a ribosome. The ribosome reads the three-letter combinations of the genetic code from the messenger RNA and creates a protein with the matching sequence of amino acids.

10.7 STUDY QUESTIONS

1. Draw the chemical structure for the amino acid isoleucine. Label the central carbon, the carboxyl group and the amino group.

2. Draw the chemical structures for glycine and tyrosine linked together by a peptide bond. Label the C-terminus and the N-terminus.

3. Describe the primary structure of proteins and write out an example.

4. Describe the secondary structure of proteins and give an example.

5. Describe the tertiary structure of proteins and give an example.

6. Describe the quaternary structure of proteins and give an example.

7. Name the four nucleic acid bases that store the genetic information in a DNA molecule.

8. Name the four nucleic acid bases that are used in an RNA molecule.

9. Using the chart write a corresponding amino acid sequence for the following DNA sequence: ATGCCTGATTTCGGA.

alanine	glutamic acid	glycine	asparagine	methionine	proline	phenylalanine
CGA	GAA	GGA	GAU	AUG	CCU	UUC

10. Describe the function for the protein machine RNA polymerase.

Appendix A: Building molecules using covalent bonds (HCNOPS group and halogens)

To build molecules using covalent bonding for the HCNOPS group, the following rules apply:

1)	Hydrogen atoms only have 1s orbtials; no hybrids, no *p* orbitals.	
2)	C,N,O,P, and S always have four orbitals, which may be a combination of hybrid orbitals and *p* orbitals.	
3)	Those electrons not involved in bonding are called lone pairs. A lone pair is a filled hybrid orbital and it does not participate in bonding.	
3)	An atom chooses its hybridization according to the number of other atoms to which it is bonded plus its lone pairs.	
4)	Every pair of overlapping half-filled orbitals forms a bond.	

Some facts about each atom:

Carbon	has no lone pairs, four valence electrons, and four available orbitals, so the four electrons occupy four half-filled orbitals
Nitrogen	has one lone pair and one more valence electron than carbon, so at least one orbtial must be filled
Oxygen	has two lone pairs and one more valence electron than nitrogen, so two hybrid orbitals must be filled
Phosphorus	similar to nitrogen
Sulfur	similar to oxygen
Halogens (F, Cl, Br, I)	all have three lone pairs each, and only one half-filled orbital

According to rule 3, the type of orbitals an atom has depends on how many other atoms and lone pairs surround the atom. Whenever an atom is surrounded by four "things" (either other atoms or lone pairs), it will have four sp^3 hybrid orbitals. If it is surrounded by three things, it will have three sp^2 hybrid orbitals plus one "left-over" p orbital (oriented perpendicular to the plane of the three sp^2 orbitals). If an atom has only two things around it, then it will have two sp hybrid orbitals and two "left-over" p orbitals (oriented perpendicular to each other and to the sp hybrids).

Number of atoms plus lone pairs	Orbitals	Example
2	(2) sp hybrid orbitals + (2) p orbitals	N in N_2
3	(3) sp^2 hybrid orbitals + (1) p orbital	O in O_2
4	(4) sp^3 hybrid orbitals	N in NH_3

A.1 Methane, CH_4

In methane a carbon atom is surrounded by four hydrogen atoms. Carbon has no lone pairs, and therefore, it has four half-filled sp^3 hybrid orbitals. The half-filled orbitals of the H atoms overlap with the half-filled sp^3 hybrid orbitals of the carbon atom to yield four sigma bonds. The molecule has a tetrhedral shape with bond angles of 109.5°.

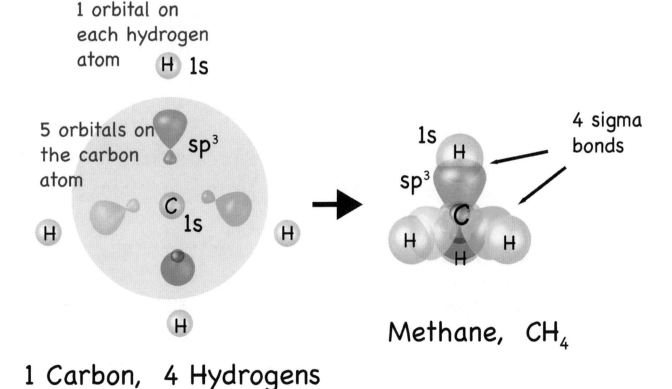

1 orbital on each hydrogen atom   H 1s

5 orbitals on the carbon atom sp^3 C 1s   H   H

1s sp^3 H   C   H   H   4 sigma bonds

Methane, CH_4

1 Carbon, 4 Hydrogens

A.2 Ammonia, NH₃

In ammonia a nitrogen atom is surrounded by three hydrogen atoms and one lone pair. This gives nitrogen four "things" it is surrounded by. This means that it has four sp^3 hybrid orbitals. One hybrid orbital is a filled "lone pair" that is not involved in bonding. The other three sp^3 hybrid orbitals are half-filled and are involved in bonding with the three H atoms. The three half-filled $1s$ orbitals of the hydrogen atoms overlap with the three half-filled sp^3 hybrid orbitals of the nitrogen atom to form three sigma bonds. The molecule is tetrahedral like methane except it has a lone pair instead of a fourth hydrogen.

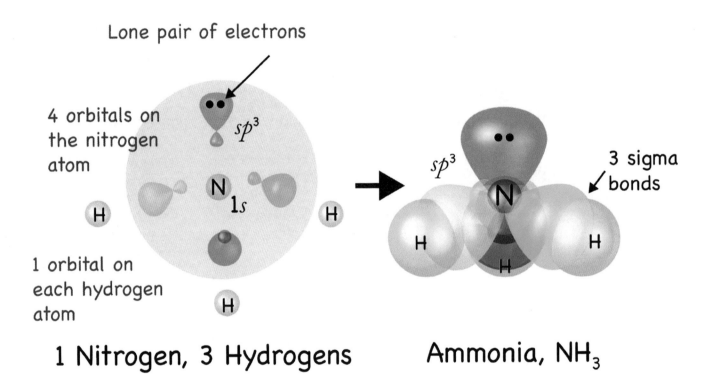

1 Nitrogen, 3 Hydrogens   **Ammonia, NH₃**

A.3 Molecular oxygen, O₂

In molecular oxygen each oxygen atom is next to its partner and each oxygen atom has two lone pairs of its own. So, each oxygen has three "things" around it, and therefore, has three sp^2 hybrid orbitals plus one "left over" p orbital.

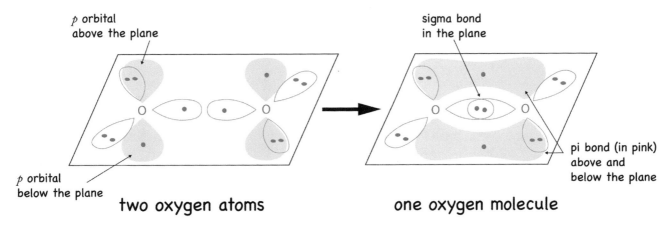

two oxygen atoms   one oxygen molecule

Two of the sp^2 hybrid orbitals on each oxygen atom must be filled for the two lone pairs. (Leftover p orbitals are never used for lone pairs.) When the two oxygen atoms are brought together, their half-filled sp hybrid orbitals overlap to form a sigma bond. But at the same time, their half-filled p orbitals also overlap to form a pi bond. So O_2 has a double bond—one sigma bond and one pi bond. Double bonds are very common and are always formed with one sigma bond and one pi bond.

A.4 Molecular nitrogen, N_2

Like the oxygen atoms in molecular oxygen, each nitrogen atom in molecular nitrogen is next to its partner. But nitrogen atoms have only one lone pair, so each nitrogen atom has only two things around it. Therefore, each N has *two sp* hybrid orbitals and *two* "left over" p orbitals.

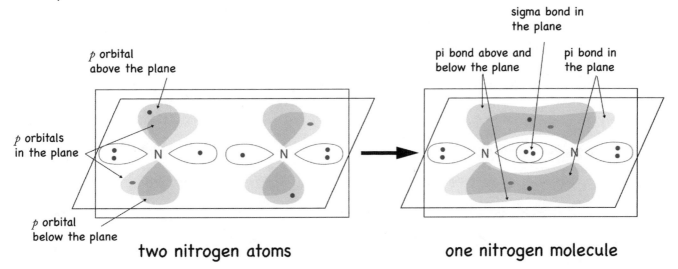

two nitrogen atoms   one nitrogen molecule

One of the *sp* hybrids on each N must be filled for the lone pair, but the remaining *sp* hybrid and both leftover *p* orbitals are half-filled. When the atoms are brought together, the half-filled *sp* hybrids form a sigma bond, and each pair of half-filled *p* orbitals also forms a pi bond. Therefore, molecular nitrogen has a triple bond, formed from one sigma and two pi bonds. Triple bonds are not very common, but are always formed of one sigma and two pi bonds. Triple bonds represent the greatest number of bonds that molecules form. There are no quadruple bonds.

A.5 Acetylene, C$_2$H$_2$

In acetylene the atoms are all arranged in a line, with the two hydrogens on the ends and the two carbons in the middle. That means each C atom has two other atoms around it (and no lone pairs), so it must be *sp* hybridized with two leftover *p* orbtials.

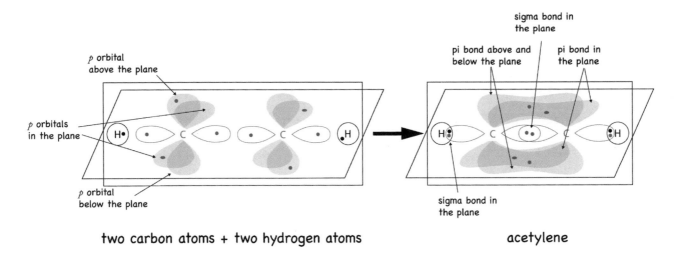

two carbon atoms + two hydrogen atoms   acetylene

The 1*s* orbitals on the hydrogens form sigma bonds with the *sp* hybrid orbitals on the carbon. The two remaining *sp* hybrids form a sigma bond between the carbons, and both pairs of "left over" orbitals overlap to form pi bonds. Except for the hydrogens on the ends, this is just like N$_2$! There is a triple bond with one sigma bond and two pi bonds. The two hydrogens on the ends are necessary because carbon has one less electron than nitrogen. Thus, it doesn't have a lone pair at the ends and needs to have them "capped" by hydrogens. But, while N$_2$ is a very inert molecule that almost never reacts, acetylene is a very reactive molecule that is used in torches to weld and cut steel. So, the fact that two molecules have a simlar bonding structure does not mean their chemistries will be similar.

A.6 Carbon Dioxide CO$_2$

In carbon dioxide the carbon is in the center, and the two oxygens are at either end, all in a straight line. Each oxygen atom has two lone pairs, so they are both *sp^2* hybridized with one leftover *p* orbital each. The carbon atom has no lone pairs, so it is *sp* hybridized with two leftover *p* orbitals.

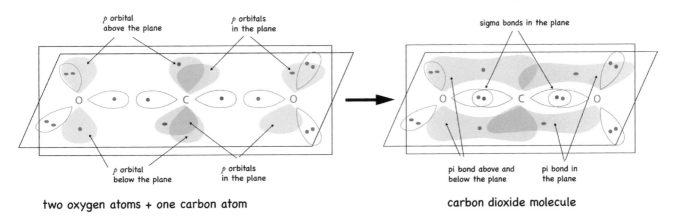

two oxygen atoms + one carbon atom   carbon dioxide molecule

When the three atoms come together, the *sp^2* hybrid orbitals on either oxygen form σ bonds with the *sp* hybrids on both sides of the carbon. At the same time one pair of *p* orbitals forms a π bond with one oxygen, and the other pair forms a π bond with the other oxygen. The result is two double bonds to the oxygen atoms on either side of the carbon atom.

A.7 Putting it all together: bonding for larger molecules (Glycine H$_2$N-CH$_2$-COOH)

The important thing to notice is that the same concepts that work for small molecules can be used to build bigger molecules. Using the examples we have investigated and using the rules we know about covalent bonding, we are ready to build a larger molecule, glycine. Glycine is one of the amino acids necessary for all living things.

The first step is to draw the molecule and assign hybridizations.

Next, draw the orbitals. The *p* orbitals can be hard to draw, so we leave them out for now. This shows us all the sigma bonds in the molecule.

Next, draw the bonds and lone pairs, but leave the orbitals out. This is called the *s* framework for a large molecule like glycine.

Finally we draw in the *p* orbitals and form the pi bonds.

This gives us the full bonding picture for the molecule. Almost any large molecule composed of atoms in the HCNOPS and halogen groups can be built this way.

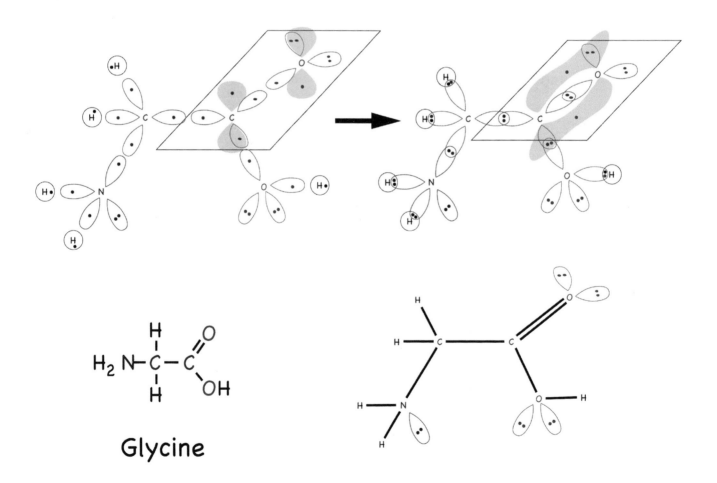

Glycine

Appendix B: Structural and empirical formulas

Name	Structural formula	Empirical formula

sodium bicarbonate
(baking soda)

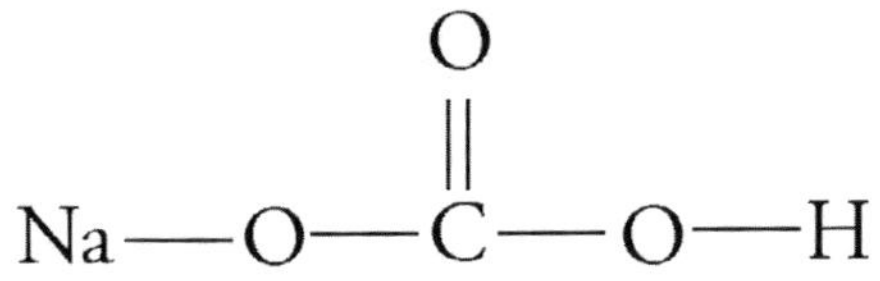

$$Na-O-\overset{\overset{\textstyle O}{\|}}{C}-O-H$$

$NaHCO_3$

acetylene
(used in welding
and cutting torches)

$$H-C\equiv C-H$$

C_2H_2

sulfur dioxide
(produced by burning
low grade coal)

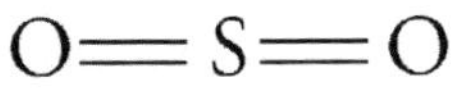

$$O=S=O$$

SO_2

ethyl alcohol
(found in alcoholic drinks)

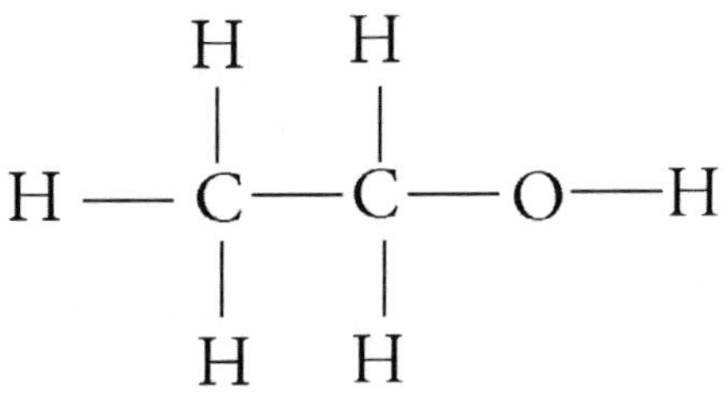

$$H-\overset{\overset{\textstyle H}{|}}{\underset{\underset{\textstyle H}{|}}{C}}-\overset{\overset{\textstyle H}{|}}{\underset{\underset{\textstyle H}{|}}{C}}-O-H$$

C_2H_6O

phosphoric acid
(found in soda pop)

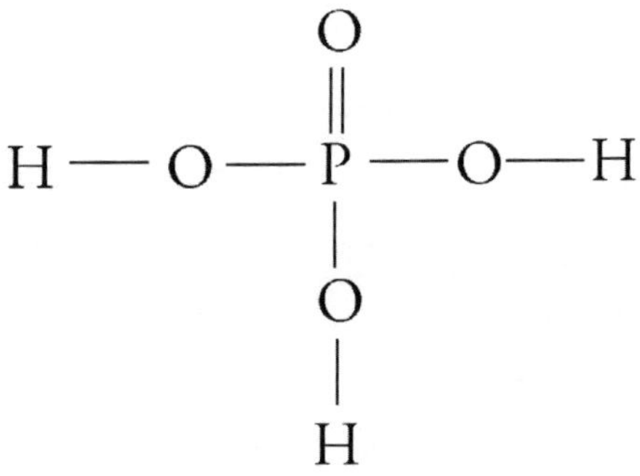

$$H-O-\overset{\overset{\textstyle O}{\|}}{\underset{\underset{\textstyle O}{|}}{P}}-O-H$$
$$|$$
$$H$$

H_3PO_4

formaldehyde
(used to preserve tissues)

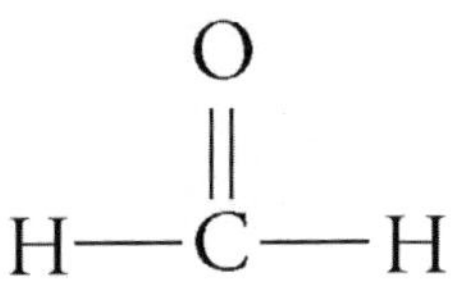

$$H-\overset{\overset{\textstyle O}{\|}}{C}-H$$

CH_2O

Appendix C: pH

pH is used to indicate how powerful an acid solution is. pH is a number that is defined by:

$$pH = -\log [H^+]$$

where $[H^+]$ is the molar hydrogen ion concentration.

A pH of 7 is "neutral," neither acidic nor basic. A pH below 7 is acidic and a pH above 7 is basic.

The pH equation comes from the fact that protons move back and forth in pure water, migrating from one water molecule to another water molecule. When protons migrate, they create hydrogen ions (H^+) and free hydroxyl ions (OH^-). The hydrogen ions don't stay free, but instead hydrogen bond to other water molecules creating hydronium ions (H_3O^+).

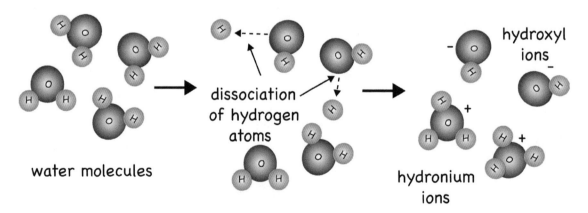

So, a solution of water does not really look like a mixture of intact H_2O molecues, but rather a mixture of hydronium ions (H_3O^+) and hydroxyl ions. Sometimes the pH is written as the concentration of hydronium ions, so the equation would look as follows:

$$pH = -\log [H_3O^+]$$

For simplicity and because the concentration of hydrogen ions (H^+) is exactly the same as the concentration of hydronium ions, only the hydrogen ion (H^+) is written.

So, where do the numbers for pH come from? Well, in pure water, the hydrogen ion (H^+) and the hydroxide ion (OH^-) concentrations are related to each other by the following:

$$[H^+][OH^-] = 1 \times 10^{-14} \text{ M}$$

This means that the hydrogen ion concentration multiplied by the hydroxyl concentration equals 1×10^{-14} M (moles per liter). This number comes from the fact that experimentally, in pure water, the hydrogen ion concentration $[H^+]$ and the hydroxyl ion concentration $[OH^-]$ are both equal to 1×10^{-7} M. In other words, in pure water:

$$[H^+] = 1 \times 10^{-7} \text{ M}$$

and

$$[OH^-] = 1 \times 10^{-7} \text{ M}$$

When these are multiplied together we get the concentration of pure water which is $[H+]$ $[OH-] = 1 \times 10^{-14}$ M. We can now see that when we plug the value for the hydrogen ion concentration of pure water into the equation for pH, the pH is 7.

$$pH = -\log [H^+] = -\log [1 \times 10^{-7} \text{ M}] = 7$$

Now we can see that when the concentration of hydrogen ions is increased by adding an acid, the pH decreases. When the concentration of hydroxyl ions is increased by adding a base, the pH increases. [The hydrogen ion concentration can be found by subtracting the hydroxyl ion concentration from 1×10^{-14}].

[H$^+$]	equation	pH	
1×10^{-1}	pH = –log [1×10^{-1} M]	1	Acid
1×10^{-2}	pH = –log [1×10^{-2} M]	2	
1×10^{-3}	pH = –log [1×10^{-3} M]	3	
1×10^{-4}	pH = –log [1×10^{-4} M]	4	
1×10^{-5}	Neutral pH = –log [1×10^{-5} M]	5	
1×10^{-6}	pH = –log [1×10^{-6} M]	6	
1×10^{-7}	pH = –log [1×10^{-7} M]	7	Neutral
1×10^{-8}	pH = –log [1×10^{-8} M]	8	
1×10^{-9}	pH = –log [1×10^{-9} M]	9	
1×10^{-10}	pH = –log [1×10^{-10} M]	10	
1×10^{-11}	pH = –log [1×10^{-11} M]	11	Base
1×10^{-12}	pH = –log [1×10^{-12} M]	12	
1×10^{-13}	pH = –log [1×10^{-13} M]	13	
1×10^{-14}	pH = –log [1×10^{-14} M]	14	

Appendix D: Dimensional analysis

In science you will often be required to use different kinds of units to do a variety of calculations. You will find yourself needing to convert the value in one unit into a new value with a different unit. For example, you may need to convert moles to grams, liters to milliliters, or Newtons to joules. The process of converting one value with a given unit into another value with a different unit is called dimensional analysis.

The best way to learn dimensional analysis is to do as many examples as you can. This appendix shows you how to set up and solve a dimensional analysis problem and gives you examples for practice.

Example 1:

How many grams of sodium are in 2 moles?

1. The first step when doing dimensional analysis is to decide what it is that the question is asking.

    In this example, you need to find grams.

2. The second step is to list what you know.

    You know you have 2 moles. From the Periodic Table, you know that the molecular weight of sodium is 23 grams/mole.

3. The next step is to understand what you know.

    You have a known quantity (2 moles of sodium) and you want to find an unknown quantity (grams), and you have a conversion factor (23 grams/ mole). The conversion factor tells you how to convert your known quantity to your unknown quantity. In this case it tells you how to get from moles to grams.

4. Next you have to set up your equation.

You need to write out your equation so that your known units cancel, leaving your unknown units behind. Remember that units in the denominator will cancel units in the numerator. To set up your equation, put the unknown units of your conversion factor in the numerator and the known units in the denominator, and multiply by the known quantity. This will give you the unknown quantity. Since we have 23 grams/ mole for our conversion factor and we want grams, we will leave the 23 grams in the numerator with moles in the denominator. [If we wanted moles, we could write the converstion factor as 1 mole/23 grams. This puts moles in the numerator and grams in the denominator.] Your equation now looks like this:

$$\frac{23 \text{ grams}}{1 \text{ mole}} \times 2 \text{ moles} =$$

When we multiply the conversion factor (23 grams/mole) by the known quantity (2 moles), the unit "moles" will cancel, leaving the unit "grams" behind. We multiply the integer values together (23 x 2) to get an integer value (46) with grams as the unit.

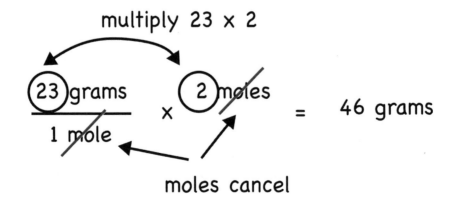

If we have a conversion factor, we can use this technique to convert one type of units to another.

Example 2:

How many liters (l) is 200 milliliters (ml)?

Following the steps outlined earlier, we see that the question (step 1) is asking for liters. We know that (step 2) we have 200 milliliters and that 1000 milliliters equals 1 liter.

So our conversion factor is

1 liter/1000 milliliters

When we multiply the conversion factor (1 liter/1000 ml) by the known quantity (200 ml), the units "milliliters" will cancel leaving the unit "liters" behind. We multiply the integer values 1 and 200 and divide by the integer 1000. This gives us 0.20 liters.

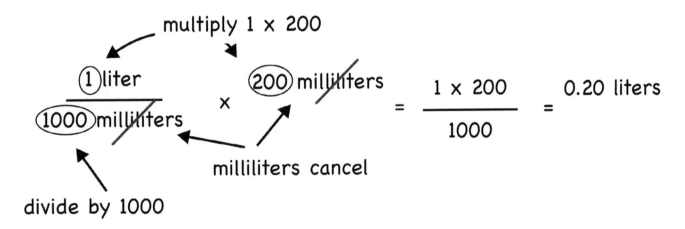

Therefore 200 milliliters equals 0.2 liters.

Appendix E: Amino acid "R" groups

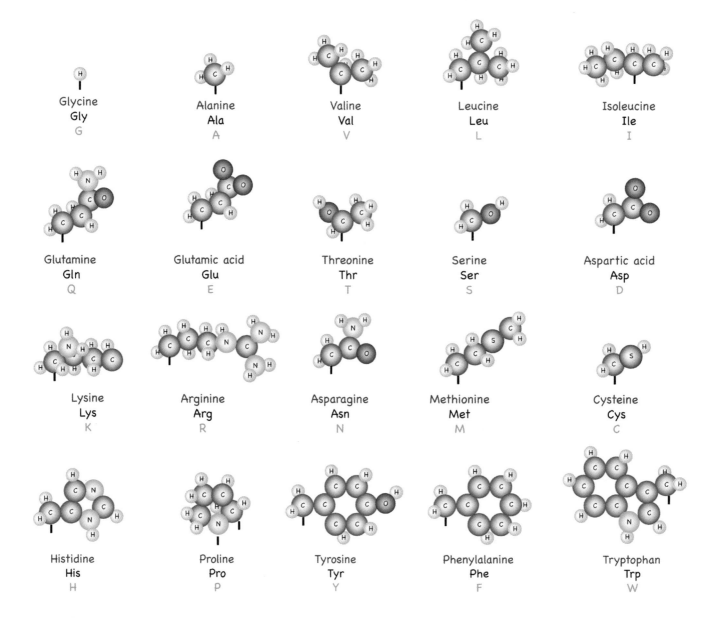

Glycine
Gly
G

Alanine
Ala
A

Valine
Val
V

Leucine
Leu
L

Isoleucine
Ile
I

Glutamine
Gln
Q

Glutamic acid
Glu
E

Threonine
Thr
T

Serine
Ser
S

Aspartic acid
Asp
D

Lysine
Lys
K

Arginine
Arg
R

Asparagine
Asn
N

Methionine
Met
M

Cysteine
Cys
C

Histidine
His
H

Proline
Pro
P

Tyrosine
Tyr
Y

Phenylalanine
Phe
F

Tryptophan
Trp
W

Appendix F: Amino acid codons (RNA)

Alanine (Ala)	Arginine (Arg)	Asparagine (Asn)	Aspartic acid (Asp)	Cysteine (Cys)
GCU GCC GCA GCG	AGA AGG CGU CGC CGA CGG	AAU AAC	GAU GAC	UGU UGC
Glutamic acid (Glu)	**Glutamine (Gln)**	**Glycine (Gly)**	**Histidine (His)**	**Isoleucine (Ile)**
GAA GAG	CAA CAG	GGU GGC GGA GGG	CAU CAC	AUU AUC AUA
Leucine (Leu)	**Lysine (Lys)**	**Methionine (Met)**	**Phenylalanine (Phe)**	**Proline (Pro)**
CUU CUC CUA CUG UUA UUG	AAA AAG	AUG	UUU UUC	CCU CCC CCA CCG
Serine (Ser)	**Threonine (Thr)**	**Tryptophan (Trp)**	**Tyrosine (Tyr)**	**Valine (Val)**
UCU UCC UCA UCG AGU AGC	ACU ACC ACA ACG	UGG	UAU UAC	GUU GUC GUA GUG

STOP
UAA UAG UGA

Appendix G: Atomic radii

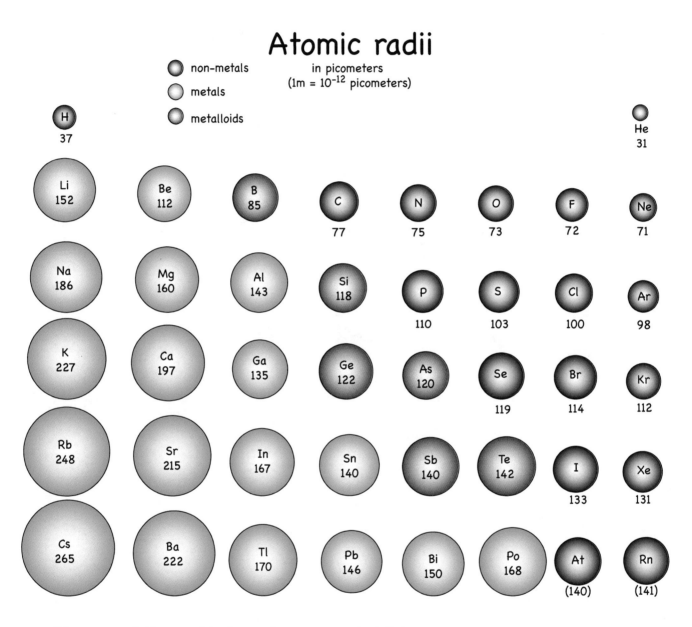

Atomic radii

in picometers
$(1m = 10^{-12}$ picometers$)$

- non-metals
- metals
- metalloids

Values were compiled from several chemistry texts, internet sources, and periodicals.

Appendix H: Ionic radii

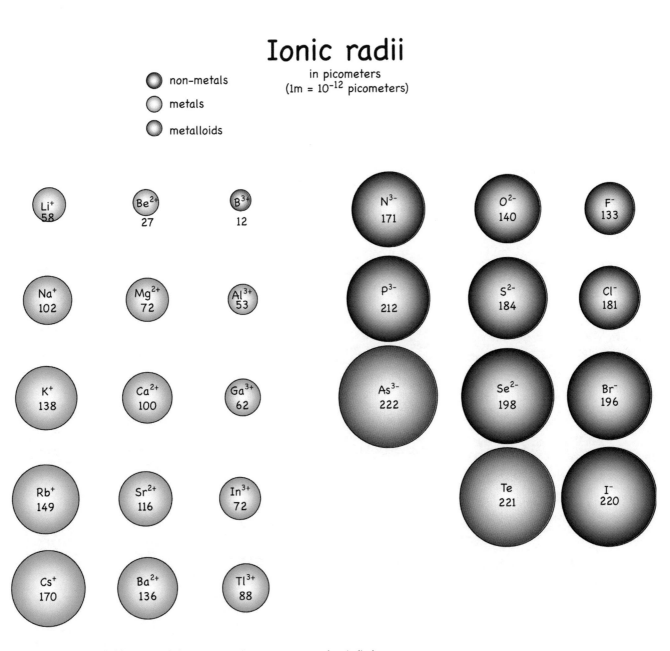

Ionic radii

in picometers
(1m = 10⁻¹² picometers)

Values were compiled from several chemistry texts, internet sources, and periodicals.

GLOSSARY-INDEX

A • the symbol for adenine, 209.

α [al'-fə] -carbon • the central carbon atom of an amino acid that bonds to both the carboxylic acid group and the amine group, 198-199.

α-glycosidic [al'-fə glī-kō-sid'-ik] bond • a bond between two monosaccharides that has the oxygen pointing downward, 171-174.

amu • atomic mass unit, 8.

ATP see adenosine triphosphate.

acetic acid [ə-sē'-tik a'-səd] • the acid found in vinegar, 60-64, 69, 78-79, 82.

Acetyl CoA [ə-sēt'-əl kō-ā] • a molecular "intermediate" involved in certain metabolic pathways, such as the citric acid cycle. An intermediate is a molecule created from other molecules and then converted into different molecules during the process, 2.

acid • any of a number of molecules whose pH in water is below 7, 78-91.

acid-base reaction • an exchange reaction between an acid and a base with a salt as a product, 78-85.

acidity [ə-sid'-ə-tē] • the property of being an acid with a pH in water below 7, 96.

addition reaction • molecules are linked together using double bonds as the functional group, 184-185.

adenine [a'-də-nēn] • one of the four nucleic acid bases that make DNA and RNA; has the symbol A, 209-213, 215-216.

adenosine triphosphate [ə-de'-nə-sēn trī-fäs'-fāt] • one of the main energy molecules found in living things — the end phosphate gets removed during chemical reactions, providing chemical energy, 2.

aerosol [ar'-ə-säl] • a mixture made of liquids or solids mixed into a gas, 114, 115.

alanine [a'-lə-nēn] • an amino acid with a methyl "R" group, 199.

alchemists [al'-kə-mists] • an early group of mystics, scholars, and inventors who, over several centuries, developed much of the experimental data that eventually became modern chemistry, 3-4.

alcohols • a class of organic compounds that contain a -OH group attached to a carbon atom, 150, 158.

aldehydes [al'-də-hīdz] • a class of organic compounds that contain a -CH=O functional group, 150, 151, 159.

alkali [al'-kə-lī] • a substance having the properties of a base; derived from the Arabic word *al-gili* which means "ashes of saltwort," 78.

alkali metal • an element that reacts strongly with water and is found in the left-hand column of the Periodic Table, 19, 40.

alkanes [al'-kānz] • a class of organic compounds that contain only carbon and hydrogen with single bonds, 150-152.

alkenes [al'-kēnz] • a class of organic compounds that contain one or more double bonds between adjacent carbon atoms, 150, 151, 153.

alkynes [al'-kīnz] • a class of organic compounds that contain one or more triple bonds between adjacent carbon atoms, 150, 151, 153-155.

amides [ə'-mīdz] • a class of organic compounds that contain a -C=O-NH- functional group, 150, 161-162.

amine [ə'-mēn] • one of a class of organic compounds that contain a -NH₂ functional group, 150, 158-159.

amine [ə'-mēn] group • a functional group in an amino acid, 198.

amino [ə-mē'-nō] acid • a molecule that has a central carbon attached to two functional groups—amine and carboxylic acid (the amino acid proline is an exception), 198-205.

amino acid polymer • a protein, 194, 200-205.

amylopectin [a-mə-lō-pek'-tən] • a branched polysaccharide made of linked glucose monomers, and one of two carbohydrates that compose starch, 173-174.

amylose [a'-mə-lōs] • a linear polysaccharide of linked glucose monomers which spirals into a helical coil and is one of two carbohydrates that compose starch, 173.

analytical chemistry • the subdivision of chemistry that "resolves" the chemical composition of substances, 4.

anions [a'-nī-ənz] • ions that contain one or more extra electrons than the neutral atom and are negatively charged, 46-47.

anticodon [an-tī-kō'-dän] • a set of three bases on transfer RNA that connects with a codon of three amino acids on messenger RNA, 218.

aqueous [ā'-kwē-əs] • any solution whose solvent is water, 85.

arginine [är'-jə-nēn] • an amino acid that is basic, 199, 236.

aromatic [a-rə-ma'-tik] • an organic compound that contains a benzene ring, 150, 156-157.

Arrhenius [ə-rē'-nē-əs], Svante (1859-1927) • A Swedish chemist who came up with a method for defining acids and bases by noting the release of hydrogen ions (acid) or generation of hydroxide ions (base), 81.

Arrhenius acid • any substance that releases a hydrogen ion, 80-84.

Arrhenius base • any substance that generates a hydroxide ion, 80-81, 84-85.

asparagine [ə-sper'-ə-jēn] • an amino acid that contains an amide functional group, 199, 236.

aspartic [ə-spär'-tik] acid • an acidic amino acid, 199, 236.

atom • the smallest distinctive chemical unit of matter, 5.

atomic mass • each proton and each neutron has a mass of 1 amu, 8.

atomic mass unit (amu) • used when measuring the mass of an atom, 8.

atomic number • the number of protons in an element, 18.

atomic weight • atomic mass, 9.

Aufbau principle • a rule for filling electron orbitals that states the order in which they are filled, 33-38.

azeotropy [ā-zē-o'-trō-pē] • when two liquids have similar vapor pressures and cannot be completely separated by distillation, 135.

β [bā'-tə] • the Greek letter beta used in scientific terminology.

β-glycosidic [bā'-tə glī-kō-sid'-ik] bond • a bond between two monosaccharides that has the oxygen pointing upward, 171-172.

β-pleated sheet • the sheet-like structure that forms when polypeptide backbones line up next to each other; a protein secondary structure, 204.

baking soda • see sodium bicarbonate.

balanced equation • when the number of atoms for each element are the same on both sides of a chemical equation, 63-67.

barrel • a protein tertiary structure formed primarily by pleated sheets lined up side by side in a barrel shape, 204-206.

base • any of a number of molecules whose pH in water is above 7, 78-91.

base pairs • the "rungs" in the middle of a double helix that connect two strands of DNA by means of hydrogen bonds, 213.

basicity [bā-sis'-ə-tē] • the property of being a base, 96.

benzene [ben'-zēn] • an aromatic hydrocarbon with a ring of six carbon atoms and six hydrogen atoms shaped in a hexagon with alternating single and double bonds, 156, 157.

bilayer [bī'-lā-ər] • a cell membrane made of two layers of molecules stacked on top of each other in opposite directions, 123-124.

biochemistry • the subdivision of chemistry that is concerned with the molecules of life, 4, 5.

branched • a polymer that forms side chains, 181-182, 185-187.

C • the symbol for cytosine, 209.

C-terminus • the end of a protein chain that contains the carboxyl group, 201-202.

carbohydrates [kär-bō-hī'-drātz] • molecules containing both carbon and water, and the most abundant class of biological molecules found in all living things, 165, 168-172.

carbonyl [kär'-bə-nil] • a carbon atom that is double bonded to an oxygen atom, 159.

carboxylic [kär-bäk-si'-lik] acid group • a functional group [-COOH] in an amino acid, 198.

cations [kat'-ī-ənz] • ions that have one or more fewer electrons than the neutral atom and are positively charged, 46.

cellulose [sel'-yə-lōs] • a structural polysaccharide found in plants, 172.

central genetic machinery • the system of DNA, RNA, and proteins that uses the genetic information in the DNA to create new protein machines, 196.

chain termination • side reactions that terminate (end) a linear polymer chain, 185.

chair conformation • the shape of a molecule where the ends of a ring have buckled and folded in opposite directions, 170.

chemical bonding • the attraction of opposite electrical charges in atoms that holds molecules together, 26-28.

chemical equation • a written description of a chemical reaction that shows what happens to molecules or atoms when they react with each other, 61-67.

chemical formula • a written description of a chemical reaction, 61.

chemical property • the property of an atom or molecule that results in chemical reactions, 129.

chemical reaction • the process by which bonds between atoms are created or destroyed, 60.

chitin [kī'-tin] • a structural polysaccharide found in the exoskeletons of some creatures like spiders and crustaceans, 173.

cholesterol [kə-les'-tə-rōl] • the most common steroid; found in the brain and spinal column tissues; the major component of animal plasma membranes, 176.

chromatography [krō-mə-tä'-grə-fē] • a separation technique that utilizes the differences in mobility of components through a solid, 138, 139.

citric [si'-trik] acid • a mild acid found in different fruits such as grapefruit and oranges, 80.

citric acid cycle • the main metabolic pathway that living things use to "burn" (or utilize) energy storage molecules, releasing essential energy molecules and other biochemical precursors that cells need for living, (also called the Krebs cycle, or the TCA [tricarboxylic acid] cycle), 2.

codon [kō'-dän] • a set of three nucleotides in a strand of DNA that is an amino acid or gives a start or stop command, 215.

coenzyme [cō-en'-zīm] • a helper molecule that helps an enzyme perform an enzymatic reaction, 167.

colloid [kä'-loid] • a heterogeneous solution that may look like a homogeneous solution but that has particles larger than individual molecules, 114–115.

column chromatography • a type of liquid chromatography in which the stationary phase is placed in a column and the mobile phase is passed through the column, 139.

combination reaction • a type of chemical reaction where two atoms or molecules combine to form a single product, 70–72.

complementary sequence • the RNA copy of DNA that is made with complementary base pairs, 215–216.

compound • a chemically bonded pure substance composed of only one kind of molecule, 15, 110.

concentrated solution • a solution containing a relatively large quantity of molecules of solute, 86–91.

concentration • the number of moles of a substance in a given volume of a solution, 86–91, 96–101.

condensation polymer • a polymer formed by a condensation reaction, 189–191.

condensation reaction • a chemical reaction in which two monomers combine to form a new molecule, giving off a by-product such as water, 189–191.

conformation • the shape of a molecule, 170.

control site • the part of DNA that determines what type and how much of each protein is made; also controls various cell activities, 211.

copolymer • a polymer made of more than one type of monomer, 180, 181.

core electrons • electrons that are buried in the subshells and do not participate in chemical bonding, 39, 44.

covalent [kō-vā'-lənt] bond • a chemical bond in which the valence electrons are shared between atoms, 45, 51.

Crick, Francis • along with James Watson, discovered the structure of DNA in 1953, marking the birth of modern molecular biology, 208.

cross-link • a covalent bond between two polymer chains, 183, 185–186.

cytosine [sī'-tə-sēn] • one of the four nucleic acid bases that make DNA and RNA; has the symbol C, 209–213, 215–216.

d orbital • five atomic orbitals; four that are shaped like a clover leaf, and one that is a combination of a dumbbell and a donut, 29, 30.

DNA (deoxyriboneucleic [dē-äk'-si-rī-bō-nü-klā-ik] acid) • a polymer that provides long-term storage of genetic information in cells; contains all of the instructions for making proteins, 194–197, 205, 207–218.

DNA polymerase [pə lim' ə rās] • a protein that makes a copy of the DNA to be used in making a new cell, 197.

decomposition reaction • when one type of reactant molecule breaks apart (decomposes) to form several new molecules as products, 72–73.

delocalized [dē-lō'-kə-līzd] • not being "localized" or found in any one particular place in space, 157.

deoxygenate [dē-äk'-si-jen-āt]• to remove oxygen from a molecule, 208.

deoxyriboneucleic acid • see DNA.

deoxyribose [dē-äk-sī-rī'-bōs]• a deoxygenated monosaccharide found in DNA, 208.

dilute solution • a solution containing a relatively small quantity of molecules of solute, 86–91.

dimer • two identical molecules that are linked together, 185 (Fig. 9.6).

disaccharide [dī-sak'-ä-rīd] • a sugar made of two monosaccharides that are connected, 171.

displacement reaction • a type of chemical reaction where an atom from one molecule removes, or displaces, an atom from another molecule, 73–74.

dissolve • when a solute is mixed into a solvent causing the solute's molecules to break apart from each other to form a homogeneous mixture, 115–116, 118–122.

distillation [dis-tə-lā'-shən] • a physical separation technique that utilizes the differences in volatility to separate compounds in a mixture, 135.

domain • in a protein, a tertiary structure made of clusters of 100-200 amino acid monomers folded into a compact unit, 205.

double helix [hē'-liks] • the ladder-like structure of DNA—two chains of nucleic acid polymers that are twisted around each other and are connected by nucleic acid bases, 212–213.

elastomers [i-las'-tə-mərz] • polymers with the ability to stretch and spring back to their original shape, 184.

electron [i-lek'-trän] • a negatively charged particle that is in an orbital outside the nucleus of an atom, 5-6, 28-57.

electron cloud • the space that surrounds the nucleus of an atom and is occupied by the electrons, 5-6, 28.

electron configuration • the arrange``ment of the electrons in an atom, 38.

electron density • the concept that one electron is more probable in some places than in others, but is not located in any one place, 31.

electronegativity [i-lek-trō-ne-gə-tiv'-i-tē] • the measure of the ability of an atom to draw electrons toward itself, 116-117.

elements • the different atoms, 13.

empirical [im-pir'-i-kəl] formula • a type of chemical formula that shows the number and kind of atoms in a molecule, 61.

emulsion [i-məl'-shən] • a type of heterogeneous mixture where a liquid is mixed together with a liquid, 115.

endpoint • the conclusion of a chemical reaction, 100.

enzymes [en'-zīmz] • large protein molecules that carry out various metabolic functions, such as breaking down food molecules inside cells; RNA polymerase and DNA polymerase are enzymes, 2, 167.

equivalence [i-kwi'-və-ləns] point • the point in a titration where the amount of acid (or base) added equals the amount of base (or acid) present in the original solution, 101.

erythrose [i-rith'-rōs] • a simple sugar tetrose that has four carbon atoms, 170.

esters [es'-tərz] • a class of molecules with the functional group -C=O-O- that provide an easy way to hook two big molecules together, 150, 161-162.

ethene [e'-thēn]• see ethylene.

ethylene [e'-thə-lēn] (ethene) • a simple alkene with a double bond functional group that allows monomers to be hooked together, 180, 185, 188.

evaporation [i-va-pə-rā'-shən] • a physical separation technique that utilizes the difference in volatility between compounds, 134.

exchange reaction • a type of chemical reaction where one atom from one molecule changes place with another atom from another molecule, 74-75.

extraction [ik-strak'-shən] • a physical separation technique that utilizes the difference in solubility between compounds, 138.

fats • nutrients that are a major source of energy, an essential component of cellular membranes, and aid in the absorption of fat-soluble vitamins, 174.

filtration [fil-trā'-shən] • a physical separation technique that utilizes differences in physical size, 132-133.

foam • a heterogeneous mixture of gas mixed into liquid, 114, 115.

free radical • an unbonded electron that is very reactive, 184-185.

fructose • a monosaccharide that combines with glucose to form sucrose (table sugar), 171.

functional group • on a larger molecule, a special site at which chemical reactions occur, 147, 149.

G • the symbol for guanine, 209.

galactose [gə-lak'-tōs] • a six carbon monosaccharide that is a simple sugar, 171.

gas chromatography • a separation technique where the mixture is dissolved in a gas, 139.

gene • the part of DNA that codes for protein, 210-211.

genetic code • the sequence of codons that contains the information that cells need to make proteins, 210.

gluconeogenesis [glü-kō-nē-ō-jen'-ə-səs] • a process inside living cells that produces carbohydrates, 169.

glucopyranose [glü-kō-pī'-rə-nōs] • a circular glucose molecule, 170.

glucose [glü'-kōs] • a simple sugar with six carbon atoms (a hexose); combines with fructose to form sucrose (table sugar), 170.

glutamic [glü-ta'-mik] acid • an amino acid that is acidic, 199, 236.

glutamine [glü'-tə-mēn] • an amino acid that contains an amide functional group, 199, 236.

glyceraldehyde [gli-sər-al'-də-hīd] • the simplest sugar with three carbon atoms (a triose), 170.

glycerol [gli'-sər-ôl] • a small three-carbon carbohydrate that is the parent molecule for triglycerides, 174.

glycine [glī'-sēn] • the simplest amino acid with a hydrogen as the "R" group, 191, 199, 236.

glycogen [glī'-kə-jen] • the primary storage polysaccharide found in animals, 173-174.

glycosidic [glī-kō-sid'-ik] bond • the bond between two monosaccharides, 171.

guanine [gwä'-nēn] • one of the four nucleic acid bases that make DNA and RNA; has the symbol G, 209-213, 215-216.

halogen • an element that melts or vaporizes at a low temperature and is found in the next-to-last column of the Periodic Table, 19, 41, 46.

helix (plural, helices) [hē'-liks, hē'-lə-sēz] • a spiral coil; in a protein secondary structure, the cylindrical coil that forms when the backbone of a polypeptide twists, 173, 203.

heptose [hep'-tōs] • a simple sugar with seven carbon atoms, 170.

heterogeneous [he-tə-rə-jē'-nē-əs] • meaning "other kind;" for mixtures, a mixture that is not the same throughout, 111-113.

hexose [heks'-ōs] • a simple sugar with six carbon atoms, 170.

histidine [his'-tə-dēn] • an amino acid that has a five-membered imidazole ring, 199-200, 236.

homogeneous [hō-mə-jē'-nē-əs] • meaning "same kind;" for mixtures, a mixture that is the same throughout, 111-112.

homopolymer [hō-mō-pä'-lə-mer] • a polymer made up of identical repeating monomer units, 180.

hybrid [hī'-brəd] orbital • an orbital that is a combination of two or more different orbitals, 53-54.

hydride [hī'-drīd] • a compound of hydrogen, 165.

hydrogen bond • a very weak chemical bond that forms when a hydrogen atom is bridged between two electron-loving atoms, 211.

hydrophilic [hī-drə-fi'-lik] • "water loving;" any substance that will dissolve in water, 120-122.

hydrophobic [hī-drə-fō'-bik] • "water hating;" any substance that will not dissolve in water, 121-122.

hydroxyl [hī-dräk'-səl] • a molecule made of one hydrogen atom and one oxygen atom, 159, 170, 174.

imidazole [i-mə-da'-zōl] • a molecule with a five-membered ring; the parent molecule for histidine, 200.

indicator [in'-də-kā-tər] • for acid-base titrations, a substance that is added to a solution and changes color as the pH changes, 99.

inert gas • a gas that is unreactive with any element; a noble gas, 20.

inorganic chemistry • the branch of chemistry that deals mainly with compounds that are not carbon-containing 145.

ion [ī'-ən] • an atom that has gained or lost an electron and has a negative or positive electric charge, 45-50.

ionic [ī-ä'-nik] bond • a chemical bond in which valence electrons are not shared between the two atoms, 45, 47, 116-119.

ionic solid • a substance in which the ions are organized in arrays of alternating cations and anions, 49-50.

ionize • when an atom or molecule gains or loses electrons causing it to have an electric charge, 90.

isomers [ī'-sō-mərz] • two molecules that have the same atoms but different structures, 147-148.

ketones [kē'-tōnz] • molecules that contain the functional group -C-C=O-C-, 150, 159.

KEVLAR [kev'-lär] • a strong polymer made of two different monomers with different functional groups, 180-181.

kinesin [kə-nē'-sən] • a molecular machine that transports cargo along microtubules inside cells, 198.

lactose [lak'-tōs] • a simple disaccharide sugar molecule found in milk that is made of a glucose molecule and a galactose molecule, 171.

law of conservation of mass • in a chemical reaction atoms are neither created nor destroyed, only rearranged to make other molecules, 64.

leucine [lü'-sēn] • a hydrophobic amino acid, 199, 236.

linear polymer [li'-nē-ər pä'-lə-mer] • a polymer that has monomer units that are connected to each other one after another, end to end, 181-182.

lipids [li'-pədz] (fats) • nutrients that are a major source of energy, an essential component of cellular membranes, and aid in the absorption of fat-soluble vitamins, 174.

liquid chromatography • a separation technique where the components of a mixture are dissolved in a liquid and passed over a solid stationary phase, 139.

lysine [lī'-sēn] • a basic amino acid, 199, 236.

mRNA (messenger RNA) • a temporary copy of DNA, 196, 215-218.

macromolecular [ma-krō-mə-le'-kyə-lər] • particles that are small but often visible; found in homogeneous mixtures, 112.

main group • on the Periodic Table, the group of elements located on the right-hand and left-hand sides, 20.

malic [ma'-lik] acid • a type of acid found in certain vegetables such as rhubarb, 80.

mass • the property that makes matter resist being moved, 7-11.

matter • anything that occupies space and has mass, 7.

physical chemistry • the subdivision of chemistry that is concerned with how natural forces are involved in molecular bonding, 4, 5.

physical property • a property of a substance, such as melting point or boiling point, that does not result in chemical reactions but can be used to separate different substances from mixtures, 129-131.

pi [pī] bond (π bond) • a covalent bond formed by the side-to-side overlap of two atomic orbitals, 52-53, 225-228.

pleated sheet • the sheet-like structure that forms when polypeptide backbones line up next to each other, 203-204.

polar [pō'-lər] • a molecule or bond where the electronegativities of the atoms are not equal resulting in two differently charged "poles"—a positive pole and a negative pole, 117-118.

polarity [pō-lar'-i-tē] • the quality of a molecule having poles with opposite electric charges; , 116-118.

polyamide [pä-lē a'-mīd• a homopolymer with a single repeating monomer unit; nylon is a polyamide, 180.

polyester [pä-lē-es'-tər] • a condensation polymer formed by hooking monomers together with ester linkages, 190.

polyethylene [pä-lē-e'-thə-lēn]• a homopolymer made of repeating units of ethylene monomers, 180, 185-188.

polymer [pä'-lə-mər] • a molecule made up of many repeating units, 179-191.

polymerase • see DNA polymerase.

polypeptide [pä-lē-pep'-tīd] • a chain of amino acids, 203-204.

polypeptide backbone • a linear molecular chain that consists of three repeating atoms, NH-CH-CO, to which the amino acids are attached, 203-204.

polyprotic [pä-lē-prō'-tik] acid • an acid that can release more than one hydrogen atom (proton), 82-83, 105.

polysaccharide [pä-lē-sa'-kə-rīd]• a long chain carbohydrate composed of many saccharides, 172-174.

polysaccharide, storage • a carbohydrate used for storing energy, 172.

polysaccharide, structural • a carbohydrate involved in the structure of cellulose and chitin, 172.

polystyrene [pä-lē-stī'-rēn]• a homopolymer with a single repeating monomer unit; styrofoam, 180, 188.

polyvinyl chloride (PVC) • a homopolymer with a single repeating monomer unit, 180, 188.

potassium [pə-ta'-sē-əm] chloride • a salt sometimes used as table salt, 20.

precipitates [pri-sip'-i-tātz] • solids, 133.

primary structure • the sequence of amino acids in a protein chain that determines what kind of machine a protein will become, 201-202.

products • the new molecules formed by a chemical reaction, 60.

promoter • the control site on DNA where RNA polymerase binds to the DNA, 216.

protein • a polymer made of amino acids that is necessary for the overall functioning of biological cells, 194-206.

proteosome [prō'-tē-ō-sōm] • a highly complex protein machine used by cells to break down other proteins, 206-207.

proton [prō'-ton] • a positively charged particle in the nucleus of an atom; a hydrogen atom that has lost its only electron, 5-7, 33-34, 48-49, 82-83.

purine [pyur'-ēn] • a nucleic acid base having two rings fused with each other, 210.

pyrimidine [pī-ri'-mə-dēn] • a nucleic acid base having a single ring, 210.

quaternary [kwä'-tər-nə-rē] structure • two or more protein chains that work together to make a single machine, 206-207.

"R" group • the group of atoms in an amino acid that makes it unique. The "R" group can be anything from a single hydrogen atom to a complicated ring of atoms; can stand for any organic group of atoms in a molecule, 162, 175, 199-200.

RNA (ribonucleic acid) • a nucleic acid polymer that provides short-term storage of information that is copied from DNA; involved in making proteins, 194-197, 207-218.

RNA polymerase [pə lim' ə räs] • a protein that makes a temporary copy of the DNA, 196-198.

random coil • a compact ball resulting from the random folding of a long-chain polymer, 181.

reactants • the original molecules before a chemical reaction takes place, 60.

recrystallization • a separation technique where one component of a mixture is separated from another component based on their differences in temperature-dependent solubility, 137.

ribonucleic [rī-bō-nü-klā'-ik] acid • RNA, 194-197, 207-218.

ribose [rī'-bōs] • a simple sugar with five carbon atoms (a pentose), 170, 208.

ribosome [rī'-bə-sōm] • a complex molecular machine made of both proteins and RNA that is used to build new proteins from an mRNA code, 196, 200-201, 216-218.

σ bond • see sigma bond.

s orbital • a simple spherical orbital that holds up to two electrons, 28.

sp hybrid orbital • a type of hybrid orbital that is a mixture of a single *s* orbital and a single *p* orbital, 54-57.

sp^2 hybrid orbital • a type of hybrid orbital that is a mixture of a single *s*-orbital and two *p*-orbitals, 54-57.

sp^3 hybrid orbital • a type of hybrid orbital that is a mixture of a single *s*-orbital and three *p*-orbitals, 54-57.

saccharide [sa'-kə-rīd] • a sugar, 169.

salt • a compound containing a halogen and an alkali metal; the product of an acid-base reaction, 19-20, 47, 78-80.

saturated fats • fats that are solid at room temperature and do not have double bonds in their hydrocarbon "R" groups, 175.

saturated solution • a solution that has the maximum amount of solute dissolved in a solvent, 120.

secondary structure • in a protein, a helix or pleated sheet that forms as the protein begins to fold, 203-204.

sequence • the order of amino acids in a protein chain that determines what kind of machine the protein becomes; the primary structure of a protein, 201-202.

side chains • atoms that dangle off the main backbone of a polymer and affect its properties, 187.

sigma bond (σ bond) • a covalent bond formed by the overlap of two atomic orbitals, 51-52.

simple sugars • the smallest carbohydrates, monosaccharides, 169.

sodium bicarbonate [sō'-dē-əm bī kär' bə nāt] • baking soda, 60-64, 69, 78-79, 82.

sodium chloride • table salt, 20, 70-72.

solid emulsion • a colloidal mixture of a liquid mixed into a solid, 114, 115.

solid foam • a colloidal mixture of a gas mixed into a liquid, 114, 115.

solubility [säl-yə-bil'-ə-tē] • the ability of one substance to dissolve in another, 115.

soluble [säl'-yə-bəl] • when a molecule or compound can dissolve in another substance, it is soluble, 115.

solute [säl'-yoot] • the substance that dissolves, 115-116.

solution • a type of homogeneous mixture in which one substance has been dissolved in another, 86-91, 113-116, 119-120.

solvent [säl'-vənt] • the substance that the solute dissolves into, 116.

starch • the primary storage polysaccharide that is found in plants and animals, 173-174.

stationary phase • in chromatography, the phase that the mobile phase is passed over, 138-139.

steroids • nutrients involved in bile acids, sex hormones, and the formation of animal membranes, 175.

stoichiometric coefficient [stoi-kē-ō-me'-trik kō-ə-fi'-shənt] • the number that is placed in front of a molecule in a chemical equation that shows how many molecules of that type are involved in the reaction; used to balance chemical equations , 63-67.

stoichiometry [stoi-kē-ä'-mə-trē] • literally, "the measure of components" in a chemical reaction; shows how many molecules of each reactant and product are involved in a chemical reaction, 62-67, 97.

structural formula • a written description that shows how atoms fit together in a molecule, 62.

subsaturated solution • a solution that has less than the amount of solute able to dissolve in a given solvent, 120.

subshell • one or more orbitals of the same type, 30.

sucrose [sü'-krōs] • table sugar; a disaccharide of a single fructose and a single glucose, 171.

supersaturated solution • a solution that has more than the maximum amount of solute dissolved in a solvent, 120.

surfactants [sər-fak'-təntz] • a broad category of molecules that contain a hydrophobic tail and a hydrophilic head, 122.

synthetic chemistry • the subdivision of chemistry that "puts together" new molecules, 5.

synthetic fibers • polymers created by chemists that can be drawn out into long, thin fibers, 184.

T • the symbol for thymine, 209.

tRNA • transfer RNA, 214-218.

tannic [tan'-ik] acid • a type of acid that is found in some teas, 80.

tartaric [tär-tə'-rik] acid • a type of acid that is found in grapes, 80.

tertiary [tər'-shē-er-ē] structure • the folding of a protein into domains and barrels which occurs after the secondary structure is organized; determines the overall shape of a protein and is critical for protein function, 204-205.

tetroses [te'-trō-səs] • simple sugars with four carbon atoms, 170.

thermoplastic • a polymer that is hard at room temperature and softens when heated, 184.

thymine [thī'-mēn] • one of the four nucleic acid bases that make DNA; has the symbol T, 209-213, 215-216.

titrate [tī'-trāt] • see titration.

titration [tī-trā'-shən] • the process of using a known solution to find out the concentration of an unknown solution, 98-106.

transcription • first step in making a new protein—RNA polymerase copies a piece of DNA, 215.

transfer RNA (tRNA) • molecules that play an important role in the synthesis of new proteins, 214-218.

transition metals (transition elements) • the group of elements in the middle of the Periodic Table that have their outermost electrons in *d* shells, 20-21.

translation • the process of copying DNA into a messenger RNA molecule, 216.

triglyceride [trī-gli'-ser-īd] • a derivative of glycerol in which the hydroxyl hydrogen has been replaced with a carbon, an oxygen and an "R" group, 174.

trioses [trī'-ō-səs] • simple sugars with three carbon atoms that are the smallest monosaccharides, 169.

U • the symbol for uracil, 213.

unsaturated fats • are liquid at room temperature and have double bonds in their hydrocarbon "R" groups, 175.

uracil [ü'-rə-sil] • one of the four nucleic acid bases that make RNA; has the symbol U, 213-214.

valence [vā'-ləns] electrons • those electrons that occupy the outermost electron orbitals and that are involved in chemical bonding, 44.

valine [va'-lēn] • a hydrophobic amino acid, 199, 236.

vinegar • a dilute solution of acetic acid, 78-79, 82.

vitamin • an essential molecule found in foods that is required for the healthy functioning of living things, 165, 167-168.

volatility [vä-lə-ti'-li-tē] • the ability to become a gas, 134.

Watson, James • along with Francis Crick, discovered the structure of DNA in 1953, marking the birth of modern molecular biology, 208.

X-ray crystallography [kri-stə-lä'-grə-fē] • a technique that allows an image of large molecules to be reconstructed by using the scattering of radiation, 208.

Pronunciation Key

a	add	f	fit	ng	sing	t	take
ā	race	g	go	o	odd	u	up
ä	palm	h	hope	ō	open	ü	sue
â(r)	air	i	it	ô	jaw	yoo	few
b	bat	ī	ice	oi	oil	v	vase
ch	check	j	joy	oo	pool	w	way
d	dog	k	cool	p	pit	y	yarn
e	end	l	love	r	run	z	zebra
ē	tree	m	move	s	sea		
ə	a in above	n	nice	sh	sure		

Made in the USA
Charleston, SC
21 March 2014